Dina

With

[signature]

3 October '98

HUGH CORTAZZI. MY 2ND COUSIN —
BROTHER OF THEO CORTAZZI
WHO MARRIED DINA. I BELIEVE
DINA & THEO HAD TO GET PERMISSION
TO MARRY AS IT IS ILLEAGEL FOR
1ST COUSINS TO MARRY AND NOT
NORMAL FOR 2ND COUSINS ???

JAPAN AND BACK
AND PLACES ELSEWHERE

Otemachi district, Tokyo, c.1990. Courtesy *Sankei Shimbun*

Japan and Back
AND PLACES ELSEWHERE

A MEMOIR

Hugh Cortazzi

GLOBAL ORIENTAL

JAPAN AND BACK
AND PLACES ELSEWHERE

A Memoir by Hugh Cortazzi

First published 1998 by
GLOBAL ORIENTAL
P.O. Box 219
Folkestone, Kent CT20 3LZ

*Global Oriental is an imprint of
Global Books Ltd*

ISBN 1-901903-20-6

British Library Cataloguing in Publication Data
A CIP catalogue entry for this book is available
from the British Library.

Set in Garamond 11.5 on 12.5 pt by Bookman, Hayes
Printed and bound in England by Bookcraft Ltd, Midsomer Norton, Avon

Contents

For Elizabeth

Preface

When I retired from the Diplomatic Service in 1984, I decided that I would not write my memoirs, not least because in the past I have found most diplomatic memoirs tedious. I changed my mind after a few years, partly because friends urged me to do so, and partly because, while my memory was still reasonably fresh, I wanted to review what my life had amounted to. I have never kept a diary and I feared that inevitably as time passed my recollections of a full life would all fade into insignificance, or worse a complete blur. Perhaps the facts that I recall are indeed insignificant and my memoirs like those of other ex-diplomats will be perceived as both tedious and trite. However, I console myself with the thought that 'such is life'. Maybe a few friends, family and diplomatic historians or students of Anglo-Japanese relations will find something of interest in this memoir.

In every walk of life the individual has to depend on the help and cooperation of his colleagues. I must start, therefore, by recording my thanks to all with whom I worked. It is not possible to mention them all, but my appreciation to the unnamed is as sincere as it is to those I have named. I must emphasize, above all, the very special contribution of Elizabeth, my wife, without whose help, tolerance and patience I could not have achieved what little I did.

I am grateful to a number of friends who have read and commented on various versions of these memoirs. In particular I want to express my thanks to Nobuko Albery, Carmen Blacker, Haruko Fukuda, Michael Loewe, Kosuke Matsumura, Ian Nish, Paul Norbury and Lew Radbourne for their comments and suggestions. I have tried to take account of many of their comments, but any errors or misjudgements are entirely my responsibility.

One reader noted that 'I' was used too frequently. I am conscious that '*Surtout le moi est haïssable*', but it is not easy to avoid the first person singular in a memoir. Another commented that I was too apologetic. But I have spent so much of my life in Japan where apologies are an unavoidable element in social relations. So I shall not apologize for being apologetic.

CHAPTER ONE

A Beginning

——————————— oOo ———————————

EARLY YEARS

I was born on 2 May 1924 in Sedbergh which was then a village in the West Riding of Yorkshire near the border with Westmoreland. Sedbergh is now in the county of Cumbria.

The Cortazzi family had come to Britain in the early nineteenth century. My great-great-grandfather had been born in Smyrna (Izmir) in 1793 and was the son of the last Venetian Consul there (this was a hereditary post). Following the Treaty of Campo Formio in 1797, which abolished the ancient Republic of Venice and led to the absorbtion of Venice into the Austro-Hungarian Empire, my great-great-grandfather appears to have adopted the nationality of his mother who was an English-woman. He became a merchant working in the Levant and at Odessa in southern Russia. He was allegedly expelled from Russia for lending money to the Polish rebels. He moved to London, took a house in Edwardes Square and became involved in the Stock Exchange where he lost his remaining fortune in Spanish bonds. My great-grandfather and grandfather were both clerks in what became the Westminster Bank. Britain in the nineteenth century was more hospitable to immigrants and refugees than it became under the eighteen-year period of the Conservative administration which ended in 1997.

Apparently originating in Constantinople around the end of the first millennium, the Cortazzi family subsequently migrated to Crete in the twelfth century. Two Cortazzi brothers are said to have led a revolt in 1212 against the Venetians who had bought the island from the Byzantine Empire. The Cortazzis, however, seem to have remained as landowners in Crete during the Venetian rule of the island and only moved to Venice in the late seventeenth century after Crete fell to the Turks.

My father, (Frederick Edward) Mervyn Cortazzi, was born in Croydon in 1888. He was the only son of my grandfather, Edward Cortazzi, who was born in 1864. Edward Cortazzi had two brothers, Harry and Arthur, and four sisters, three of whom lived with my great-uncle Harry in a large house at Sanderstead. We used to visit my great-aunts regularly but I only have limited memories of them. They were Lena, Olga and Beatrice, all of whom lived out their lives as spinsters. They were kind to us as children and I remember their generosity when at Christmas-time I used to receive a postal order for what was then the very princely sum of 12/6. Lena had a gammy leg. Beatrice clearly had been beautiful as a young woman. Olga was always rather a sad figure. I should like to have known the private stories of these ladies living with their bachelor brother in a truly Victorian environment and way of life. It is a fact, for example, that they had an old samovar which they had inherited perhaps from their grandfather who might have bought it in Odessa in the early part of the nineteenth century.

My great-uncle Harry, who worked in the city, seemed happy enough to devote himself to providing a home for his sisters. He was kind to children, but remote and set in his ways. My great-uncle Arthur remains a shadowy figure. All I can remember of him, apart from the fact that he had only one lung and was always in poor health, was an occasion when I was four or five and he invited the family to Croydon Airport. My mother and elder brother were treated to a brief flight in a biplane for, I think, the sum of 5/-. I cried bitterly because I was thought too young to go in an aeroplane. My mother, who did not enjoy the experience, never flew again as far as I am aware. Even in the 1930s aeroplanes were rare and when at dame school we heard an aircraft engine droning above we would rush to the window to look at this strange bird.

My father had four sisters all of whom were strong characters. Before the First World War his eldest sister Trixie married Jan Roosenschoon an English language teacher in Holland, who used to visit us in Sedbergh almost every year in the 1930s to fish for trout in the local brooks and rivers. My first visit abroad, probably when I was about five years old, was to Holland to visit Jan and Trixie in Amsterdam. I was fascinated by the railway crossings where the gates rose in the air rather than opening outwards as was the case in England before the war. They both suffered badly during the Second World War and the Nazi occupation of Holland. Jan died shortly after the end of the war but Trixie lived into her nineties.

My father, who went to Wallington Grammar School near Croydon, managed to get to Cambridge (from, I think, 1910-1913). He studied French and German at Queens' College. He enjoyed his time there and only got Third Class Honours. He was not greatly ambitious and having a natural bent for teaching sought a job as a master at a public school. He was employed first at Framlingham and then in 1920 was appointed a master at Sedbergh. During the First World War he served in the Royal Scots, first in Scotland and later in France where he suffered in one of the German gas attacks in 1917. He was not incapacitated for long but the damage suffered by his lungs combined with heavy smoking probably exacerbated the emphysema which he suffered in old age.

He was a good language teacher, but at Sedbergh he and Neville Gorton, later Bishop of Coventry, were put in charge of a new sixth form called 'Clio' where, in addition to history taught by Gorton, the boys studied elementary economics and politics under my father's guidance. My father was not an expert in either subject but he read widely and had broad and liberal interests which enabled him to bring out the intellectual qualities of his pupils – many of them going on to Oxford and Cambridge, often with scholarships or exhibitions. Among his ex-pupils were members of the Indian Civil Service, including Philip Mason, who became Joint secretary for Defence to the Indian Government towards the end of the war, later headed the Race Relations Commission and wrote extensively about India. Others became home civil servants, lawyers and businessmen.

My father suffered the great disappointment of not being made a housemaster. His teaching abilities and his understanding of young men would have served him well in such a role, but while competent at games he did not disguise his dislike of the over-emphasis on sport at the school (its motto was 'Dura Virum Nutrix' i.e. 'Hard Nurse of Men'). His political views were also probably too liberal for the average north-of-England parent. Moreover, he had not himself been to a public school and my mother's family had been in 'trade'.

My mother, Madge Miller, was born in 1893, also in Croydon. Her father owned a small department store in Croydon which disappeared before the Second World War. I can only remember visiting the store once. I enjoyed myself in the toy department, but I understand that after my mother's father died it had gone from bad to worse. I do not know when she and my father first met, but it must have been in Croydon before the First World War. They married in August 1920 when my father was appointed to Sedbergh. There had been some opposition to the marriage in my father's family on the grounds that my mother's family were shopkeepers whereas the Cortazzi family were allegedly of higher class, my grandfather being a bank clerk. Today, such snobbery hardly seems credible, but I have no reason to doubt what I was told.

My elder brother, Theodore, was born in Sedbergh in 1921. I was the second child. My mother wanted more children, but she was disappointed and in the mid 1930s she had to have a hysterectomy and thereafter suffered a great deal from hot flushes and other problems of the menopause. She was a very loving mother and immensely kind to all with whom she came in contact. I never knew my mother's father who was reputed to have drunk more than he should have done, but we saw much of my grandmother who after the death of my mother's father married a Mr Manton, a button manufacturer on a small scale from Birmingham. I never met him, either, but we used to visit and stay regularly with granny Manton who had a house on a park at Moseley outside Birmingham. My mother's brother, Philip, became a clergyman. Her younger sister, Betty, married a rubber planter in Malaya. He was captured by the Japanese in 1941 and sent to work on the Burma-Siam railway. Like so many other Japanese prisoners of war he was cruelly treated by his Japanese captors. He was repatriated to Britain at the end of the war, but died while still in his fifties.

SEDBERGH

Sedbergh school in those days was narrow-minded and snobbish. The snobbery was absurd considering that most of the school's pupils were from northern manufacturing families. The school, like so many public schools, had been established in the early sixteenth century for the education of local boys. It still took a few 'day-boys' from the area, but 'day-boys' were definitely second class citizens as far as the school was concerned and were often treated with contempt by the boarders who lived in houses with 50-60 pupils in conditions which were at best spartan.

In the years between the two world wars the educational hierarchy and the snobbery which went with it was such that many jobs were available only to those who had been at the right schools. University meant Oxford or Cambridge to most people, and before the war all the masters at Sedbergh were graduates of one or the other. The London School of Economics implied socialism and the rest of the universities were regarded with some contempt by those who did not know them. It seems strange to me that my father never contemplated teaching in a state school or a grammar school, but this was a reflection of the time and of the probably slightly higher salaries paid to masters at public schools than to teachers in secondary schools. (The term 'master' was used by public schools while those who taught in government schools were mere 'teachers'!).

The school dominated the village. Most of the school buildings dated from the late Victorian era to the early years of the twentieth century. The only building of any age was the old school which had been turned into the school library. It was here that my father's sixth-form 'Clio' met. One of his duties was to act as librarian for the school and, as a result, the library was well provided with books on history and contemporary affairs. I found a great deal of interest in the library where I spent as much time as I could. Browsing and helping with library chores enabled me to read fairly widely in both history and English literature.

The village of Sedbergh stood near the junctions of the Lune and the Rawthey rivers. It was surrounded by bleak fells and dominated in particular by Winder, a fell (hill) of some 1200 feet, up which boys at the school were expected to run in some 20 minutes. Farming was fairly primitive. There were a few cattle and some ploughed fields, but in the main this was sheep-farming country. The winters as I remember them were long, cold and wet and I saw no joy in running or walking on the fells in such conditions.

The main street contained the usual number of pubs including the White Hart and the Bull which considered themselves a cut above the rest. There was an uninspiring selection of shops including a couple of grocers, greengrocers, and butchers, one stationer/bookshop, a shoe shop and a chemist. There were a few gas lamps and I can still remember the gas lighter doing his rounds as the evening set in. Milk in the late 1920s and early 1930s was brought to our houses in pails and delivered by a horse-drawn milk cart.

There were two doctors in addition to the school doctor. They generally made up themselves the medicines which they prescribed. There was no universal health service and the local doctors often gave their services free to patients who could not afford their fees. Hospital facilities in the neighbourhood were limited. When at the age of four I had an abcess in the middle ear I was taken by car to hospital in Manchester some 80 miles away, and it is perhaps not surprising that I caught bronchial pneumonia and was lucky to survive in those days before there were any antibiotics. My mother's hysterectomy was also performed in Manchester. Manchester still recalls to me those hospital times. There were occasional cases of mastoiditis as well as meningitis at school, and as a result, some boys died or became deaf. There was much concern about tuberculosis and polio, but few precautions were taken.

There was no dentist practising in Sedbergh before the war, so we had no choice but to travel some distance to find one – either in Kendal, or even on some occasions in Windermere (19 miles away). I hated going to the dentist. The old-fashioned mechanical drill could be very painful and there were no pain-killing injections available for children in those days.

Sedbergh before the war had a railway station one mile from the village. To get to Sedbergh by rail it was necessary to change at Tebay or Lowgill on the main line from Euston to Carlisle. The line was one of the many which were abolished in the Beeching years of the 1960s.

Towards the end of the 1930s a small cinema was established in Sedbergh near the gas works. Before that we used occasionally to go to the cinema in Kendal, ten miles away over the hills. On special occasions we might go as far as Lancaster if it was a particularly good film. I can just remember silent films. We were of course excited by the first colour films. I think that the first film I saw in colour was the final section of a costume drama about the Rothschilds. Newsreels helped us to learn a little about the world outside England and were for us an important part of any cinema visit. When war broke out in September 1939 London's Old Vic Theatre and Sadlers Wells Opera came to Kendal on visits but in the years before the war the only plays or pantomimes we saw were when we were taken to see a performance during our periodic visits to relations near London or in Birmingham.

The wireless was important for keeping in touch with events especially during the war. My father read the *Manchester Guardian* every day and the *New Statesman* and the *Spectator* at the weekend.

On Sundays we had the *Observer*. I began reading newspaper articles when I was about 12 and inevitably took an increasing interest in events as Britain prepared for war. Events such as the death of King George V and the abdication of King Edward VIII were followed with great interest by all of us. My father as a liberal was much concerned by what he heard of the Nazis in Germany and the Fascists in Italy and I remember a row at school when a right-wing minor politician (Kenneth de Courcy) gave a lecture to the sixth forms and received a frosty reception from boys who had learnt to think for themselves and question authoritarian pro-Fascist sentiment. The Munich Agreement was initially welcomed with relief, but my father realized that war was becoming unavoidable.

We lived for a time in a three-storey semi-detached house and later in a two-storey detached house near the village. Neither had central heating, which was the normal situation in those days, and both had only one bathroom. We only had a refrigerator shortly before the Second World War, and that was quite special. But we usually had a maid or a char (home-help) and we had a telephone. Our telephone number was Sedbergh 66. All calls had to be made via the exchange and to call the exchange, after unhooking the receiver, you had to wind a knob which rang a bell at the exchange. Trunk-calls to Birmingham or London were expensive and had to be booked in advance if you did not want an often interminable delay.

Not all the masters at Sedbergh in those days had cars and there was not much motor traffic in the village. As my mother had inherited a small amount of money on the death of her father, my mother and father were, however, able to own a motor car. The first one I remember was a very upright model. It had a new signalling device which consisted of a model hand which could be manipulated from the inside. Cars did not of course have either heaters or radios in those days and driving was slow and tedious especially for young children. To change gear it was necessary to double declutch. I recall being much impressed by a friend's father's car which with its fluid fly-wheel was the precursor of the automatic cars. Neville Gorton who owned an old open car was reputed to have had to drive in reverse gear to get up one of the nearby slopes. Like many other clergymen of my acquaintance he was otherwise a fast and dangerous driver.

The car was a boon for holidays as we usually visited my mother's mother in Birmingham and then my father's father in Redhill whence he had moved from Croydon when he retired from the Westminster Bank. In those days it took all day to drive from Sedbergh to Birmingham although the distance was only 160 miles. We drove via Lancaster, Preston, Wigan, Warrington and Wolverhampton through much of the 'Black Country'. This was a depressing drive at any time, but especially in the days of the Great Depression when we would see the unemployed vainly waiting for non-existent jobs or for the pubs to open. Once, I think in 1937, my father took the car to France and we drove as far as Annecy but unfortunately I was very sick there with food poisoning.

Although the country round Sedbergh is hilly and there were few flat roads, the limited amount of traffic made bicycling fairly safe and I used my bicycle a good deal for exercise and enjoyment. After war broke out the bicycle became essential.

SCHOOL

I cannot remember much about my first dame school to which I went at the age of four. Apparently, I quickly learnt to read and took pleasure in demonstrating my ability reading out signs as we passed in the car. At the age of six I was sent to a local prep-school in Sedbergh run by a Mr Gladstone, descendant of the great Victorian Prime Minister. My brother had gone there and I suppose my parents thought that this would help me to settle down. In fact I was so miserable and home-sick that I became ill and had to be taken away. I then went to another dame school run by a Miss Tetley. She was a good teacher, strict but also kind. I can still remember the problems I had with spelling. Why should 'with' be spelt without an 'h' after the 'w' while 'which' had one! In order to memorize such spellings I had to make cards and stick them up in my bedroom.

At the age of nine I was sent to Cressbrook, another private prep-school at Kirkby Lonsdale some 10 miles away. I was a little less unhappy here although in my first term I got whooping cough and all boys with the disease were segregated in a house temporarily acquired for the purpose. I shall not forget one horrible boy who tried to force the smaller boys to burn their bottoms on the paraffin stove which was the only means of heating our temporary dormitory that winter.

When I came home for the Christmas holiday I seemed slow and run down. Eventually, after X-Rays at the General Hospital in Lancaster some 26 miles away, tubercular glands in the lower abdomen were diagnosed as a result of drinking tuberculin-infected milk. The cure in those days was rest in bed for six months or more and quantities of grade A tuberculin-tested milk. I was away from school for two terms. It was tough on my parents and boring for me to remain in bed for six months especially as I did not feel particularly ill. I learnt innumerable games of patience and devoured all the boys magazines my mother could buy. These included *Hotspur*, *The Magnet* and *The Gem*. The stories were popular and of no literary value but they helped to widen my horizon and develop my reading ability. My father and mother also read a great deal to me. I recall particularly my enjoyment of *The Three Musketeers* and *The Count of Monte Cristo* by Dumas.

When I returned to Cressbrook I was inevitably fat as a result of months of rest in bed and feeding with Grade A milk. Not surprisingly, I was no good at games, but I began to make quite fast progress in class. I was not as miserable as I had been, but I remember once being dragged along the floor on my bottom into which some largish splinters of wood became imbedded. I was too ashamed to confess what had happened and it was only after I got home at the end of term and my mother found the festering wound which the doctor had to cauterize that I told what had happened. The teachers were all unqualified except for the owner/headmaster, F.N. Dowson, but they were adequate for teaching elementary subjects.

I am not sure why my parents decided to take me away from Cressbrook and to enter me for Sedbergh as a day boy, but it may well have been to save money on boarding fees. In the summer term of 1936 I was the youngest boy at Sedbergh school, being just 12 years old. It was not helpful to be the son of a master, especially as I was still fat and no good at games. I did not enjoy my time at Sedbergh. Most of the teaching was old-fashioned, and science (the so-called 'Modern Side') was generally regarded as being appropriate for the less intellectually gifted. The Classical Sixth form was the top form of the school, with the Modern Language Sixth and 'Clio' coming very definitely in second place. When J.H. Bruce Lockhart took over as headmaster in late 1936 he put more emphasis on modern languages as he was a gifted teacher of French. He also did his best to encourage music at the school, but he was a rugby enthusiast and a firm believer in the dictum *'mens sana in corpore sano'*. So Sedbergh continued to be primarily a place where the hearty flourished and the intellectual was looked down upon.

Attempts were made to force me to play games and to make me enter Sedgwick House as a boarder. I resisted these efforts vigorously. My parents, who were not well off, were reluctant to have to meet the cost of boarding fees which at that time amounted to between £120 and £150 a year. At best, my father's salary was, I think, £650 a year. My elder brother was a boarder and was due to go to Oxford in the autumn of 1939, having been awarded a music scholarship at Keble College. My parents would have to give him an allowance out of their very limited income. So they, too, resisted these pressures, but I became increasingly ostracized by my fellows.

My great enjoyment was reading. I spent all my pocket-money on books and especially enjoyed the great classical novelists of the nineteenth century. Indeed, I was so fascinated by Dickens that I became for a time a subscriber to the *The Dickensian* magazine. Before the war, Nelson Classics were 1/6d a volume and were 6d cheaper than the Everyman and World Classics series at 2/- each, but Nelsons did not have as wide a selection as the others. So, sometimes I bought books in other series. Then in 1939 the first Penguins appeared at 6d each. Sadly, only too soon as a result of inflation and war, prices began to rise quickly.

Apart from the holidays which I have mentioned in France

and in Holland, we went twice to Switzerland on package holidays organized by Thos. Cook and Sons. These took us to lakes Lucerne and Lugano, and on a later occasion to Lake Thun. From Lugano I remember that we went on a day trip to Milan where I doubtless saw Italian fascists but all I can recall is a little steam train and Italian peasants smelling of garlic. It was exciting to cross the Channel and have a continental breakfast on the station at Basle. Although I had crossed the Channel about four times before the war my knowledge of Europe was generally limited to what I had read in books and journals and my horizon was a narrow one. My parents were much more broad-minded than many of their contemporaries in Sedbergh but it was difficult in a place like Sedbergh to escape from insular prejudices. They were both practising Anglicans and I was brought up in the Anglican faith. I was duly confirmed and accepted willingly the practices of the Anglican Church during my school days, although I found the Christianity taught in the school chapel increasingly unconvincing.

☐

In 1939, the situation looked so threatening that no plans were made for a holiday abroad. Instead, we went that August to Bude in Cornwall. We had to hurry home as my father had joined the Royal Observer Corps as an auxiliary and he was expected to be on duty at his post in Sedbergh. I remember taking him a thermos of tea and sandwiches on the morning of 3 September and hearing Mr Chamberlain announce that we were at war with Germany. Nobody knew quite what to expect. We had been issued with gas masks and for a few days we tried to remember to take them around with us. Children from northern towns which seemed likely to be German bombing targets were evacuated to Sedbergh and other country districts and there were the usual stories about bad behaviour, dirt and home sickness. But the evacuees soon returned home and the winter of 1939/40 passed without local incident. The phony war had little effect on us.

I had taken my school certificate in the summer of 1939 and

was now preparing to take my Higher Certificate in 1941. I decided to specialize in French and German, having an apparent facility for languages. A German refugee, Dr Steinberg, came to Sedbergh as a temporary teacher in 1940. He was a great deal more knowledgeable than our usual teachers. A Mr Gairdner was my main teacher of French. He was a great enthusiast for Corneille. He was not a bad teacher, but his attitude to me was not encouraging. I remember him saying in the early part of 1941 that I was useless and would never make the grade.

After the withdrawal from Dunkirk in 1940, life became increasingly restricted. The car was given up and we had to rely on our feet or on bicycles. I was a member of the OTC (Officer Training Corps) at school and joined the Home Guard. Pill boxes were established at strategic points throughout the country. All sign posts were taken down and local maps were no longer available for sale. The black-out was even more strenuously enforced. But the only aircraft which came near Sedbergh were those that had lost their way. My father and I, who sometimes stood in for him at the Royal Observer Corps Post in Sedbergh, however, studied aircraft recognition to help us identify enemy aircraft.

In the winter of 1940/41, my father's father and my mother's father came to live with us in order to escape the bombing raids; we soon had a full house of relatives and other evacuees. Indeed, our house was always full until near the end of the war. This put a great strain on my mother who was not in the best of health, and on our resources generally, although living in the country as we did we escaped some of the worst of the food-rationing.

My brother, unfortunately, failed his exams at Oxford, having neglected his studies as he became involved in Roman Catholicism under the influence of the Dominicans. In 1941, he was called up and eventually became a Lieutenant in the Royal Artillery. He had wanted to become a monk but gave this idea up when he met his cousin Dina (granddaughter of great-uncle Arthur). They were married quickly and had two children shortly after the war, but the marriage did not last. Theodore in due course went out to Costa Rica as a tutor, remarried twice and had a further five children. He died in 1998.

In 1941 J.H.Bruce Lockhart, realizing that I was a misfit at Sedbergh, encouraged me not to stay on at school hoping for a place at Oxford or Cambridge but to try for St Andrews University in Scotland, where I could go at the age of 17. In due course, I went up to St Andrews to take the examination. This meant changing trains at Lowgill and again at Carlisle where I waited for a train to Edinburgh. Here it was necessary to change stations. The final change was at Leuchars junction for St Andrews. The journey took a full day but was at least a change from the restricted life of Sedbergh in wartime. I was attracted by what I saw of St Andrews and impressed by the students in their red gowns. No-one, least of all myself, expected that I would win more than a place. I was astounded and delighted, therefore, when a telegram arrived informing me that I had been awarded a Harkness scholarship to study modern languages (French and German).

I managed to get in five terms at St Andrews (enough for a war degree) combining French and German with Geography and Economics. I certainly enjoyed my brief time there. I had a study-bedroom to myself in St Salvator's Hall. I felt liberated from the narrow-minded atmosphere of Sedbergh, but I was innocent and shy. Fortunately, I was able quite quickly to make a number of close friends. They were from all sorts of different backgrounds. I soon found that in Scotland some of the brightest had been at high schools rather than public schools. Indeed, it seemed that boarding public schools were not only the exception in Scotland but also rather looked down upon by those who had been at such good day schools as the Edinburgh and Glasgow Academies or George Watson's in Edinburgh.

We spent many evenings discussing into the small hours every aspect of life and culture. We drank China tea and huddled over the small coal fires which were the only means of heating our study-bedrooms. I used to hoard the small quantities of coal provided, wrapping up the pieces in brown paper parcels and storing them in the cupboard until it was my turn to provide a place for our talks. The fires were not easy to start and we had to devise ways of getting the fires to draw, for example, by holding up sheets of paper. Once I left a drawer up against the fire in an attempt to get it to burn. Without thinking, I slipped out to the loo and was horrified on my return to find that the drawer was ablaze. Fortunately, I was able to extinguish the fire and disguise the damage I had done.

I joined the Amateur Dramatic Society and enjoyed trying to act. I was never any good and my 'rector', T.M.Knox, the Professor of Moral Philosophy, who was a porky conservative Hegelian scholar, read me a lesson on not wasting my time on such frivolous activities. Professor Knox, who later became Principal of the University was rather intimidating and I dreaded having to visit him. He meant well and I am sure his advice was usually sound, but I do not think he helped me to overcome my shyness.

We worked hard, cramming the best part of three years work into five terms. We also had to spend a day-and-a-half a week in military training. Food was scarce and we made up when we could afford it by buying packets of chips for 4d. We had little money. In addition to my scholarship of £100 a year I had a grant from Sedbergh of £25 a year. This had to cover university fees, board and lodging as well as books. I used to buy cheap second-hand books at a second-hand shop run by a Mr Small. My small library grew quite quickly as I was able to buy second-hand classics for a few pence. I have always found it difficult to pass a bookshop without going in and I rarely come out without one or more books.

While at St Andrews I tried hard to improve my physical fitness and served conscientiously in the University OTC (Officer Training Corps), in particular, in the signals section. But I could not pass the physical tests required for entry to officers' training and realized that I would not be of much use in the army.

☐

I cannot recall anyone telling me anything much about the world outside Europe at school although through reading Kipling I became interested in India and I learnt a little about the Far East from former pupils of my father when they visited him at Sedbergh. I also realized the growing threats of war in Asia from reading the newspapers. I regretted the almost total emphasis at school on English and European history and wanted to know more about other countries.

I suppose that I began to think in my early teens what I should do when I grew up. I was first attracted by the idea of joining the Indian Civil Service, but it was already clear that the British Raj was approaching its end and I soon realized that even if I could pass the stiff examinations there would probably be no long-term future in that service. Then early in the war Anthony Eden, as Foreign Secretary, announced that after the war the Diplomatic Service would be reformed enabling men without private means to become British diplomats. I decided that I wanted to join the diplomatic service when I had graduated from university. I never wavered from this ambition.

I had learnt practically nothing about Japan at school or university. Inevitably, we heard about Japanese aggression in China and I recall seeing film shots of the Nomonhan incident in 1939 involving Japanese and Soviet troops, but I had no inkling in my school days that Japan would feature so fully in my life as an adult. Two events set me thinking about Japan and about studying Japanese. One of these was a talk given to the combined societies of the university in, I think, January 1942 shortly after the sinking of the *Prince of Wales* and the *Repulse*, but before the fall of Singapore to the Japanese. The talk was given by Professor Sir D'Arcy Wentworth Thompson, a famous scholar who was still Professor of Zoology although he was then over 80. In addition to being a biologist of world renown and a Fellow of the Royal Society, he was an outstanding mathematician and classical scholar. Rumour had it that when some fifty years earlier the chairs of Greek, Mathematics and Zoology had fallen vacant in the university he had applied for all three and could have filled any one of them. D'Arcy, who was a commanding figure with a flowing white beard and encyclopaedic knowledge, described a visit which he had made to Japan towards the end of the nineteenth century and spoke in particular of his impressions of Japanese gardens. It took some courage at that time in the war to speak in such civilized terms about aspects of our Japanese enemy. I feel sure that D'Arcy, who spoke movingly and mellifluously, was trying to make us realize that Japan, despite what the Japanese Imperial Forces were doing, had a valuable civilization from which we too could learn and which in the battles ahead we should not forget.

The second event was the announcement about scholarships for young men with linguistic ability to come forward to study difficult languages including Japanese. I considered applying for one of these scholarships but the Principal of the university, Sir James Irvine, dissuaded me. He urged me to stay on at the university as long as I could so that I could at least get a war degree. He thought rightly that there would be other opportunities for me to study a difficult language.

Over the winter of 1942/3 I learnt that the the Royal Air Force was indeeed looking for volunteers to study Japanese. Accordingly shortly before my nineteenth birthday and before I was called up compulsorily for the forces I volunteered to join the RAF. I was duly accepted and in May 1943 I began my initial training as an aircraftsman (general duties) second class. I was first sent to an initial training camp at Arbroath, which was by no means easy, but it helped me to get to know all sorts of people from different walks of life. I was not impressed by the absurdities of spit-and-polish discipline; nor did I care for the barbarities of bayonet practice, but this period of training was quite soon over even if at the time it seemed endless.

During this time, I was asked to speak to the local Rotary Club. As the Wing Commander in charge of the initial training unit was a member of the club I suppose he must have put my name forward having noted that I had been studying at St Andrews University. I had spoken occasionally in debates but this was my first 'public speaking' experience. I spoke to the Rotary Club on some aspects of Germany. It seemed to go down well as I was asked to speak again. This time I chose to speak on 'Forgotten Scotsmen; James Boswell and Tobias Smollett'. This did not go down at all well. Boswell and Smollett were not popular in puritanical Arbroath. Moreover, the Scots do not like to think that any of their great men could conceivably be 'forgotten'.

From Arboath I was sent to a transit camp near Rugby to await orders. The weeks I spent there were frustrating as, of course, we were not told anything about what was in store for us. However, in September 1943, I received my posting to Air Ministry Unit which was housed in flats in Hallam St., London W.1, which had been converted into barracks. My study of the Japanese language was now about to begin.

STUDYING JAPANESE

At this stage in the war courses in Japanese at the School of Oriental and African Studies (SOAS), off Malet Street and behind the main University of London buildings, were of three kinds. The shortest course of six months was for servicemen who were to be used in helping to decipher Japanese cables and would either be employed at the Government Communications centre at Bletchley, Hertfordshire, or in India. The other two courses were for interrogators and translators, each course lasting approximately one year.

I was instructed to join the SOAS interrogator's course, presumably because I had been studying modern languages and had obtained some limited ability in spoken French and German. There were students from all three services at the school. However, partly because the required vocabulary varied between the services, we were often segregated into different groups. Our main class, which included men from all three services, consisted of some 8-12 pupils. We spent some six to eight hours every day, except for Saturdays and Sundays, at the school. Some teaching was done each day in class, where periodic tests were held to check on our progress, but we also had many one-to-one sessions to practise the spoken language and learn to repeat phrases which had been recorded on gramophone records (the old 78 rpm type, of course).

We began by studying McGovern's *Elementary Japanese Grammar*. This was one of the very few text books available at the time. It was out of date and not a good introduction to Japanese, but the school had to make do with what they had got. As we were to be interrogators all the teaching at this stage was in the roman script. As soon as possible we were introduced to romanized texts prepared by staff at the School. I can still remember one text designed. I suppose, to show how in conversation phrases can be elided. This included a conversation between two Japanese serving with Japanese forces in South China. One soldier tells another that his piles (haemorrhoids) etc had disappeared after he came there (*'ji no warui no nanka kesh'tond'yatta yo'*).

The texts used on the gramophone records, which we had to repeat after hearing each phrase, began with simple questions and answers, such 'are you going out?' (*'Anata demasu ka*) with the reply 'Yes I am going out' (*Hai, demasu*). It seems strange now that we should have been taught to use the word *'anata'* for 'you' in this way as in practice in Japan the word *'anata'* meaning 'you' is avoided. Even *'hai'* for 'yes' is marginally misleading. Perhaps as these words were in McGovern's grammar that is why we learnt them in this way. Or was this a throw-back to the late nineteenth century when foreigners used to say *'O-hayoo, anata'* meaning 'Good morning to you'?

The Japanese teaching staff came under the general supervision of Professor Eve Edwards, the Professor of Chinese, a somewhat formidable blue-stocking but a kindly figure. They were headed by Frank Daniels, Reader in Japanese at SOAS, and by Major General Piggott, a former military attaché in Japan and already something of a legend because of his pro-Japanese tendencies.

Frank Daniels had been in the naval attaché's office in Tokyo and had then become a teacher of English at Otaru in Hokkaido. He had married a Japanese lady, Otome, who was also brought in as one of our teachers. She was rather shy, but having no children of her own took a great deal of care of those of us who showed any interest in things Japanese. She wrote beautifully in Japanese long hand and was working on a dictionary of *'sosho'* ('grass' script). This was produced and printed in rough form in 1944. It was a boon to those of us who were faced with trying to decipher Japanese hand-written texts.

Other teachers included serving officers, who had acquired

some knowledge of Japanese, such as Squadron Leader Lomax, and former missionaries, such as Canon France. There were also as the year progressed some exceptionally gifted students who had been on the first course for civilian students under the government scholarship scheme. One of these was Ron Dore. But the most valuable teachers were Japanese nationals who had been released for this purpose from internment on the Isle of Man. They were headed by Yanada, who had graduated in Economics from Tokyo University, and by Matsukawa, a charming and cultured man who was getting on in years. Both of them had English wives and had settled in Britain. There were also a couple of former Japanese businessmen from the world of shipping called Takaira and Shimizu. Finally, there were some Canadian *nisei* who had the rank of sergeant in the Canadian army and who took us for individual conversation practice. I remember a Sergeant Yamaguchi and a Sergeant Yamamoto. (We none of us cared for Sergeant Yamamoto who, we thought, sneered at us in an arrogant way; I met him again many years after the war working for the Japanese Embassy's consular section.) The arrangements at SOAS and the personalities have been described in some detail by Sadao Oba in his book translated into English as *The Japanese War* (Japan Library, 1995).

It was essential if we were to make progress in the spoken language that we should have maximum practice. The amount of time which we could have with individual teachers was inevitably limited. So an RAF friend, Stuart Gibb, and I used to try out our spoken Japanese with one another in public places, for instance making comments in Japanese on fellow passengers in buses and on the underground. Fortunately, in war-time London many foreign languages could be heard and no-one understood what we were saying.

It was soon apparent to me that we could not hope to master the spoken language and become competent interrogators let alone interpreters if we did not learn something of the written language. There were far too many Japanese compounds with the same sounds. We needed to know the Chinese characters used in such compounds if we were to make sense of romanized texts. It also became clear that without a knowledge of the written language we should be lost in conversations on technical or complicated subjects. We accordingly pressed for the inclusion of the teaching of characters into our course. Our views coincided with those in authority in the school although not with the service authorities. At first, we had to try to teach ourselves the syllabaries and simple characters. I remember taking a Japanese primary school reader (*tokuhon*) home to study over the Christmas period in 1943. I was much puzzled by long texts in the Japanese syllabaries because there was no indication where words began and ended. In order to memorize characters we produced our own character cards with the character on one side and the reading(s) on the other.

In early 1944 our plea for the inclusion of a study of the written language in our course was accepted and we became the first joint course in spoken and written Japanese. To cope with the extension of our syllabus, the length of our course was extended from twelve to fifteen months. Accordingly, we began to receive lessons in the written as well as the spoken language, but it was made clear to us that in our case the written language was to be subsidiary to our studies of the spoken language and that we were still destined to become interrogators rather than translators. By the autumn of 1944 the numbers studying Japanese had expanded so much that the premises at SOAS were no longer adequate and some now moved into temporary premises in old houses in Sussex Square which had escaped earlier bombing raids.

I became fascinated by the written language and determined to master as much of it as I could, but I soon realized that to understand Japanese properly I needed to have at least a basic knowledge of Japanese history and culture. So I bought a few books about Japan and read as much as I could in the limited time available. Fortunately, we had occasional lectures from outsiders on aspects of Japan. One lecture which I shall never forget was by John Pilcher, a member of the Japanese consular service working with the Ministry of Information in London. He told us about his experiences in Japan before the war when he had studied the language in Kyoto. He gave us one of his superb imitations of a kabuki actor.

The RAF was the only one of the three services which refused to permit their language students to stay in digs and kept us in barracks. Our quarters in converted luxury flats in Hallam street were far from luxurious. I shared a room with five others. We slept in double-decker bunks and the only furniture consisted of a wooden table and four very uncomfortable upright wooden chairs. We had to get up at reveille, strip our beds, pile up the 'biscuits' (hard sections of mattress) and clean the room for inspection. We took our mess tins to breakfast and attended a morning parade. Sergeant Fletcher, who was in charge of us, clearly regarded us as a 'shower' – a bunch of hopeless cases – and did not understand the difficulties we faced trying to study Japanese in these circumstances. He accordingly did his best to make life extremely tiresome. After parade, we made our way across to SOAS, returning for our midday meal in the mess and also for the evening high tea. There was a great deal of homework to be done in order to ensure that we passed the frequent tests which were held at the school. If we did not pass we would soon be RTU (returned to unit). The only alternative to studying in our room was to go to the NAAFI canteen, but this tended to be noisy and smoky.

Occasionally, we had Saturday parades and even some church parades on Sundays when we would be marched to a nearby church. It was sometimes possible to get a weekend pass. This enabled me to visit one of my father's three sisters who lived in Redhill and Reigate. We had home leaves at Christmas, Easter and in the summer, and were given travel vouchers to enable us to get home by rail. In those days, servicemen had to wear uniform at all times and were liable to be stopped by the military police who would demand to see one's pass and identity card. If you were AWOL (absent without leave) you could be arrested.

As aircraftsmen 2nd class general duties (known as AC2GD) we received at the weekly pay parades every Friday the sum of 21 shillings which was the lowest weekly pay of anyone in the services. At pay parades, when your name was called, you had to shout out the last three figures of your service number (in my case double six eight), go up to the desk, salute smartly and take your money. Our pay had to cover things like toilet items, refreshments and supplementary food in the NAAFI (at this time I did not drink beer or spirits), as well as travel in London. It left us with little money for amusements, but seats in the gallery at London theatres in those days were cheap and many theatres gave concessions to serving men and women in uniform. Whenever I could I would go with a friend to see some of the fine productions staged at London theatres in the period 1943/44. We saw performances by Gielgud, Olivier and Donald Wolfit. I particularly admired Gielgud as Hamlet and Wolfit as King Lear. We also managed to get to a number of classical concerts at the Albert Hall. Despite the war, bombings and the black-out London was still culturally very much alive, but there was a shortage of food and we simply could not afford to go to such restaurants that were endeavouring to carry on.

We did not escape all the dangers and discomforts of war, however, and had to take our turns as fire-watchers doing duty on the roof in case there were any fire-bomb raids. If we were not on this duty we were expected, whenever the air-raid siren sounded, to move down to the air-raid shelters in the basement. This often meant at best disturbed nights. The winter of 1943/44 was relatively peaceful, but in the spring and summer of 1944 London was the target of a series of attacks by flying bombs, the so-called V1s. The flying bombs seemed at first, at least, to have no difficulty in evading London's defences which consisted of fighter aircraft stationed in Kent, anti-aircraft guns and barrage ballooons which were clustered round the south eastern part of London. There were an increasing number of casualties from these bombs and damage was extensive. Whenever we heard the drone of the flying bombs we listened apprehensively for the time when the engine cut out and wondered where the bomb was going to fall. If you were on fire-watch duty you could do nothing but pray for those who might be hit by the bomb.

Our studies increasingly suffered as a result of these disturbances and for a time in the summer of 1944 we were allowed to go into digs. But the disadvantage soon outweighed the advantages. An RAF friend and I were placed in digs in Cricklewood and in order to get to SOAS we first had to take a bus and then the underground from Finchley Road to Euston Square. The underground was frequently disrupted and this would make us late for classes. Moreover, our landladies, who disliked having anyone billeted on them, were far from friendly. I remember one Welsh landlady by the name of Evans who was reluctant to let us have baths and who, I thought, did not allow us our fair share of the rations to which we were enitled from the ration books which we handed over to her.

From the autumn of 1944 London also became the target of the V2 rockets. These were in some ways even more frightening as you had no warning of when and where they might strike. One V2 fell in the middle of Tottenham Court Road as we were returning from SOAS for lunch at the Hallam Street barracks. I had managed to reach the corner of Fitzroy Square when the bomb burst. I threw myself on the ground and was sufficiently far away from the bomb to escape injury. But two other RAF students were less lucky and were killed.

At the end of 1944 we had completed our 15 months' study and were apparently regarded as sufficiently competent to go on active service. The war against Japan in the Far East was becoming more intense and we were said to be needed urgently in South East Asia. I cannot recall being issued with any kind of certificate of proficiency, but something must have been inserted on our records, because in January 1945 I and other RAF students who had completed the course with me were promoted to the rank of acting Sergeant and received our orders to proceed to South East Asia. We thought that we had been posted to Headquarters South East Asia Command in Colombo. A few of us, including myself, after a brief embarkation leave at home, were told to report in late January to RAF Lyneham in Wiltshire to board an aircraft bound for Colombo.

INDIA: 1945

After a delay of 24 hours I and two other RAF Sergeant interpreters, as we were termed, were given seats on an RAF York air-craft (a converted Lancaster bomber) bound for Colombo. We were by far the most junior people among the 20 or so passen-gers. Our flight took us over France well to the south of the fight-ing. This was the first time I had ever flown and also the first time I had been abroad since before the war. Our first stop was at Mal-ta where we spent a night in transit quarters, but managed to make a quick visit in the dark to Valetta which had suffered so much in the war-time siege of the island. The next day we flew to Cairo where again we were able to hitch a lift into the city for a few hours. After the London black-out and the shortages of con-sumer goods Cairo seemed a different world. It was also a cultur-al shock to come in contact for the first time with a Middle Eastern bazaar. We flew out of Cairo at midnight and I was as-tounded by the sight of the city still fully lit up.

Our next stop was the RAF station at Shaibah, in the desert, near the Persian Gulf. From there we flew on to Karachi. Here, although we were expecting to go on to Colombo, we were sum-marily taken off the flight and consigned to Mauripur transit camp near Karachi airport to await further orders. This was a great disappointment as we were looking forward to reaching Ceylon and starting on some productive work. We feared that we were being discarded and would be left to rot! Mauripur in the desert was a dump where gippy tummy was endemic. Three weeks there was more than enough, although we were able to hitch the odd lift into the city and enjoy roast chicken and apple pie with cream (luxuries unknown in war-time London) in a local Chinese restaurant.

Eventually, we received our orders and four of us were ordered to report to the RAF Officer Cadet Training Unit (OCTU) which was located at Poona in the Deccan. This meant a two-and-a-half-day train journey. We went first through the Sind desert to Hyder-abad where we changed trains onto a different gauge on the line to Ahmedabad. There we changed again for Bombay. At Bombay we had to make our way with our kit to a different station to catch the Deccan express to Poona. We were fortunate in getting sec-ond class compartments most of the way. There was no such thing as air-conditioning, of course, but for the crosssing of the Sind desert we were able to get a block of ice which, placed under the ceiling fan, helped to keep us cool as it melted. There was nothing, however, that we could do about the dust and the smuts from the engine except wipe away as much as we could with wet rags. We got our meals either at restaurants on stations or, when there was a restaurant car on the train, we accessed it by getting out of the train and walking along the platform to it – the trains having no corridors. The bustle, the dirt and the beggars, combined with occasional signs of anti-British feeling, did not make India seem an attractive place.

In Karachi we had discarded the pith helmets which had been issued to us before leaving, although no-one in the services in India wore such headgear. Indeed, it was asserted to us by the more experienced that only Indian clerks wore such things. Instead, we had taken to wearing khaki shorts in order 'to get our knees brown' and demonstrate that we were not innocents straight out from Blighty (as Britain was called by servicemen in India). We bought tin trunks to carry our kit and save it from white ants which we were warned to expect in most barracks. We had to get porters to carry these. This did not present a problem but the constant demands for baksheesh, even when one had given a reasonable tip, were jarring.

At Poona we found the RAF OCTU housed in what had been the Parsee orphanage. Here we had to rehearse our marching and drill as well as improve our physique through exercises and gym. We also had to learn about the rudiments of administration and military law. I did better in the more academic aspects of the course than in the 'square bashing' and physical side. After six weeks we passed out of the OCTU, but immediately reverted from officer cadet to our previous rank of Acting Sergeant. Officer commissions could only be issued on the authority of the Air Ministry in London when they had received reports of performance at the OCTU.

I was posted to the headquarters of Combined Services Detailed Interrogation Centre (India) (CSDIC(I)) in the Red Fort in Delhi. The journey consisted of first going back to Bombay and then taking the famous 'Frontier Mail' train to Delhi. I arrived in Delhi in April in time for the hottest season of the year. I was sent to the sergeants' mess and housed with some twenty others in a barrack room on the top of an old building in the Fort. These old buildings were primitive and seemed an inferno in the Delhi summer. The latrines were outside the building (a descent of three floors) and washing facilities were limited. I found it very difficult to sleep on my 'charpoy', a bed made of wooden posts over which a rope net was strung and on which 'biscuits' were placed as a base for any other bed-clothes one might have. These were carried around in what was called a bed-roll. If I got out of bed at night and touched my tin trunk it still felt baking hot. Daytime temperatures in May were up to 117° Fahrenheit. The butter in the mess was reduced to rancid oil and the food in this heat was unappetizing. I drank quantities of 'nimbu-panee' (lime or lemon and water) to assuage my thirst and avoid dehydration and heat stroke, but it was acid stuff and my stomach suffered as a result. The only way to keep cool in the office was to sit behind bamboo screens onto which water was constantly being splashed by coolies and which, as it evaporated under the ceiling fans, helped to make the offices tolerable.

I passed my twenty-first birthday in Delhi without any celebration. On VE day that May I watched the victory parade at Connaught Circus in New Delhi and wondered what was in store for us as the Allies concentrated on the defeat of Japan. How long would the war go on? Would the Japanese fight to the bitter end? Eventually, in late May, my commission as an acting Pilot Officer on probation came through and I was able to move out of barracks in the Red Fort to an RAF Officer's mess outside the old city of Delhi.

My work as an interrogator began as soon as I had arrived, but there were very few Japanese prisoners and much of my time was taken up with questioning members of the Indian National Army (INA) who had been captured in Burma. I felt a strong antipathy towards these men, thinking at that time that they were traitors who had betrayed their salt. This was an understandable emotional reaction, but many of those who served in the INA were forced to join or were simply gullible. I had little under-standing of or sympathy at that time for the Indian independence movement.

I had had no training in interrogation techniques and I doubt if what I learnt from these interrogations was of much use to British intelligence. But I remember one Japanese officer who was able to give me an account of the position on the Burma Thai border in the area of Chiengrai which at least improved my geo-graphical knowledge. What I was able to report about the state of communications between northern Siam and Burma may, I sup-pose, just have been marginally helpful to our forces in Burma.

From time to time I had to take my turn as duty officer and inspect the cells and prisoners' quarters. I do not think that the prisoners were badly treated, but their days in the Fort must have seemed long and comfortless. The Japanese prisoners, most of whom were ordinary soldiers, had little to say and it was very difficult to make contact with them. One question on the POW form we had to fill in concerned their religion. We found their answers puzzling as we were ignorant of, for example, the rela-tionship between Shinto and Buddhism.

I was glad to have started work, but realized that we were un-able to contribute much if anything to the intelligence picture. I looked forward to getting away to one of the mobile sections of CSDIC(I) which operated with front-line units. But the cam-paign in Burma was largely over and plans were being developed for a landing in Malaya. This campaign which was given the code name 'Operation Zipper' was to be launched by 14 Army which had been withdrawn from Burma and was regrouping in South-ern India. It was now commanded by General Dempsey who had come out from Europe to relieve General Slim. The CSDIC(I) unit to be attached to his Headquarters was No 5 CSDIC(I) Mo-bile Section which was under the command of Major Eric Crane who had been brought up in Japan and had had a Japanese mother. In July 1945 I was appointed a member of his section which, in August 1945, was ordered to proceed to 14 Army head-quarters at Secunderabad near Hyderabad.

We left Delhi in a convoy of jeeps and trucks early on the

morning of 15 August 1945. I was sent on ahead to Agra to check on our billets, driving a jeep for the first time. Unfortunately, I was an inexperienced driver and when my jeep boiled dry in an Indian village I stupidly put well-water into the cylinder which cracked. On eventual arrival in Agra I feared that I would be court-martialled! However, the news of the Japanese Emperor's surrender broadcast had come through. My CO seeing me look-ing so dejected poured my mess tin full of whisky and com-manded me to swig it down. With this help (my first but by no means my last whisky) I recovered my equanimity and we went off to celebrate by viewing the Taj Mahal in hazy moonlight!

My jeep was no longer serviceable and Major Crane decided to send me and a couple of other officers ahead by train to 14 Army headquarters. It was far from clear what was going to happen to the proposed operation for a landing in Malaya in the new cir-cumstances. At Secunderabad I was introduced to General Dempsey, the C-in-C 14 Army, and found myself appointed as his personal interpreter. As I had never been to Japan and my knowledge of Japanese was strictly limited I was not a little con-cerned about whether I was up to the job.

Tactical Headquarters 14 Army, to which I was attached, was immediately despatched to Madras. Here, I had my first rickshaw ride before boarding a troopship in a convoy of ships carrying troops towards Malaya and the Morib beaches where it was planned that we should land. As we feared attacks by Japanese *kamikaze* aircraft we maintained a strict black-out and watch. However, when we reached the Malacca Straits tactical HQ 14 Army was ordered to Singapore. Here we encountered no oppo-sition and landed safely at the beginning of September 1945.

I was not sorry to have left India. The atmosphere in the last years of the Raj was uncongenial and I had found India a pro-found cultural shock.

SINGAPORE: SEPTEMBER 1945 TO JUNE 1946

My task, initially, was to help with liaison between tactical head-quarters and the Japanese command at Raffles College in Singa-pore. The British authorities insisted that there should be a gap in both time and space between Japanese withdrawal and Allied occupation. This was understandable as there was a great deal of suspicion that some members of the Japanese forces at least might not obey the Imperial command to surrender. But it ensured that there was an ample opportunity for looting. The Japanese had prepared inventories of requisitioned properties in readiness for handing over to the British, but widespread looting by Chinese and, sad to say, by members of the Allied forces, rendered the inventories useless. General Dempsey's personal staff concentrated on finding and taking over a large house, and ensuring that it was provided with such luxuries as were available from other properties which they helped to loot. The Singapore water supply which had been neglected during the Japanese occupation was not working properly and electricity was also disrupted. Conditions in Singapore were therefore chaotic for some time after the British forces arrived.

I had very little to do with General Dempsey but I had to work for the Brigadier General Staff (BGS). I shall never forget trying to interpret at a meeting between the BGS and the acting Japanese Commander-in-chief General Itagaki who was later hanged as a major war criminal. At one point, I asked General Itagaki to explain something which I had not properly understood. The BGS then bawled me out and told me that my job was not to ask the General questions but to interpret word for word what he said! Fortunately, one of the Japanese side's interpreters helped me out of this difficult moment.

I was present in the crowd at the formal Japanese surrender ceremony held on the Padang, the area in front of the government offices in Singapore, on 12 September 1945 but I was not involved as interpreter. This responsibility fell to Wing Commander Boyce who interpreted between Admiral Lord Louis Mountbatten and General Itagaki representing Field Marshal Terauchi, the Japanese C-in-C who was said to be dying of tertiary syphilis at his headquarters in Saigon.

At about this time, I received a telegram from home telling me of the sudden death of my mother in a hospital in Kent. I was devastated by the news as I had been very close to her and had been looking forward to the time when we would meet again. At first, I was inconsolable. I realized how much her loss would mean to my father, who had been devoted to her, and I did what I could to help him during this period by writing to him almost every day. That summer, my father had retired from Sedbergh where the retirement age was 55 (he was approaching 57, but had been asked to stay on until the end of the war and then leave so that places could be found for officers returning from war service). He had moved in August 1945 to Cranbrook in Kent where he had been appointed a master at the school there. He needed to go on working, not least because his pension from Sedbergh after 25 years service was only £250 a year. (This was never increased despite inflation and hardship. Once when he visited Tokyo as an MP, I complained to the late Sir Wavell Wakefield who was chairman of the governors of Sedbergh school about the meanness of the school authorities to faithful servants of the school, but had no response. I have accordingly never responded to appeals from the school for funds.)

I did my best at this time to try to get news of my uncle (George Lewis Hinde), the former rubber-planter, married to my mother's younger sister Betty and who had been a prisoner-of-war on the Burma-Siam railway. I discovered that he had been released, but did not manage to see him before he was repatriated. I did, however, succeed in contacting my Dutch cousin by marriage who had been in Surabaya with his wife and children when the Japanese captured Java. He, too, had been on the Burma-Siam railway and his family had had a bad time in Japanese camps. These experiences did nothing to reduce my prejudices against the Japanese which had been reinforced by allied propaganda during the war, but I still hoped to discover a different side to Japan and the Japanese people.

As Japanese forces were ordered to congregate near Kluang in Malaya for screening prior to allocation for various duties in the area before repatriation I had little to do at 14 Army Headquarters and was transferred to South East Asia Translation and Interrogation Centre (SEATIC) which had come to Singapore from Colombo and assumed CSDIC(I)'s duties. We were stationed in requisitioned properties in Dalvey Road, Singapore, near Raffles College.

SEATIC was anything but a normal military unit. We were all temporary officers from the three services and included Indian army officers, some of whom had the inevitable chips on their shoulders and occasionally tried to pull rank. We even had a few Gurkha soldiers as guards. Our officers' mess was unhierarchic and fairly democratic. Some officers were just waiting to be demobilized (demob-happy was the phrase); others, like myself, were enjoying new experiences. One of our senior officers was a Lt Colonel Heaslett, the son of an Anglican Bishop in Japan who had been a medical doctor before he had been transferred to Intelligence and had become CO of one of CSDIC(I)'s mobile corps. Heaslett was an experienced tease. He saw me as the innocent that I was and I was inveigled by him into playing bridge. The stakes were high by my standards and I lost consistently. Eventually, I pulled out, just able to pay my debts. I have never played cards since for any significant sums. Indeed, I have never been a gambler.

After my six month's probation was over I was appointed to the rank of Flying Officer and eventually in 1946 to Acting Flight Lieutenant (equivalent of a captain in the army), despite the fact that I had had a silly accident driving a jeep too fast up a slope in Dalvey Road one day. The jeep turned over. I was shaken, but not injured. After this experience I really learnt how to drive, practising on 15-cwt trucks and eventually on a 3-tonner.

As an officer in SEATIC I was involved immediately after the end of the war in various war crimes investigations. One day, I was shocked to read that a Japanese major whom I had been interrogating had committed suicide leaving a note confessing to the brutal murder of some RAF officers at Changi. Among senior Japanese officers whom I interviewed, together with other British officers, including the late Louis Allen, was Colonel Fujiwara of the *Fujiwara* and *Hikari kikan* which were Japanese intelligence organizations operating in South East Asia. (After the war, Fujiwara joined the Japanese Ground Self-Defence Force and became Chief-of-Staff. I reminded him of our earlier meeting when, as Ambassador to Japan in the early 1980s, I entertained him to dinner to meet the British Army Chief-of-Staff, General Stanier, who was then visiting Tokyo.)

In October 1945 I was sent with a Royal Navy radar officer to Palembang in southern Sumatra to investigate Japanese radar. Such Japanese radar equipment as had been allocated to South East Asia had been concentrated around Palembang as part of the Japanese efforts to protect their supplies from the oil fields in southern Sumatra. My knowledge of radar was practically non-existent and I certainly did not know the Japanese technical terms. However, I soon found that this did not matter as the technical people found a common language in diagrams and blue prints. At that time, Palembang was still administered by the Japanese army, as the only allied force to have reached the town was a group from members of the British Force 136 who had been operating behind Japanese lines. This meant that, much to the annoyance of Dutch internees awaiting repatriation, we were escorted around by armed Japanese soldiers.

Back in Singapore, the work was limited and I had not a great deal to do, but I thought that there might be some interest in the history of Japanese air operations and defences in South East Asia in the final years of the war. Accordingly, I spent most of my time interviewing senior Japanese army air force officers and Japanese naval staff in order to draw up a report on the state of Japanese air defences at the end of the war and also to produce a historical survey of the decline of Japanese air defence capacity in the area.

The Japanese navy in South East Asia had very few aeroplanes left by the end of the war and Japan's main air defence capability was in the hands of Japan's Third Air Army which was commanded by Lt General Kinoshita. I had many meetings with him and his senior staff officers trying to piece together what their plans and resources had been. General Kinoshita was always courtous to me as a junior officer who was inevitably ignorant of Japanese forms and the structure of the Japanese forces. Kinoshita took charge of the surrendered Japanese forces in Malaya, following the despatch to Tokyo of General Itagaki to stand trial for war crimes. Pending repatriation, Japanese forces were sent to the island of Rempang off Singapore. On one occasion, I visited him on the island acting as interpreter to a senior British officer inspecting the position of the Japanese. We found that they had worked hard to make life tolerable on the island and that discipline had been maintained in difficult circumstances.

Life for us in reoccupied Singapore had its compensations. Towards the end of 1945, I remember going to Singapore's only theatre to see John Gielgud in *Hamlet* and Ralph Richardson in *The School for Scandal*, if I remember correctly. They both came to a boozy meal in our mess. I managed once to get by jeep with a friend to Kuala Lumpur and to Fraser's Hill to the north of the Malayan capital. This was an interesting trip in the days before the roads in Malaya were made unsafe by communist bandits. But I felt that I was largely wasting time. I really wanted to get to Japan to use and improve my knowledge of Japanese.

I lobbied hard for a posting to British Commonwealth Forces in Japan. These were being formed in the early months of 1946. As a result of this lobbying I met Air Vice Marshal Claude Bouchier (popularly known as 'Boy') who was to command the British Commonweath Air Forces in Japan (BCAIR, Japan). I was summoned to interpret for him while he watched a Japanese war propaganda film. My effort was not particularly good, but at least I was not vetoed when my name eventually came up for appointment to Japan.

JAPAN: JUNE 1946-AUGUST 1947

In June 1946, I finally received my orders to proceed to BCAIR Headquarters in Japan as an acting Flight Lieutenant for intelligence and security duties. I looked forward to reaching Japan and to obtaining first-hand experience of the country whose language I had begun to study some three years earlier.

I had found Singapore much more agreeable than India. Was it, I now wonder, because its atmosphere was more British? I do not think that I gave much thought at that time to the future of British possessions in the East. I was forced to recognize that the Japanese occupation had given a boost to independence movements, but I felt sure that the Japanese record as an occupying power had been such that no-one would choose Japan as the preferred colonial power. What I learnt of Japanese behaviour in Singapore after the British surrender in 1942, and their maltreatment of Chinese, was more than sufficient to justify local feelings of hostility towards the Japanese military. Furthermore, it seemed from all I heard about Indonesia that Dutch colonial rule had often been harsh and repressive, and I was far from impressed by what I learnt of French rule in Indo-China and of the arrogance of the French colonists.

I was put on an RAF flight from Singapore to Hong Kong. The aircraft was that old war-time work-horse, a Dakota or DC3. The seats consisted of web benches down the side. The aircraft was not pressurized and flew at a relatively low level. We ran into tropical thunderstorms on the way and these forced us almost down to sea level. Altogether, it was an uncomfortable and bumpy flight. I was glad when we reached Saigon where we stopped for the night and for refuelling, leaving the next day for Hong Kong. Here I had to wait some days for a seat on a flight to Japan.

Hong Kong was very hot and sticky without air-conditioning. The city was beginning to recover from the Japanese occupation. The population was relatively small although the streets seemed to teem with people. The only 'high-rise' building was the pre-war Hong Kong and Shanghai Bank on the island. The old Peninsular Hotel was an officers' mess. Many of the buildings on the Peak had been looted and were derelict, although the Peak tram was working. It was interesting to be in Hong Kong at this time, but I was eager to get to Japan.

Eventually, I was put on another Dakota flight bound for BCAIR Headquarters at Iwakuni in Yamaguchi prefecture. A Dakota could not, however, fly to Japan without refuelling. So we flew first to Shanghai where we spent a night. I remember little of Shanghai in 1946 except that inflation was at its height and a million yuan bought nothing. The next day, we left for Japan. It was the middle of the rainy season and our pilot could not at first find his way through the clouds. Eventually, when it was far too late to turn back (our fuel was running low), the pilot found the straits of Shimonoseki which we passed through at a low level – fortunately above the cables linking Honshu and Kyushu. The pilot tried twice to land at Iwakuni but driving rain and cross winds caused him to divert to the alternative airfield at Bofu (Hofu or Mitajiri, also in Yamaguchi prefecture, but further west than Iwakuni). This was manned by the Royal Australian Air Force (RAAF) who entertained us royally before sending us on the next day by train to Iwakuni.

IWAKUNI

I duly reported to the Squadron Leader responsible at BCAIR for intelligence. He had practically nothing for me to do and I was instructed to join the RAF Provost [RAF Police] and Security Flight in the city of Iwakuni. My main responsibility was for security matters, but there were no signs of trouble from the Japanese population of Iwakuni and the surrounding area. They were all preoccupied with finding enough to eat at a time when Japanese food supplies were very short with many people, especially in the big cities, close to starvation. Moreover it was clear that the Japanese people had accepted the fact of Japan's defeat and were ready to cooperate with the Occupation authorities.

There were two other Japanese-speaking officers and a number of NCOs (RAF and RAAF) working with me. We did our best to find things to do. We visited schools and factories allegedly looking out for relics of Japanese militarism and checking on the dismantling of industrial machinery to be packed off to South East Asia as reparations. We began what we called a security survey of Iwakuni, but which became in the end something of a social survey, although none of us were trained social scientists.

I found that I had to help out with provost (i.e. military police) duties, especially where these involved Japanese nationals. There were a few cases of larceny by Japanese and a large black market soon developed involving not only NAAFI goods but also such common items as sugar. Some enterprising Australian officers arranged to off-load sugar from merchant ships on their way to the base at Kure and smuggle the sugar ashore before flogging it through Japanese middlemen at about £1 per lb, a huge sum in those days. They were eventually caught and court-martialled, but got away with a reprimand and loss of seniority. The Japanese offenders got terms of imprisonment. This imbalance in punishment seemed wrong to me then and still more so now.

We were supposed to be subject to strict 'no fraternization' rules which meant that we were not allowed to meet or talk to Japanese nationals except in the course of duty. These rules were plain silly and the Japanese linguists took no notice of them, arguing rightly that if they were to do their job as intelligence and security personnel they must have contacts with Japanese. The fact that we fraternized was condoned by senior officers although I once nearly got into trouble with the Air Vice Marshal whom I came across one day while out driving my jeep. He accused me of misuse of a military vehicle but, as he was enjoying himself having a picnic with some officers including WAAF (Women's Auxiliary Air Force) personnel and was using official vehicles, he sensibly did not pursue the matter.

I helped a local group of Japanese who wanted to practise English and learn more about the world. Among those involved were a medical doctor, Fujimura, and his dentist friend, Dr Ichioka, with whom I kept in touch for many years until they died. We kept an eye on the local theatre which performed occasional Kabuki pieces. I also remember one chamber concert where a Japanese violinist and pianist performed moderately well.

Iwakuni is famous for its fine old arched wooden bridge, the *Kintaibashi* ('the bridge of the brocade sash' which was the subject of wood-block prints by Hokusai and Hiroshige). The countryside around, especially the Nishiki (brocade) river valley, which runs down to Iwakuni and thence into the sea was beautiful, especially as the autumn colours developed. I particularly recall one visit into the hills behind Iwakuni that autumn when a couple of other officers and I went partly by jeep and then, when the track became impassable, on foot, to visit the former daimyo of Iwakuni, Kikkawa, who had made what the family considered an inappropriate marriage. (Today, their castle has been rebuilt on a hill behind Iwakuni and turned into a tourist attraction.) On another occasion, we went on a hunt for wild boar. I am glad to say that we never found any as I was armed with a .303 rifle and was not a good shot at the best of times.

Some of us spent the Japanese New Year of 1947 at the house of the mayor of Hongo, a village in the Nishiki valley behind Iwakuni. He gave us a jolly time with lots of illicit saké! The Americans suspected him of being a Communist and we were not popular with American local government officials in Yamaguchi city (capital of Yamaguchi prefecture) who resented any attempt to interfere in what was their preserve. I recall once having to drive by jeep over some absolutely vile rough roads to Yamaguchi to explain myself about some activity which the Americans regarded as interference in matters which were their responsibility as representing military government. Having eaten humble pie we all got horribly drunk to demonstrate Anglo-American friendship and confirm that no ill-feelings had been left. This incident underlines the powerlessness of the British Occupation authorities in the area allotted to them by the Americans. The area consisted initially of the Chugoku region prefectures of Yamaguchi, Hiroshima, Okayama, Shimane and Tottori and the four prefectures which formed the island of Shikoku.

One day in August 1946, I was instructed to accompany a VIP visitor on a visit to Hiroshima. He was a a senior member of the British Foreign Office, Rob (later Sir Rob) Scott who had been interned by the Japanese in Singapore during the war and had suffered badly from being kept in solitary confinement for some time in Changi jail. However, he did not show any rancour and felt moved by what he saw of Hiroshima as any one must have been who visited the city so soon after the atomic bomb. The people still seemed dazed by the effects of the bomb and the hillsides around remained scorched and bare as a result of the blast. Inevitably, we discussed the rights and wrongs of the decision to drop the bomb. It seemed to us then that the bomb had probably in the end saved both Allied and Japanese lives by providing the excuse for the Japanese to surrender. I was not so sure that the second bomb on Nagasaki was equally justified. I have continued on many occasions to debate the rights and wrongs of the use of atomic weapons. My initial reaction was inevitably rather shallow as I did not have all the facts. Now, I still think that in the circumstances at that time President Truman's decision was understandable and may have been justifiable in the absence of clear indications that the Japanese were then prepared to agree to unconditional surrender. Whether it was wise for the allies to insist on unconditional surrender is a different issue.

Rob Scott, who later was one of my first bosses on joining the Foreign Service (see below), and I were glad to get away from Hiroshima. On our way back to Iwakuni by jeep we stopped at Miyajima-guchi and went across on the ferry to take a quick look at the fine old shrine of Miyajima which remains my favourite among the three most famous Japanese beauty spots (the so-called Sankei being Miyajima, Ama-no-Hashidate and Matsushima). I managed a couple of other visits to the island while I was stationed at Iwakuni.

The only other visit which I made other than to Yonago (see below) was to Beppu in Oita prefecture in Kyushu where I had to go to check on the behaviour of RAF personnel who used this hot spring resort on R and R (rest and recuperation) leaves. I thought Beppu one of the most vulgar places I have ever visited and my attitude towards the place has never changed!

YONAGO

In January 1947, the officer in charge of the Provost and Security Flight at Yonago, next to the RAF base at Miho (there were only three stations in BCAIR in Japan: these were Iwakuni, Bofu and Miho), was thought to be going round the bend and I was instructed to take charge of the flight, although I had had no training or experience in provost law matters.

I welcomed the change, seeing it as a good opportunity for me to get to know another part of Japan. Moreover, while at Iwakuni I had had to live in barracks, at Yonago I had to be off the base and a room had been requisitioned for the unit commander at the Tokoen Hotel, a Japanese inn at the small country hot spring resort of Kaikei Onsen on Miho bay. I remained at Yonago except for a few visits to Iwakuni and one to Tokyo (see below) until I left Japan for demobilization in August 1947.

Life in Yonago was full of interest. At 22 I was in command of my own unit some way from headquarters. I had to supervise the administration and the discipline of the flight as well as take charge of patrols and crime investigations. I got to know quite a number of Japanese in Yonago including professional people and officials. Nosaka, the Mayor of Yonago, had a difficult job, but he did it well. I regarded him as very much the old-fashioned Japanese gentleman. Interestingly he always wore formal Japanese male dress (*haori* and *hakama*). Dr Higuchi Tazu was a formidable lady doctor in charge of the local health office. I came in touch with her first because of the need to ensure that the prostitutes in the red light district were kept free from venereal disease. But I recall doing what I could to help with medical emergencies, including getting penicillin from the RAF medical centre at Miho for Japanese who might otherwise have died. Another friend was Dr Isaka Ryonen who was the brother of the proprietor of the Tokoen who grew his own vegetables. I was given some of these and they seemed so delicious after the tinned and dried vegetables which came with our rations. There were practically no fresh foods in our diet and I suffered that summer from a series of nasty boils.

I came into conflict with Group Captain Christie, the officer commanding the station at Miho, on at least one occasion. We had discovered that one of the military police sergeants at the base had taken the law into his own hands and was enjoying himself confiscating black market goods to use for his own purposes and then meting out punishments at his own whim of so many strokes of his cane on the culprit's bottom. I reported our investigations to BCAIR headquarters and was told to forward the case to them before submitting it to the Group Captain who, the Judge Advocate General Squadron Leader Boyd thought, would attempt to deal with the case himself and not refer it, as he should, to a court martial. Christie was furious. He summoned me and threatened to have me court-martialled. Eventually, he was forced to back down as I received the Judge Advocate General's backing and that of the Squadron Leader in charge of the Provost and Security Flights in Japan.

Another serious case involved a learner driver who, in an accident when he was driving a truck too fast on a narrow street in Yonago, killed two schoolchildren. He was eventually court-martialled but in my view was let off very leniently as he had been responsible for a fatal accident which should never have happened. I also remember an occasion involving a chase through the Japanese countryside after a New Zealand airman who had threatened people with a gun. Eventually, we caught up with him at Tamatsukuri hot spring resort to the west of Matsue in Shimane prefecture. Fortunately, by then he had sobered up and as he was in the bath at the time was in no position to put up violent resistance.

There was an Indian army battalion stationed at Tottori to the east of Yonago (Tottori was the capital of Tottori prefecture). On one occasion when the RAF Dentist at Miho was absent I had to visit the battalion's Indian dental officer to have a tooth removed. The battalion did not take kindly to interference by RAF policemen in their area and I got the distinct impression I was not a popular visitor. As well as this battalion, there was an Indian Army Service Corps depot based in Yonago. This latter unit caused us quite a lot of trouble as their men were constantly in trouble in the red light district and regularly involved in black market offences.

I only had one brief spell of leave in Japan. This consisted of about five days in Tokyo where I stayed at the Marunouchi Hotel which had been allocated by the Americans for use by British Commonwealth officers. I wandered round the ruins of Tokyo noting with distress the hovels and sheds under the railways in which many Japanese still sought shelter. I saw with shame the black market at Ueno and compared the life-style of the Japanese with that of the American servicemen with all the luxuries available to them at the American PX store. I went by train (in the section reserved for servicemen) to Kamakura and wandered round the temples admiring especially the Daibutsu and the Hachiman shrine. As I had failed to get a sandwich from the hotel before leaving I survived on a very sour *natsumikan* (a large sour orange) which was the only item of food I could buy.

I found the countryside around Yonago just as, if not more attractive than that around Iwakuni. Matsue, an old castle town where Lafcadio Hearn had lived and taught at one time, Miho no Seki, an ancient shrine by the sea, Izumo Taisha, one of Japan's oldest and most famous Shinto shrines, and Mt Daisen which rose behind Yonago, all seemed to encapsulate in different ways Japan's love of nature. I had become fascinated by Japanese temples and shrines and I wanted to learn more about Japan, its history and culture. I also wanted to improve my Japanese.

I came to like many Japanese and to appreciate their genuine kindnesses. I did briefly wonder at one stage whether after demobilization I should try to stay on in Japan. I admired Japanese *'en-ryo'* (reserve/humility) where it was genuine and the courtesy of the older generation and of educated Japanese generally. But I recognized that my attachment to Japan was based on a romantic and unrealistic view and that there were darker sides to Japanese life as shown by the behaviour of members of the Japanese military in China and South East Asia. Some of my prejudices had been dissipated and I was inclined to accept that, for instance, Japanese cruelty to prisoners of war had been largely due to indoctrination and force of circumstances rather to any innate qualities in the Japanese. But I had been brought up to believe in individual freedom and a liberal society and I did not care for Japanese conformism. I also knew that as an officer in the occupation my position had been privileged and these advantages could not be maintained. Moreover, I was ambitious and determined to succeed if I possibly could in my chosen profession, but before I could do so I had to pass into the Foreign Service, as the Diplomatic Service was then called.

□

In the autumn of 1946 I had been offered the chance of early demobilization enabling me to return to St Andrews University on a government Further Education and Training Scheme (FETS) grant. I turned this down and indeed when my number for demobilization came up in the natural way in the spring of 1947 I applied for a six-month extension. I wanted to have longer in Japan and thought probably correctly that the experience of being a unit commander would stand me in good stead later in life. The pay as an acting Flight Lieutenant on Indian rates (I had been commissioned in India and was paid as if I was serving there) was also not bad and there was little to spend my salary on. In fact when I was demobilized in late-1947 I had managed to accumulate some £600 which was a fair sum in those days and provided me with a cushion against possible future financial difficulties.

I had completed my application to join the Foreign Service under the post-war reconstruction provisions as soon as I was able to do so. The rule that an applicant had to have had a first or second class honours degree was waived for service applicants who only had to show through references that they would have got such a degree had they had the opportunity to complete their course and sit the examination. They also had to show ability in one foreign language. St Andrews University readily provided suitable references and I was able to sit the preliminary written examination in Iwakuni in early-1947. The examination included fairly simple mathematics as well as questions and essays on contemporary themes. My maths was not good and as I had been abroad for over two years and had had access to little more than the *Manchester Guardian* weekly I did not do particularly well in this examination. However, I was not failed outright and as a borderline case I was told that I would be given a special interview on my return to London which would determine whether I was allowed to go on to the full Civil Service Selection Board, including the 'Country House' weekend of tests and interviews. I was disappointed but not totally downcast by this setback which in fact made me all the more determined to gain what experience I could in Japan.

By mid-1947 with the forthcoming withdrawal of the Indian Division following Indian and Pakistan independence it was clear that the British occupation force could not be sustained on any scale and would have to be run down. I realized that it was time to leave and start a new life. I was sad to leave Yonago and my Japanese friends there on that day in August 1947 when I entrained for the British naval base at Kure, but I knew that it was high time I moved on. At Kure I joined the P & O ship *Strathnaver* which had been turned into a troopship and was overcrowded with members of the services returning to Britain for demobilization.

Looking back over fifty years later on my time with the occupation force, it is difficult to distinguish between impressions formed at the time and judgements which came from further experience of Japan and a study of Japanese history. But a few impressions which have not changed with time remain.

Japanese people in 1946 and 1947 had been reduced to penury and food was very short. Most people had to put all their efforts into scraping together such limited supplies of food as were available on rations and in the black markets which were to be found everywhere. If we visited a school we might be offered as refreshment some sweet potatoes. We were reluctant to accept these knowing how short of food the children were, even those living in farming districts. Living accommodation, especially in the cities, was very hard to find as so much had been destroyed in fire and high explosive saturation bombing. Such heating as there was came from charcoal *hibachi* and *kotatsu*. In the Sanin district in which Yonago was situated snows in winter were heavy and the cold could be quite severe. In the countryside there was an almost total absence of farm machinery and farming was, to say the least, primitive. I remember seeing Japanese peasants flailing rice with hand flails. Human manure, transported in what were euphemistically called 'honey buckets', was the universal fertilizer.

Transport was appallingly crowded and slow. As members of the occupation forces we had special coaches on trains, but most trains were stopping ones. It took the best part of a day and a night to get by train from Iwakuni to Yonago. It was necessary to take the main line from Iwakuni station towards Osaka and change at Okayama (the capital of Okayama prefecture which like most Japanese cities had been practically destroyed by air-raids during the war), wait there for some hours and then pick up a slow train on the Hakubi line leaving in the early hours and taking some 4-5 hours to reach Yonago through the mountains. Buses were equally crowded and were mainly run on charcoal. Even main roads were largely unmade up, dusty and full of potholes.

It is hardly surprising that in the circumstances politics were at a low ebb. The Japanese people seemed fatalistic in their attitude towards the Occupation. I recall attending and giving a speech at a meeting marking the introduction of the new constitution on 3 May 1947, but I do not remember either much enthusiasm or any opposition. Little was said about the Emperor although I recall that at the Tokoen there was a special bath which the Emperor had used on a visit and in which ordinary mortals were not allowed to bathe (I was once allowed the privilege!).

Japan's role in the war was generally avoided by Japanese with whom I spoke. The main focus was on Japanese returning from the occupied territories, especially Manchuria, and Japanese still held in Russian camps. There were many ex-servicemen, often limbless, begging near shrines but few if any signs of anti-foreign feelings. On my brief visit to Tokyo in February 1947 I spent a few hours at the trial of major war criminals but did not find it very interesting and I felt that most Japanese were fairly indifferent to the trial which they doubtless viewed as victors' justice.

The Korean communities, especially in the Yonago area, were vociferous and viewed with suspicion by the Japanese. Koreans were certainly extensively involved in the black market and Koreans whose origin was from the North were viewed as Communist Party supporters. The Communist threat was taken increasingly seriously, especially towards the end of my time with the occupation forces, but there were no strikes or demonstrations in our area.

As members of the Occupation forces we were not directly affected by the economic reforms of the Occupation. We had our own forces' currency which we used in the NAAFI and in the mess (e.g. to pay for drinks). The vouchers were denominated in sterling. We only used yen in limited local purchases of souvenirs. The rate of exchange when I first arrived in Japan was 60 yen to the pound, but the exchange rate was pretty meaningless. We read in English papers about the fears in Lancashire of the likelihood of 'unfair competition' from Japanese sweated labour, but this was all very remote from our life.

At the time, I tried to justify to myself the British role in the Occupation, but as we were excluded from military government it was difficult to see what we were contributing towards such ideals as the development of democracy in Japan. Indeed, by our non-fraternization policies and occasional demonstrations of military power, as well as by the operation of military courts, our actions could have been regarded as counter-productive. In fairness, it must be said that the RAF Judge Advocate General, Squadron Leader Boyd, did his best to see that the Occupation courts behaved justly and fairly. However, we had to rely to a considerable extent on the local Japanese police who had not been retrained in democratic policing. Their treatment of suspects was sometimes brutal and arrests were often made on suspicion rather than adequate evidence.

On the whole, looking back, I think that the main contribution of the British Commonwealth Occupation Force in Japan was a political one. It reminded the Americans that we were still in those days a power of some importance in the Far East. We were also useful to the Americans if only as a counterweight to the Russians, who resented their exclusion from the Occupation. (They would dearly have liked to occupy the northern island of Hokkaido and consolidate their gains in Sakhalin and the Kuriles.)

I doubt whether the Japanese made a great deal of distinction between us and the Americans. If they did it was not always in our favour. The Americans were much less stiff and fraternization was not discouraged by their authorities. It seems to me that the non-fraternization policy was the biggest mistake of the British Commonwealth Occupation Forces. Our prisoners had suffered greatly but so had American prisoners, especially in the Philippines. Our unfriendly attitude, which was to last many years, was a barrier to closer Anglo-Japanese relations. This period of frosty relations and mutual suspicions contrasted sadly with the close and friendly relations which had developed especially in the early years of the twentieth century, beginning with the first Anglo-Japanese alliance of 1902.

SCHOOL OF ORIENTAL AND AFRICAN STUDIES (SOAS): 1947-49

The journey home from Kure to Southampton in an over-crowded troopship was boring and uncomfortable. I had an upper bunk in what had been the swimming pool with some 50 others. There were very few chairs and much of the time we had to sit around on the deck reading and playing cards. The Red Sea was particularly hot and I tried sleeping on deck, but as the decks were swabbed down with sea water early in the morning I did not find this altogether satisfactory! We stopped briefly in Hong Kong, Singapore and Bombay where still more troops were put on board.

On arrival at Southampton, I was sent to the RAF demobilization centre and given a civilian suit of clothes and a soft hat. The suit was of poor quality and I threw the hat away as soon as I could decently do so, but clothes were still rationed and as I had no alternative I had to use the suit. I was then given a travel warrant to take me to my father's home in Cranbrook, which in those pre-Beeching days still had a railway station. My father had re-married in 1946 and I met my step-mother, Marjorie, for the first time. We took an instant dislike to one another. She was jealous of my relationship with my father and disliked any kind of intellectual discussion. I particularly deplored the way in which she had discouraged my father from pursuing his interests in music. He had been a competent pianist and had taught himself the clarinet, the bassoon and then the cello. Under her influence he had entirely given up his music. I had never had any intention of re-maining long at home but the atmosphere was such that I was determined to move away as quickly as I could.

While I was waiting for my qualifying interview before I could take the Civil Service Selection Board (CSSB) examinations I

decided to pursue the option of going back to SOAS and studying there for an honours degree in Japanese. For this purpose I
applied for and was awarded a Further Education and Training
Scheme (FETS) grant of £250 a year for two years. (These were
grants for ex-servicemen whose education had been interrupted
by war service to enable them to go to university or undertake
further training.) Accordingly, I enrolled in late October at
SOAS. I had been given exemption from the first year course in
Japanese because of my wartime studies. Among those studying
with me was Pat O'Neill, later to be one of the Professors of Japanese at SOAS, and Ken Gardner, who later joined the Oriental
Printed Books and Manuscripts Department at the British Museum (now the British Library).

I was successful in the preliminary interview for the Foreign
Service. The next step was the CSSB series of interviews and examinations over a two-day period at Stoke Dabernon in Surrey.
The written papers were mainly psychological tests. We also had
to take part in discussion groups and deal with the imaginary
problems of an island state. Each of us had to write down not
only our own assessments of ourselves but also of other members
of the group. Finally, we had three interviews including one with
a psychologist. I did sufficiently well in these tests to go on to the
final interview before the Civil Service Selection Board then
housed in what was until recently the Museum of Mankind in
Burlington Gardens. There were about nine members on the
board including a trade unionist and a member of the Foreign
Service. The chairman was the First Commissioner of the Civil
Service, Sir Percival Waterfield. Questions ranged widely and included ones about my attitude towards the use of the atomic
bombs at Hiroshima and Nagasaki. One question from the
Chairman of the board was, I thought, 'off-side'. He asked
whether I did not think that St Andrews University was rather
like an extended sixth form at a public school. I decided that the
question did not deserve more than an answer of 'No Sir!'. My
final marks were 230 which was just under the pass mark of 240
for entry into the Foreign Service (candidates were marked out of
300 in stages of 5: I never saw any evidence that those with high

marks necessarily did better in their careers!). I was naturally disappointed as I had set my heart on joining the service, but I could reapply for a second chance. I decided to do so but determined first to complete my honours degree course at SOAS.

I found it very difficult to make the change from being a unit commander on a reasonable salary to being a penurious student on a futher education grant living in at best spartan accommodation. After a brief spell in a guest house in Bayswater, I moved to the 'International Language Club' which was close to the station at East Croydon. I had a largish but very cold and barely furnished room in a Victorian house. I did what I could to make it comfortable, but could only afford a single bar electric fire. My father gave me a threadbare carpet and after a lot of searching I managed to find an armchair. New furniture at that time was, like almost everything else in post war Labour-controlled Britain, rationed. The food was at best indifferent and fairly sparse, but at the club I met many foreign students, including a number of congenial Indians. One problem about living in East Croydon was commuting to London. The trains were frequent and fast to Victoria but I could not afford a season ticket all the time. The alternative was to bicycle up to SOAS or take the tram which still ran as far as Kingsway and took much longer, but was a great deal cheaper than the train.

The staff at SOAS were keen and interested in developing Japanese studies in Britain under the reforms proposed by the Scarborough Commission. But under Frank Daniels Japanese studies at SOAS tended to be remote from the modern world. Certainly, neither he nor others at SOAS had much if any idea about what graduates might do after completing their courses other than seeking an academic post, but applicants for such posts needed to win first class honours.

I worked very hard, but found Japanese classical texts difficult and much of the course unrewarding. The main exception was Japanese history where Bill Beasley (later Professor) encouraged my interest in modern Japanese history. Charles Dunn who had only just graduated himself did his best to take us through the history of Japanese literature, but I felt that he was only just keeping ahead of us. Yanada and Matsukawa who had stayed on as lecturers in Japanese after the war-time courses ended were, of course, very competent in the Japanese language, but there were few suitable textbooks and language learning aids did not exist at that time. Frank Daniels was absorbed in his work on a Basic English-Japanese dictionary and on the snake myth in Japanese folklore. He was shy and sometimes discouraging as he found it difficult to make contact with his students. I am sure he wanted to be helpful but did not know how. Otome Daniels, his wife, was outstandingly kind.

One element in the honours degree course was the writing of a mini-paper on a Japanese theme. I chose to study and write about haiku. I quite enjoyed this element in the course. Frank Daniels was, however, unfortunately not of much help and his comments on my paper were vague and did not seem to lead anywhere.

In the summer of 1948, assisted by a £15 present from an uncle, I went on a cycling holiday in France with one of my cousins and her husband. We took a train as far as Dijon and cycled from there through the Jura mountains and into the Alps. We managed to cross the Col du Galibier, but I was exhausted by the climb and very glad to reach a cheap inn after free-wheeling down the other side in the dark. Eventually, we picked up a bus at Sisteron to Marseilles and had a couple of days on one of the beaches near Marseilles before returning home third class (the third class carriages had wooden benches). It seemed a long journey! France was quite cheap in those days and rationing was less severe than in England. I particularly enjoyed the *vin ordinaire* which we drank everywhere! In the following summer after graduation I joined a small party of students, including Ron Dore, on a cycle tour along part of the Pyrenees from Bayonne as far as Pau. This was equally tough but good fun. On the way back I made my first visit to Paris, staying in student accommodation.

Ron Dore and I wrote a joint letter to *The Times* in 1948 complaining about the attitude of the American authorities in occupied Japan regarding the import of books in English into Japan. It seemed to us absurd that we were not allowed to send books from Britain to our friends in Japan. This letter was duly published and led to an invitation from John Pilcher who was still involved in information work in the Foreign Office to visit him. Ron and I called at his office in Carlton House Terrace and he introduced us to his assistant, Tommy Lyell, who had so little work to do that he spent his time knitting.

I had decided by early 1949 that if I failed to get into the Foreign Service and could get a good enough degree I would try for an academic career. I was accordingly very disappointed when I only succeeded in getting an Upper Second Class Honours. I was even more disappointed when my second application to join the Foreign Service also failed. I was awarded the same mark of 230 as on the first attempt. The CSSB took the line that my degree in Japanese was of no interest to the Foreign Office who preferred to train their own linguists.

I decided to look for a job in business. I sought the help of the university appointments staff, but they were of little or no help. British firms were generally not interested in graduates in such esoteric subjects as Japanese. When I tried Shell I saw a Mr Lovely who made it clear that they only took Oxbridge graduates. The main UK Far Eastern Trading companies in those days preferred to take young men straight from public school and did not want Japanese speakers on their staffs in Tokyo. Unilever did have a graduate training entry but were not interested then in developing business in Japan. The only company who offered me a job where I could use my Japanese was a small textile company with interests in the Far East. Looking back, I think that I made the mistake of seeking a job which would take me quickly back to Japan.

Fortunately, when I was feeling discouraged, I received a letter from the Foreign Office. They had not been able to find enough candidates with qualifying marks. They were then accepting candidates with 235 marks instead of 240 as hitherto. It was possible that they might offer places to candidates who had only got 230 marks (as I had). Eventually, I was offered a place and instructed to report to the Foreign Office in mid-October 1949. I joined the Foreign Service as a third secretary on probation on a salary which had just risen to £400 a year. (I suppose, to put this in modern terms, it is necessary to multiply the sum by 20-30 times, but it was certainly not a generous salary, although it was a good deal better than my FETS grant of £250.)

CHAPTER TWO

First Steps in Diplomacy

 oOo

FOREIGN OFFICE: OCTOBER TO DECEMBER 1949

The Foreign Service in 1949 was very different from the pre-war Diplomatic Service. In pre-war days every member of the service had had to have an adequate private income and many were old Etonians or Wykehamists. They were generally intelligent gentlemen, but they had earned for the service a reputation for lofty superiority which often irritated members of the Home Civil Service.

The post-war service consisted not only of members of the pre-war Diplomatic Service and the separate Foreign Office. It also included former members of the various specialist consular services including the China and the Japan Consular Services. The China and Japan Services had ensured that their officers were competent in Chinese and Japanese. In the case of the Japan Service they served as Japanese Secretaries and as Japanese Counsellor in the British Embassy in Tokyo providing specialist advice and help to members of the Diplomatic Service. In addition to performing consular duties, they undertook many tasks relating to commerce and shipping. The new service also included men who had served in the Department of Overseas Trade and were knowledgeable on trade matters which had tended to be ignored by members of the old Diplomatic Service. After the independence of India and Pakistan in 1947 some of the younger members of the Indian Civil and Political Services were taken into the Foreign Service as were some members of the Sudan Civil Service and in due course, as British colonies became independent, members of the former colonial civil services. With their wide experience of overseas service they brought new ideas and thinking to the Foreign Service.

Inevitably, it took time for traditional attitudes to disappear and for the various disparate elements to merge, but on the whole I think the merger went pretty smoothly and many members of the former consular services and the Indian Civil service went on to high posts in the combined service.

The post-war 'reconstruction' entrants (as those of us who joined under the special arrangements created for ex-servicemen were called) were a mixed bunch. Almost all had had war service; some had earned high battle honours. Some came straight into the service without university degrees, but many, especially those who joined in 1948/9, had gone back to university after the war and joined the service after graduation. Most were from public schools and almost all who had been to university were from Oxbridge. The Civil Service Commission tended to favour Oxbridge candidates, not least because on the whole they had the self-confidence and poise which it was thought were required for diplomacy. As a graduate from the universities of St Andrews and London I was an exception in those days. I disapproved of the apparent prejudices of the Civil Service selection boards in their choice of applicants for the Foreign Service, but once you had been accepted I do not think it mattered much, if at all, where you had been to school or university. You were judged by your abilities both in and outside the office.

The pre-war diplomats were well adapted to political work, but many were reluctant to sully their hands with trade and tended to look down on journalists. This meant that despite their intelligence and experience, they often aroused unfriendly reactions from industrial and trade visitors and from visiting or resident journalists.

There was no initial training for new entrants. The new recruit had to learn on the job. I was sent to join the 'third room' (i.e. where the desk officers sat) of the South East Asia Department. There were six of us in one office. With telephones ringing, typists coming in to take dictation and messengers almost constantly bringing papers in boxes and tubes (vacuum tubes were used in those days to send up to departments advance copies of incoming telegrams) it seemed at times like Bedlam. Among those in the third room who were destined for higher things were Reg Hibbert, who ended his career as Ambassador in Paris, and Curtis Keeble, whose last post was as Ambassador in Moscow. My job was to assist Leslie Glass (later High Commissioner in Nigeria) on Burma and on the problems of rice supplies which, after the devastation caused by war in South East Asia, were so important for the rehabilitation of the economies of these countries. Leslie had been in the Civil Service in Burma and spoke good Burmese. He was an amusing and laid-back character. The assistant head of the department was John Lloyd who had been in the Japan Consular Service, while the head of the department was Rob Scott whom I had first met in Iwakuni in the summer of 1946. The Assistant Under-Secretary was 'Bill' (later Sir Esler) Dening whom I found a formidable figure. In the two-and-a-half months which I spent in the department I do not recall meeting any Minister, let alone the Permanent Under-Secretary.

As a new boy I had to master the Foreign Office system. All papers were submitted in separate jackets which showed when they had been received and where they came from. The jackets also showed the file number allocated to the paper by the registry, who were supposed to attach all other recent papers (in their original jackets) which were referred to or which were directly relevant. The separate bundles were tied together with red tape. The desk officer to whom these were submitted had to ensure first that all relevant papers were there and then decide what action was required. He would 'initial off' (i.e. send back for filing away) any paper which in his view did not need to go higher. If, however, he thought that the paper should be seen by a superior officer he would write a brief comment on the jacket, sign his name in full and submit the paper to the assistant in the department. If a reply was required it was his job to draft a response attaching it on the top of the jacket. An important paper which needed to be submitted to Ministers had to be accompanied by a draft submission (a form of memorandum) on blue draft paper and cleared with any other departments with an interest in the subject. When approved the draft would then be retyped on crested paper and signed by the head of department before wending its way upwards. All this was based on the 'bottom-up' principle used in Foreign Office work.

Many of the papers which came to me dealt with claims for wartime losses: some of these came with letters from MPs acting on behalf of constituents. Such letters had to be given due priority and replies drafted for the relevant junior Minister.

There were large numbers of telegrams arriving all the time. These were given an appropriate circulation by the communications department. Even in the third room in the department we would have to glance through many telegrams every day where our department's interest was minimal. But through reading these telegrams and the despatches from our missions which were circulated in 'Foreign Office Print' we were able to understand more of the broader picture than was conveyed by our departmental papers.

We had to learn about the security classification of papers (Top Secret, Secret, Confidential and Restricted) as well as how to draft telegrams of instructions to our missions overseas. A few were sent '*en clair*' i.e. in plain language which anyone could read, but the majority which were classified (i.e. had a security marking) had to be sent in cipher. A small number of administrative telegrams were still sent in 'R' code but this was no real protection to the contents as there were many 'R' code books around the world.

I also had to learn the Foreign Office etiquette. All other members of the service were addressed by their surnames until you met them: you then immediately used their first names. The only people addressed as 'Sir' were Ambassadors. Ministers and the Permanent Under Secretaries (PUS) were addressed by the titles of their office i.e. Secretary of State, Minister or PUS. We signed letters to other members of the service 'Yours ever', but to home civil servants we always signed ourselves 'Yours sincerely'! In those days some official letters still went out addressed 'Sir, I am commanded by the Secretary of State for Foreign Affairs (abbreviated as SOSFA)' and signed 'I am, Sir, Your obedient servant'.

I learnt that you never knocked before entering the office of a superior and I had to try to give up the Japanese habit of bowing after Rob Scott had said to me, 'For God's sake, Hugh, stop bowing!'. The dress code was not particularly strict although casual clothes were only worn on Saturday mornings (the Foreign Office had not yet adopted the five-day week). I bought a short black jacket and striped trousers but very rarely wore them, an ordinary dark suit being considered adequate. Hardly anyone wore a bowler and I never possessed one.

SINGAPORE: 1950-51

In January 1950 I was posted to the office of the Commissioner General for South East Asia, Mr Malcolm MacDonald, based in Singapore. I flew out by a British Overseas Airways Constellation aircraft. This was long before the introduction of jet airliners and the journey took the best part of two days. Before leaving London I had been given a tropical kit allowance; so I had a few tropical clothes, but I had to get other suits made in Singapore by a Chinese tailor as soon as I could find the necessary funds. After a few days staying with the Head of Chancery (then Dalton Murray) I was allocated a bungalow in Braddell Rise. I managed to get a Chinese cook and was soon quite comfortably installed even if I had little or no equipment of my own. Later on I moved to a semi-detached house in Holland Road which I shared initially with Robin Mackworth Young, who later became librarian to the Queen; and after he left, with John Heath, who ended his career as Ambassador in Chile.

On the occasion of Robin Mackworth Young's farewell party we put up fairy lights on the lawn. Foolishly, I stood on a chair to insert a bulb and put my hand on a socket which was live. I fell to the ground thus fortunately breaking the circuit, but had to be carted off to the military hospital where it was decided that I needed a skin graft on my hand. The operation was duly conducted next day by a Lt Colonel Skinner. The graft eventually took and I was not permanently injured.

One of the first things I did in Singapore was to use part of my nest-egg in buying a car. This was a 500 cc Fiat Topolino. It was pretty small for me but it was about all I could afford and it was economical on petrol.

The Commissioner General for South East Asia had a roving brief but no direct authority over missions in the area. His influence depended largely on his personality and the access which he had to Ministers in London. Malcolm MacDonald, the son of Ramsay MacDonald, the pre-war Labour Prime Minister, had been Secretary of State for the Colonies and for the Dominions before the war. He had also served as British High Commissioner to Canada and later to India. He had considerable charm and was liked and respected by the political leaders he met in South East Asia. The colonial community in Singapore did not, however, care for his informality and his preference for local personalities over British expatriates.

Malcolm MacDonald was a politician rather than a civil servant. He used to send long telegrams of many pages marked 'Secret' and given the 'Immediate' prefix which meant that they had to be dealt with before telegrams marked 'Priority' or 'Routine'. The only marking higher than 'Immediate' was 'Emergency' later changed to 'Flash'. His long telegrams were a nightmare to the cipher officers who, in those days before machine ciphers, had to put the texts into cipher by looking up the numbers allocated to words in a book and then subtracting figures in one-time cipher pads. Assuming that the one-time pads were kept safely the texts should be undecipherable by any outside organization. Ciphering and deciphering were laborious processes even for the expert.

At the outbreak of the Korean War in mid-1950 I had to help our six cipher officers in the task of deciphering telegrams repeated to us for information. At one point we were so inundated that we asked for copies to come to us 'saving' (i.e. by bag).

The Commissioner General's office was at Phoenix Park in Singapore. This was also the headquarters of the three service Chiefs of Staff in South East Asia. One of our main tasks was to act as political advisers to the service chiefs. We accordingly served on various committees on planning and intelligence. One Foreign Office Counsellor acted as Chairman of the Joint Intelligence Committee which included representatives of MI5 and MI6.

After Dalton Murray left Singapore in early 1950 Dudley Cheke, a former member of the Japan Consular Service, was appointed Head of Chancery. Dudley later served in Japan as Consul General in Osaka and as Minister in the Embassy. He was a meticulous but kind boss. There were two Deputy Commissioner Generals, one for colonial issues and the other for foreign affairs issues. The Foreign Office Deputy, to whom I worked through the Head of Chancery, was Jack Sterndale-Bennett, popularly known as Benito. He was a little man with a shrunken arm (I think this was due to a wound which he received in the First World War) and a total work-aholic. He worked six-and-a-half days a week and occupied himself on Sunday afternoons catching up with the British papers. He was an experienced diplomat who knew how to get the best out of his juniors by sometimes seeking their views and comments on drafts. The main drawback in working for him was his reluctance to let one take any leave or even go into hospital for a minor operation. (I should have had an operation on my sinuses in Singapore but it had to be postponed until I got to Japan.)

A top-level conference was held once a year at Bukit Serene across the causeway from Singapore in the state of Johore where the Commissioner General had his residence. This was a large gathering under Malcolm MacDonald's chairmanship. Among those attending were the three Commanders-in-Chief (General Harding, Admiral Brind and Air Marshall Fogarty), the Governors of Singapore, Sarawak, North Borneo and Hong Kong, as well as the Ambassadors from Rangoon, Bangkok, Djakarta, and the heads of missions from Saigon and Manila. Dening came out from London. Dudley Cheke who was due to take the minutes was sick; so the task fell to me; it was a good experience. I thought General Sir John Harding (later Field Marshal Lord Harding) was outstanding among the service chiefs. Sir Alexander Grantham, Governor of Hong Kong, showed his contempt for the proceedings by nodding off frequently. The subjects discussed ranged from the implications of the Korean war to the prospects for British interests in South East Asia and the future of British colonial possessions in the area. I do not think that any of those present quite realized how stretched British resources were and that we could not much longer sustain an imperial presence in Asia.

Shortly before the conference ended, rioting by Moslems broke out in Singapore. The occasion was a court case involving a Dutch girl, Maria Hertog, who had been brought up as a Muslim but who was being brought back to Holland for a Christian education. A good deal of damage was done by the rioters and some British officers were killed and injured. The Singapore Governor, Sir Franklin Gimson, did not display much common sense in his handling of the riots. Fortunately, our house in Holland Road was not attacked, nor was Phoenix Park, but we had an unpleasant couple of days.

Owing to the insurgency we were not allowed to travel in Malaya. The only times I managed to get out of the island, other than to go to Bukit Serene, were a trip with a diplomatic bag to the British Consulate at Medan in Sumatra and two trips to Burma as a junior assistant to Malcolm MacDonald. Malcolm got on well with Prime Minister U Nu and even managed to charm General Ne Win, who on one occasion accompanied the party on a visit to Mandalay and Maymyo. I found the Burmese a charming people whose chances of prosperity were sadly destroyed by the military regime set up by Ne Win after U Nu was deposed.

Unfortunately, I never managed to accompany Malcolm MacDonald to Cambodia where he became absorbed by the temples at Angkor or to Sarawak where he made a study of the Dayaks and their way of life. Malcolm thought highly of the Emperor Bao Dai in Vietnam and was, I remember, furious when one of my colleagues in the Chancery, Oliver Wright, who retired after being Ambassador in Bonn and Washington, had the temerity to disagree with his chief about Bao Dai.

My work in Singapore only once brought me any real contact with Japan. In early 1951 a rice conference was held in Singapore and the Japanese Government was allowed by the Supreme Commander Allied Powers (SCAP) to send a representative. He was Mr Kitahara Hideo who in due course became Japanese Ambassador to Paris, having studied French at Lyons before the war. When I went to meet him on his arrival in my little Fiat 500 I was taken aback to find that, unlike most Japanese, he was a huge man, at least as tall as I am, and could barely fit into my tiny vehicle. It was not easy for a Japanese to visit Singapore at that time when memories of the Japanese occupation were so fresh in peoples' minds. I hope that by making him welcome I showed that not everyone in Singapore continued to loathe every Japanese.

I had gained some useful experience in Singapore but the Commissioner General's Office was not a proper diplomatic mission and the work was at times frustrating as we were generally only involved on the periphery. I was accordingly delighted when I heard that I was to go to Japan as third secretary in the United Kingdom Liaison Mission to SCAP in the autumn of 1951.

I left Singapore for London in early July 1951. I arranged to break my journey home in Bangkok and Rome where I had never been before. As I was flying KLM, having met the KLM manager in Singapore and been given a good deal, I also decided to visit Amsterdam to see my Dutch relations before going to London where I arrived in early August.

I did not have long in Britain as I was due to depart for Japan on a cargo ship of the Blue Funnel line carrying some 30 passengers and leaving Liverpool in September. I did, however, manage to fit in a brief industrial tour arranged by the Central Office of Information (COI). I chose to visit Manchester to learn about the fears of the Lancashire textile industry over Japanese competition. I also went to Stoke-on-Trent to see the Wedgwood factory and hear about the concerns of the potteries about imports from Japan. I found attitudes in both places depressingly negative towards Japan as well as protectionist. This was not exceptional on the part of British industry in those gloomy post-war years.

JAPAN: OCTOBER 1951 TO FEBRUARY 1954

When I reached Tokyo in mid-October 1951 I had completed my two years probation and was confirmed in my appointment to the Foreign Service. In due course, I received my commission signed by the Queen and countersigned by the Foreign Secretary, Anthony Eden. I was also promoted to Second Secretary.

The Peace Treaty between the Allies and Japan had been signed in San Francisco that summer. The first task of the Embassy, which at that time was still known as The United Kingdom Liaison Mission to SCAP (UKLM), was to prepare for the entry into force of the Peace Treaty as soon as the necessary ratifications had been lodged.

Sir Esler Dening who had been the Assistant Under-Secretary for Asia in London had just arrived as Ambassador. Sir Esler, who had been born in Japan (his father was a missionary, the Rev Walter Dening) had been a member of the Japan Consular Service before the war and had served as political adviser to Admiral Mountbatten in Colombo during the war. He was a clear thinker and effective draftsman, but he had a number of prejudices arising from his experiences in Japan before the war as well as a significant streak of obstinacy. He was a confirmed bachelor, tall and jowlish with a stern face and uncertain temper. His staff generally found him a formidable figure

As the junior secretary in chancery I was given a variety of tasks. In addition to some political work, and jobs requiring a knowledge of Japanese, I had to assist with the administration of the mission as the administration officer was very junior and inexperienced. There were many administrative problems. The local (and domestic) staff of the mission had become grossly inflated since, during the Occupation, they had been provided and paid for by the Japanese authorities. Housing in requisitioned properties had also been provided for all staff at no cost to HMG (His Majesty's Government).

Arrangements had to be made to streamline the local staff and pay them from public funds. This meant that many local staff members had to be asked to leave and appropriate conditions of service drawn up for those that were to be kept on. Houses had to be found for UK staff who could not be accommodated in the Embassy compound. The Foreign Office and the Ministry of Works had to be consulted on many points. Leases then had to be drafted, approved and signed. Many of the Embassy staff who found that they would have fewer local staff, or would have to live in less good accommodation, deeply resented the changes.

The accounts system had to be revamped as all local payments had to be made in yen. British Armed Forces Vouchers in sterling which we had used used in the NAAFI were no longer of use to us as NAAFI privileges were withdrawn. We banked in those days with the Tokyo branch of the Hong Kong and Shanghai Bank. Individual officers were entitled to draw an advance of salary and allowances each month from the accountant against their quarterly entitlement. At the end of each quarter the amounts which they had drawn locally were entered on a 'Life Certificate' (certifying that the officer was still alive and entitled to his salary!). This was then signed by the individual officer and sent home. In due course, up to eight weeks after the end of the quarter, the balance due to the officer was paid into his UK bank account without, of course, any interest being added to compensate for the delay in his receiving his full entitlement.

The Japanese authorities with whom I had to negotiate on administrative issues seemed to go out of their way to be difficult. They were also increasingly arrogant. I shall not forget one brutish official who received me with his feet on his desk picking his nails. He looked suspiciously at the British Embassy cheque which I produced in payment for a piece of ex-German property which the Admiralty had agreed to purchase for the Naval Attaché's use. The Japanese bureaucrat made some sarcastic comments about sterling which was weak at the time implying that he hoped the cheque would not bounce! I was angry, but I suppose attitudes such as his, after nearly six years of the Occupation, were understandable if unattractive. Certainly, Japanese bureaucracy had learnt how to be obnoxious and obstructive to foreigners. The Admiralty made a good bargain as the house only cost some £3000 at the time and when it was sold, admittedly many years later, fetched well over half a million pounds. It was difficult to persuade anyone in London that in those days, when property prices were low and rents high, property should be bought rather than leased.

One of the many problems we encountered was dealing with various Allied property claims. The Diet had passed an 'Allied Powers Property Compensation Law' and an unofficial English translation had been produced. Arthur de la Mare, the Head of Chancery, rightly considered the English version total gobbledegook. He instructed me to produce a new English translation over one weekend. I managed it with the help of one of the Embassy's Japanese translators, but anyone who has looked at Japanese legalese and knows how vague it can be will appreciate the difficulties of this task.

I read Japanese newspapers each day and did some political reporting. This enabled me to begin to understand the intricacies of Japanese politics and the potential threat from extremists on the left and right. On May Day 1952 there were Communist-inspired riots in Tokyo and cars, especially American cars, were overturned and set on fire in the area between the Imperial Palace and the Marunouchi business district. One member of the Embassy's staff who was attempting to take photographs was pursued by stone-throwing rioters, but as he was an Oxford athletics blue he managed to escape without injury. We spent a good deal of time examining evidence of Communist activities which looked menacing in those days at the height of the cold war. The Communists were at this stage under Soviet tutelage. The Socialists were increasingly split between old-fashioned Marxists, who looked for support from Communist China and spent most of their time attacking the Americans, and a more moderate faction which split away from the main party in October 1951 just as I arrived in Japan. The public sector unions including Nikkyoso, the teachers union, tended to be militant Marxists.

We were justifiably suspicious of any signs of a revival of Japanese nationalism or militarism. In fact, the extreme right while very noisy was never much of a real threat. In addition, we were doubtful about many of the pre-war politicians who returned to the political scene after they had been 'depurged' following the end of the Occupation. We were far from convinced at that time that democratic principles had taken root. Our suspicions were aroused by the calls to revise the Constitution to allow Japan to rearm and to strengthen the position of the Emperor. We were concerned about the implications of the government's moves to centralize the police and to transform the National Police Reserve into the Self-Defence Forces. We also saw dangers in the Subversive Activities Prevention Law enacted in 1952.

One of my tasks was to scan the Diet records and very occasionally I watched the proceedings from the public gallery, but I found these far less interesting than those of the House of Commons. The procedure of set policy speeches, followed by repetitive interpellations, revealed little of general interest. Yoshida Shigeru as Prime Minister showed his contempt for the Diet in various typical gestures. He seemed to go out of his way to use pre-war vocabulary and difficult Chinese compounds in his speeches to the Diet. It used to be said that he did not want to be understood and that to make matters more difficult for his listeners he would take out his false teeth before delivering a speech. This was, I am sure, a fiction.

Official communications from the Ministry of Foreign Affairs (Gaimusho) were still sent to us in the form of third person notes in Japanese. It was our task to translate these into English or arrange for them to be translated. We would then have to check the translation.

Dening occasionally gave speeches in Japanese, but he was no longer fluent in reading *kanamajiri* texts. So I had to ensure that the translations were submitted to him in roman script. Understandably, he abhorred the passive tense and care had to be taken to ensure that the texts in romaji were not too complicated.

We had English secretaries for confidential work, but lacked copying machines or modern electronic office machinery. Often, to save time, I would dictate memoranda to a typist who transcribed directly onto the typewriter. If we needed copies we had to rely on carbons. If we required more than a minimum number then the document would have to be typed on a 'skin' (wax paper) which would then be 'run off' by hand on a Roneo or Gestetner duplicating machine. These machines seemed invariably to spread ink over whatever fingers and clothing came into contact with them.

One of my most time-consuming tasks was to represent the British Mission, later (after 28 April 1952, and the entry into force of the Peace Treaty) the British Embassy, in negotiations for a United Nations Status of Forces Agreement. This should have been ready by 28 April 1952 as otherwise British and other forces in Japan in connection with the Korean war would have no legal rights and privileges. We were instructed to follow closely the terms of the US-Japan Administrative Agreement which provided for the use by American forces of facilities in Japan under the US-Japan Security Treaty which came into force at the same time as the Peace Treaty. In theory, our negotiations should have been easy. In practice, they were not. The Japanese authorities were determined to claw back as much as possible of the concessions they had been forced to make to the Americans.

Clauses involving costs to Japan were fought over word by word with the Ministry of Finance taking a very tough line. But the greatest difficulties were over articles covering jurisdiction. We sought the same exemption as had been accorded to the Americans, namely the right to try all offences allegedly committed by members of UN forces under the laws of the home state (called the 'sending' state) with any punishments pronounced by the court to be served in the home state. The Japanese authorities saw this clause as analagous to the provisions of the 'unequal' treaties of the nineteenth century, which after lengthy and difficult negotiations had been finally ended in 1899, and adamantly refused to concede on the principles involved. They were determined that having achieved independence under the Peace Treaty they would in due course force the Americans to allow the Japanese authorities to exercise juris-diction. They asserted that they were neither involved nor inter-ested in developments in Korea and the mission of the UN forces. When we argued that as the Japanese had said so often in the past 'Korea was a dagger-pointing at the heart of Japan' and that it was in their interest to help the UN forces they preferred not to hear.

The Foreign Office, who failed to appreciate the difficulties we were encountering, used to send us unrealistic instructions demanding that we always work 'under the American umbrella' i.e. let the Americans take the lead on every occasion. They were understandably very reluctant to do so. Once, when thoroughly frustrated by these instructions and in the absence of the Ambas-sador and the Head of Chancery, I drafted a telegram which was approved by the Minister, Norman Roberts. My draft perpetrated a dreadful mixed metaphor; I urged that we should 'give up flog-ging the dead horse of the American umbrella'. This led John Pilcher, who was then the Head of the Japan and Pacific Depart-ment in the Foreign Office, to send in long hand a four-page letter to Arthur de la Mare which consisted of a series of mixed metaphors. Sadly, I do not know what happened to this letter.

The negotiations on the UN Status of Forces agreement in-volved much consultation with the American Embassy and with the Embassies of Australia, Canada and New Zealand. The agree-ment, much to my chagrin, was only signed shortly after I left Japan in 1954. Before it could be agreed the Americans had in the main conceded to the Japanese demands on jurisdiction and we had accepted largely similar clauses. By then there were, of course, hardly any UN forces left to use the bases in Japan.

An ugly incident occurred in the summer of 1952. Two sailors from *HMS Belfast* which was visiting Kobe at that time were in-volved in a drunken brawl in which a Japanese taxi-driver was injured. They were arrested by the Japanese police who despite protests from the Embassy through the Japanese Ministry of For-eign Affairs refused to hand them over to the RN patrol. Despite further increasingly acrimonious protests, drafted by Arthur de la Mare and approved by Sir Esler Dening, the two sailors were duly brought before a Japanese court in Kobe and sentenced to imprisonment. But the right of the Japanese courts to exercise jurisdiction having been asserted by the Japanese government, the sailors were in due course handed over to the British authorities.

I became closely involved in this affair not least because I was on duty over one weekend and tried to arrange through the Consul in Kobe for the trial to be postponed. I remember attempting to get through to Sir Esler Dening who was staying at the Embassy villa at Chuzenji (by the lake in the mountains behind Nikko). In those days it could take hours to get through on the telephone and sounds were very weak. Dening when he eventually received my call on his return from a fishing expedition declared ominously: 'I am coming down to Tokyo.' I awaited him the following day with some trepidation because I had acted without authorization, having had to make a snap decision about seeking a postponement. I thought that if there was a postponement further representations could be made. When I saw Dening who clearly felt very irritated at having to cut short his weekend, he demanded to know whether I had consulted the American Embassy. When I replied that I did not see what they could do, he told me to go away and consult my American colleagues. They understandably said that the matter was one for us to settle. Dening never told me that I had been wrong in seeking a postponement of the trial; I suspect he felt marginally guilty for having been away and inaccessible on what might have been a crucial weekend.

Incidents such as these did not make for happy relations with the Japanese authorities. Dening and de la Mare who had both been in Japan before the war were highly suspicious of any signs of a revival of Japanese militarism and nationalism and looked with scepticism at the establishment of the National Police Reserve as a forerunner of a new Japanese army. They did not welcome the reemergence of pre-war right-wing politicians such as Kishi Nobusuke and Hatoyama Ichiro. Dening was aware of the controversial arguments about the war-time role of Shigemitsu Mamoru but his appointment as Japanese Foreign Minister was hardly a welcome one. Dening got on quite well with Yoshida Shigeru, the Japanese Prime Minister, but was inclined to be suspicious of Shirasu Jiro, Yoshida's *eminence grise*.

Dening particularly disliked John Foster Dulles whom he considered a hypocrite and prig. He also thought that Dulles had double-crossed him over the so-called Yoshida letter about the Japanese intention to conclude a separate Treaty with the Chinese Nationalists on Taiwan. Dulles had argued that the letter was necessary to persuade the US Senate to ratify the Peace Treaty. Dening, who had been responsible for advising the British Government to recognize the PRC, thought that the Japanese should be free to determine their own China policy. I shall never forget a very frosty dinner party which Dening gave early in 1952 for Dulles who was accompanied by US Senators Smith and Sparkman. I was the junior secretary on duty.

With the entry into force of the Peace Treaty we reestablished friendy relations with the Imperial Household, especially with the Grand Master of Ceremonies and his assistants. As in those days there were only a few diplomatic missions to Tokyo even junior secretaries, such as I was, were invited to imperial occasions such as duck-netting, visiting the imperial stock farm and attending imperial garden parties. We also all paraded in diplomatic uniform to the Palace on New Year's day on 1 January 1953 and 1 January 1954 to bow before the members of the imperial family and receive our rations of New Year food. As most of us did not find these titbits exactly delicious the domestic staff usually took over what we had been given. The saké was, however, excellent and the *sakazuki* (imperial saké cup), inscribed with a crane, the symbol of good fortune and long life, which we were allowed to take home with us, made a good souvenir of the occasion. The British, as one of the few surviving monarchical powers, were favoured by the Imperial Household, although there was much sensitivity about the withdrawal of the Order of the Garter from the Emperor during the war. (This was later restored before the imperial visit to Britain in 1971.)

On the occasion of the coronation of the Queen in 1953 it was decided that an olive branch should be extended and the young

Crown Prince was invited to represent the Emperor. This invitation was gladly accepted and preparations were made for an extensive tour by the Crown Prince which might echo some of the activities of the Showa Emperor during his visit to Britain in 1921 as Crown Prince. David Symon, another language officer with whom I shared a house at the time, was appointed to the Crown Prince's suite and instructed to visit the Prince and help him prepare for the visit. (David did a very good job with the Crown Prince, now the Japanese Emperor, and was, I thought, destined for higher things. Sadly he died in 1964 as a result of a blood clot brought on by a minor skiing accident.) I remember a dinner given by Sir Esler Dening in honour of the Crown Prince where one of my tasks was to ensure that the Prince's chamberlain, who suffered from a weak bladder, was given a 'comfort station' opportunity before dinner. Inevitably, as Dening was rather a remote older figure, the Crown Prince was shy and the officials from the palace a stuffy lot, this was not a relaxed occasion.

I was not directly involved with commercial and economic work at this time and did not have many opportunities to travel. I did, however, persuade Dening to allow me one official trip in the summer of 1953. On this occasion I chose to study Japanese agriculture and fisheries and the work of the agricultural and fisheries cooperatives. My journey took me first to Hachinohe in Aomori prefecture. Then after visiting an apple experimental station I visited Niigata and went over to Sado before returning via Nagano. I was impressed by the way in which the American-inspired land reform had been implemented. While Japanese farms following the reform were uneconomically small it was clear that the farmers were beginning to improve their standard of living with the help of the cooperatives. Japanese agricultural experimental stations seemed to be doing good work in improving crop varieties and productivity. The fear, after the near famines of the post-war years, was that Japan would never be able to produce enough food to feed the population which had significantly increased as Japanese returned from Manchuria and other Japanese overseas settlements and as a result of the post-war baby boom. In fact I came back from my tour with the belief that Japan might soon have a surplus of rice.

It was very difficult to get any local leave as we were so busy in the office. I did, however, on one occasion get away for some ten days. This allowed me to drive to Kyoto and to visit Nara. I also managed on other occasions brief visits to Nikko, Chuzenji, Hakone, the Fuji Lakes and Izu although I found driving the old-fashioned Morris Oxford which I had brought to Japan quite a strain because of the appallingly bad Japanese roads. Kamakura was, of course, a simple day's outing.

The commercial department in the Embassy was still small, but they were already beginning to report on Japanese economic plans, including a huge increase in the number of Japanese power stations. There were complaints from British businessmen, who had had difficulty in getting permission from SCAP (they suspected SCAP of favouring American companies) to reopen their offices in Japan during the Occupation, about Japanese quotas, tariffs and other restrictions. Companies in Britain were already moaning about unfair competition from Japanese textiles made by 'sweated labour'. The Embassy was to become increasingly involved in dealing with these complaints and with the opportunities, then very limited, for British exports to Japan.

The British trading firms in Japan were largely staffed in those days by expatriates who had lived in the colonial atmosphere of Hong Kong or other British settlements in the East. Many of them lived in Yokohama and were active members of the Yokohama Country and Athletic Club (YCAC). Some were also keen supporters of the Tokyo Amateur Dramatic Club (TADC) and of expatriate organizations such as the St George's and St Andrews' Societies. While there were naturally some congenial spirits among the expatriates I did not find much in common with the 'hearties' whose colonialist attitudes seemed to me to be out of date. Moreover, it was clear that our priority must be to extend our contacts among the Japanese.

By early 1954, it was becoming increasingly obvious that the procurements for the Korean war had given an important and necessary boost to the Japanese economy. But the Japanese economy was only just beginning to turn the corner and I doubt if anyone then thought that economic success would be achieved so quickly. Living standards were still low. Salaries were only sufficient for most people to eke out a livelihood and housing was poor. Many blocks of apartments were little more than wooden barracks, of course without central heating. Most roads outside the cities were narrow and unpaved. There were very few private cars although there were increasing numbers of 'bata-bata' as we called the three-wheeled trucks which were the main means of distribution. The dust on the roads from the growing number of dump trucks involved in construction added to the hazards of driving to avoid ruts and puddles which might at any stage lead to a broken sump. Even on the main road from Tokyo to Utsunomiya in the rainy season of 1952 I had had to get out of the car and test the depth of some puddles to make sure that we did not get bogged down. A drive on the Tokaido to Kyoto was a lengthy nightmare and it still took up to eight hours by train from Tokyo to Kobe. The telephone system was poor even in Tokyo and long-distance calls via the operator took hours to put through.

One of the most interesting and knowledgeable members of the Embassy was Vere Redman, the eccentric Information Counsellor about whom I wrote a long piece in *Britain and Japan: Biographical Portraits*, Volume II, Japan Library 1997. Another valuable member of the Embassy staff was John Figgess, then assistant Military Adviser but later Military Attaché and successor to Vere Redman as Information Counsellor in the 1960s. The mission was a large one although the corps of Foreign Service staff was small. The Head of Chancery inevitably played a key role. For the first half of my time in Tokyo, between 1951 and 1954, the post was filled by Arthur de la Mare who prided himself on being a Channel Island peasant and calling a spade a spade. He was a hard worker and could take tough decisions. He had a monumental row while I was there with an 'idiot', as Arthur described him, from Security Department. Ironically, Arthur, who was eventually to serve as Ambassador to Afghanistan, High Commissioner in Singapore and Ambassador to Thailand, became head of Security Department after his return to London from Tokyo. There he had to cope with the aftermath of the defection of Burgess and Maclean. I always got on well with him. His successor was Aubrey Halford who was one of the youngest officers to be promoted Counsellor. He had never been in Japan before and prided himself on being a member of the pre-war diplomatic service able to cope nonchalantly with any situation. He managed to hit it off with Dening and to spend much of his time in Tokyo studying and enjoying Kabuki.

The long sea voyage to Japan had given me an opportunity to brush up my Japanese. So when I reached Japan in mid October 1951 I immediately applied to take the Civil Service Japanese language examinations so that I could qualify for a language allowance. My honours degree in Japanese did not even exempt me from the first or intermediate examination. Having passed this I went on to take the higher and the advanced level examinations which I also passed. The examiner in the intermediate was Henry Sawbridge, a pre-war member of the Japan Consular Service and then Consul General in Yokohama. He had a good knowledge of Japanese but he was shy and behaved liked a rather remote schoolmaster. On his retirement from Japan he worked for a time with the Japanese Studies Department at Sheffield. He was assisted in the oral examination by Nishi Haruhiko, later to be the second Japanese Ambassador after the war in London. The subsequent examinations over a period of some six months were conducted by Arthur de la Mare, who had also been a member of the pre-war Consular Service and was then Head of Chancery in Tokyo. He was assisted by Masaki Hideki, a Japanese Foreign Service officer and subsequently interpreter to the Emperor Showa.

After the Civil Service Commission had duly recognized my qualifications and Arthur de la Mare had been transferred, responsibility for conducting the Japanese language examinations fell to me and I also sought Masaki's help in the oral examinations. To pass the higher examination it was necessary for the candidate to be able to speak Japanese reasonably fluently and to be able to do simple interpreting. Candidates also had to be able to translate newspaper articles and official documents as well as simple letters in cursive script. As a further test of their ability they had to translate a piece in English into Japanese. The advanced examination had a similar content, but more difficult pieces were set for translation and in the oral examination it was necessary to be able to interpret on a moderately complicated subject and to read and translate at sight a piece from a newspaper. On the whole, the examinations were sensible tests so long as they were based on the practical needs of the service. Unfortunately, the Civil Service Commission wanted to put all language examinations into the same format and their advisers tended to take an academic rather than a practical approach. Their administration of the examinations was also absurdly bureaucratic and slow.

I shared a house in the Embassy compound (No 6 House) in these days with David Symon and Dick Ellingworth who were language students when I arrived. We met and, when we could afford to do so, entertained many young Japanese, some of whom became good friends over the years. Some were members of the Japanese Foreign Service, but our friends were by no means limited to officials. Carmen Blacker who came to study at Keio University and whom I had known while studying at SOAS, brought us into contact with literary and artistic figures.

Although I had found my time in Tokyo interesting, I was quite glad to leave Japan in February 1954. I looked forward to developing my knowledge and understanding of the European scene and culture. I had, however, learnt a good deal from my two-and-a-half-year stint in the Tokyo Embassy. I had begun to understand something of the political scene in Japan and of diplomatic work in general. Negotiating the UN Status of Forces Agreement had been a tough assignment but a very useful experience. I found that Japanese officials who were all trained in law were meticulous negotiators and determined that the only ambiguities should be deliberate ones. We had to negotiate agreed minutes interpreting various articles and then agreed records confirming our understandings of the meanings of agreed minutes! Certainly, officials in the Ministry of Foreign Affairs had a very good working knowledge of written English.

While I had returned in 1947 from Japan with a rose-tinted view of Japan, I came back in 1954 with a fairly negative view. In particular, I had taken very much against many Japanese bureaucrats who despite their abilities seemed to be arrogant and often anti-foreign. The wheel had come full circle. But I had no wish to cut myself off from things Japanese. I hoped that when I was next posted to Japan, as I expected, and indeed wished, that I would be at some later stage in my career, I should be able to form a more objective and balanced as well as less emotional reaction to Japan and the Japanese.

I obtained a passage home on a Dutch cargo vessel (the *Hoog-kerk*) which carried up to 10 passengers and which left Yokohama in mid-February 1954. The long voyage was a good opportunity to 'recharge my batteries'. The ship had originally been due to call at Marseilles. From there I had intended to take a train to Venice which as the home of some of my ancestors I longed to see. In fact we went straight to Antwerp but I was determined not to miss the opportunity of a little travel in Europe. So I immediately set off for Venice which, in the early evening light when I arrived in late March, was stunning.

LONDON: 1954-58

Before starting work in the Foreign Office I had to find somewhere to live. For a few weeks I lived in digs in Kensington but then arranged to take over the lease of a small flat in Vincent Square. This was very convenient for the Foreign Office and had the advantage of a south-facing sitting-room overlooking the Westminster School cricket ground. The flat had two small bedrooms, kitchen and bath with old-fashioned equipment and lacked central heating, but it was good enough for a bachelor. To help cover the costs I shared the flat: one of my flat-mates was Dick Stratton (later Sir Richard and High Commissioner to New Zealand) who was best man at my wedding in 1956.

☐

My first appointment in London was as desk officer for Japan in the Far Eastern Department. My work covered the whole range of our relations with Japan. One of my tasks was to help arrange the programme for the official visit to London in October 1954 of Mr Yoshida Shigeru, the Japanese Prime Minister. This was the first visit ever by a Japanese Prime Minister to London and was a significant step in the normalization of Anglo-Japanese relations. I do not now remember all the details of the programme, but I do recall having a row with a customs officer at Heathrow who threatened to inspect Mr Yoshida's baggage. He did not do so and the arrival went off smoothly.

One of Mr Yoshida's important appointments was a speech to Members of Parliament. He was questioned aggressively by Lancashire MPs angry about the Japanese copying of British textile designs. Although he had been Japanese Ambassador in London before the war he was no longer fluent as he had had little or no practice in English for some time. His English was not good enough to cope and there was embarrassment all round. I had not been present at this meeting, but when Mr Churchill, then the British Prime Minister, heard of it he ordered that a British interpreter capable in Japanese was to attend the dinner he was giving that evening for Mr Yoshida. I was the only person available. So I raced home to change into my black tie and have a snack before presenting myself at No 10 Downing Street. It proved quite an ordeal because both Prime Ministers were over 80 and already fairly deaf. There were also many VIPs present including Anthony Eden, Clement Attlee and Herbert Morrison. I apparently managed alright as Churchill was affable when I said good-night and Yoshida the following day in the train to Southampton, where he was getting the *Queen Mary* to New York, said that he hoped his 'cockney' Japanese had not been too difficult.

Despite the contretemps at the House of Commons I think that the visit went well and was successful although nothing could induce Anthony Eden, whose son had been killed in fighting in Burma, to look with favour on the Japanese. The late Sir John Pilcher when he was head of Japan and Pacific Department (later merged with China and Korea Department to form Far Eastern Department) while I had been in Tokyo in 1953 used to say that any submission put up to Eden about Japan never induced Eden to write more than 'I do not like the Japanese'.

A major issue which caused real political difficulties while I was in Far Eastern Department was the allocation of the limited funds available under Article 16 of the Peace Treaty for compensation for former British prisoners of war (POWs). Responsibility had been given by the Article to the International Committee of the Red Cross (ICRC) to distribute the funds which were collected from the disposal of assets of the Japanese Government and of Japanese nationals in countries which were neutral during the war. The British Government appointed Sir Norman Roberts, formerly Minister in the British Embassy in Tokyo, to negotiate with the ICRC and with the representatives of the ex-POWs. Sir Norman, who was an honest and likeable man, did his best. The ex-POWs were adamant that each individual should receive a monetary recompense and that money should not be allocated to, for example, a hospital for sufferers. The ex-POWs received just some £76 each. This was very little even in those days. As Japan became increasingly prosperous the ex-POWs pressed for a more generous settlement. In terms of international law the issue had been concluded by the signature and ratification of the Peace Treaty by the British Government and the Government could only argue, as they have continued to do from time to time, for some kind of ex-gratia payment by the Japanese. The Japanese Government have rejected such suggestions not least because they feared that any concessions would leave them open to other claims. An unsuccessful attempt was made in the early 1990s to persuade Japanese business firms to make generous donations to a fund for ex-POWs but such appeals were summarily rejected. The problem has remained a source of friction until this day.

I have always felt that the Japanese Government could and should have made an ex-gratia sum available, for example, for a hospice, hospital or nursing home for ex-POWs even if they could not pay individual compensation because of the difficulty of calculating the appropriate sums so many years after the war. A generous gesture would have earned goodwill for Japan. Unfortunately, the Japanese Government have often seemed at best grudging in acknowledging their responsibilities towards ex-POWs and towards the inhabitants of territories occupied by Japan during the war. In 1995 Prime Minister Murayama's public apology was largely neutralized by the attitude of some Liberal Democratic Party (LDP) members of the government and members of the Diet from the LDP and the New Frontier Party. The repetition of this apology by Prime Minister Hashimoto in January 1998 was helpful, but it did not prevent a few ex-POWs making public protests during the State Visit to Britain by the Japanese Emperor and Empress in May 1998.

Work began at this time on the draft of a revised UK-Japan Treaty of Commerce and Navigation, but the Board of Trade had no enthusiasm for the project and their legal staff took a pedantic aproach while British industry was only interested in further restrictions on imports from Japan. (The Treaty was not concluded until 1962. For background on the negotiations see two essays in *Biographical Portraits* Vol. II.)

□

The Personnel Department in the Foreign Office, wanting to broaden my experience, transferred me at the beginning of 1955 to Information Research Department (IRD) where I was expected to cover the Asian side of the department. I protested that this would limit my experience rather than broaden it. So I was put onto the European side. My contacts with Japan now generally ceased.

The name of the department was misleading. It had been set up to counter Communist propaganda and while research into Communist activities and propaganda was an important element in the work of the department much of its effort was devoted to the production and placement of material which exposed Communist activities and intentions. While I strongly supported the purpose of the department I did not find the work altogether congenial. I thought that the department was too big and could/should be slimmed down. I also did not think it was sufficiently professional in assessing the value of its products. I did not make myself popular by pointing out on a number of occasions that the appearance of an article or news item originating in IRD in a right-wing newspaper in, for example, Latin America was of no value whatever.

IRD was staffed almost entirely by temporary civil servants who, because they could not generally be moved to overseas missions, were in practice permanently in the department while Foreign Service officers such as I was were the temporaries. This inevitably led to frictions from time to time. Some of the 'permanent' members of IRD had had experience of psychological warfare and were both experienced and able. An interesting and amusing member of the department was Robert Conquest, the poet and historian whose books, particularly *The Great Terror*, 1968, exposed in graphic detail the horrors perpetrated under Stalin.

One of the most important events during my time in the department was the Hungarian uprising. We did all we could to expose the Soviet intervention and Soviet motives. Very unfortunately this tragedy largely coincided with the abortive Anglo-French intervention in Egypt over control of the Suez Canal. Like almost every other member of the Foreign Office at the time I deplored an action which we considered both immoral and politically unwise. Only a very small number of officials were in the know and the task of putting over such case as we had was extraordinarily difficult. I could not defend in private the British action and I sympathized with those who resigned over the issue but did not feel that as a junior official I was other than a saddened spectator.

I attempted to study Communist and Marxist philosophy and at one point gave a series of lectures on this dreary subject. I also attended meetings on psychological warfare and liaised with other departments including the Security Service (MI5). At another time, I was told to follow the work of the Moral Rearmament Movement (MRA). I am not an MRA sympathizer and this led to a contre-temps with the Assistant Head of IRD, Norman Reddaway, who retired after being Ambassador to Poland. At one point he told me that I should read Trollope's *He Knew He was Right*. I felt that this was 'the pot calling the kettle black'. Jack

Rennie, the head of the department who later became head of MI6, was sympathetic. He recalled his irritation on waking up one morning after a night on the town while he was an undergraduate at Oxford and finding a young MRA man praying for his soul beside his bed.

☐

On the European desk in IRD studying the French and Italian press was a beautiful and charming girl named Elizabeth Montagu. I asked her out on a number of occasions and on 1 October 1955 we announced our engagement. We were married on 3 April 1956 (3:4:56 – a happy sequence which we only realized on the day after our wedding!). Elizabeth came from a distinguished family of British Jews. At first, her father was much upset at the idea of her marrying outside the faith, but in due course he came round. But he did not like the idea of a church wedding. I did not feel strongly on this point although my family would have preferred a religious ceremony. So we were married in the registry office at Caxton Hall in Westminster. My parents-in-law then gave a reception at the Rembrandt Hotel. We spent our honeymoon in Rome, Ischia and Positano.

I was very happy and the nervous dispepsia from which I had been suffering and which my doctor had feared might become a duodenal ulcer was soon cured. Elizabeth continued to work in the department for some months but found this and looking after our flat a strain. It was also unnecessary as I had been promoted just before we were married to First Secretary and my salary had risen to £1000 a year (perhaps £20,000 in today's money). This was not a great deal after some seven years service and was considerably less than the earnings of contemporaries in business, but I never contemplated leaving the service to enter the city. We had a little Austin car (A30) and were thus able to visit some of Britain's fine country houses together.

BONN: 1958-60

In the spring of 1958 I was posted as First Secretary in the Chancery (political division) of the Embassy in Bonn. Before leaving I had a few revision lessons in German and it did not take me long before I was reasonably fluent in the language. The Embassy in Bonn was one of our largest missions. The offices were in an ugly post-war building on the road from Bad Godesberg to Bonn in the Rhineland. Most of the Embassy staff were accommodated in houses or flats in or around Bad Godesberg. The Ambassador's residence was on the banks of the Rhine in Bad Godesberg. Sir Kit Steel, the Ambassador, was a fairly remote patrician figure whom I saw only rarely.

We were allocated a small but pleasant house in Bad Godesberg (Jahn Strasse 41) which was provided with utilitarian furniture dating back to the Allied Control Commission. We had German neighbours, including retired civil servants such as an Oberpostrat (a post office official) whose wife struck us as a caricature of a prim and proud German *hausfrau*. Bad Godesberg had been a small watering town; it was now a suburb of Bonn, itself known as the Bundesdorf (the Federal village).

The British Embassy in Bonn at that time was snobbish and hierarchical. The Head of Chancery, who was a Counsellor, and his deputy, a senior First Secretary, did not attempt to hide their contempt for the 'plebs' who doubtless included myself. I shall never forget the way they used to waste time at Chancery meetings commenting on people who lived on the wrong side of the Park, by which they meant anyone living in Bayswater. The only acceptable clubs seemed to be Whites, Brooks, Boodles or the Carlton. Their scene was not mine.

We were depressed by the unfriendly atmosphere of the mission. The camaraderie that had existed in the Embassy in Tokyo seemed unknown in Bonn. When shortly after we arrived I had to go into hospital because of a 'slipped disc', hardly anyone helped Elizabeth, who had only just learnt to drive. While in hospital I invented a game of diplomatic snakes and ladders. One snake's head was on a counter marked 'runs mini into Ambassador's Rolls': the tail was a square marked 'Posted to Monrovia'. One ladder began from a square marked 'Takes Head of Personnel Department out to Prunier's for lunch'. After I was mobile again, however, we found congenial friends in the Embassy, particularly among new arrivals. One of these was Dick Stratton who had been our best man.

In those days there were few cultural manifestations in and around Bonn. For these we had to go to Cologne, Düsseldorf or one of the state (Land) capitals like Hamburg or Munich. But the countryside around Bonn was attractive and we could get out into the country for a walk in a few minutes by car. We had the Rhine almost on our doorstep with the Ahr and the Mosel valleys not far away. Bonn was also a good place from which to visit Austria, Italy and even Greece.

The late 1950s were the heyday of the German economic miracle (the *'Wirtschatswunder'*) whose symbol was Herr Erhard, popularly known as the 'Gummi-Loewe' (rubber lion). I was glad to see that the Germans were able to laugh at themselves in the popular film of the time *'Wir Wunderkinder'* (We wonder boys). Certainly, German industry was humming again, but we often thought that the much-vaunted German efficiency was largely a myth. German promises of completing a job on time seemed to us just as unlikely to be fulfilled as similar promises in Britain. Petty German bureaucracy appeared as tiresome and dilatory as in Britain and service in shops and restaurants was no more willing than in Britain.

Anglo-German relations were fostered by growing links. One of the most important was the annual Koenigswinter Conference of British and German parliamentarians. There were many other contacts at lower levels including those fostered by the British Council. But there were sensitivities on both sides. Any action or statement made inadvertently could arouse hackles. The German press and public were, for instance, horrified when undergraduates at Oxford greeted President Heuss on a state visit to Britain with their hands in their pockets. They could not believe that this British informality was anything but an insult.

British forces in Germany at the height of the cold war were an important element in NATO and in the defence of the Federal Republic. So NATO and defence issues were a significant part of the work of the Embassy. To my regret I was not directly involved with these vital issues. My main job in the Chancery was to assist Lance Pope on internal affairs. Lance Pope, who spoke excellent German and had a German wife, had served in the Control Commission and had wide contacts especially in the governing party the CDU. He was a temporary member of the service who was 'permanent' in Bonn. While he had excellent access, especially among former Nazis, he was not a trained civil servant and his memoranda were not always reliable, particularly if he had been drinking wine and schnapps with his friends the night before. He was not keen to help me develop my contacts and, I felt, somewhat resented my position. At any rate, much of the reporting on the internal scene which fell to me was routine stuff on such boring topics as elections in the Länder (the German states). The job did, however, enable me to travel around Western Germany. I generally took Elizabeth with me at my expense and together we visited the various Consulates General and every Land in the Bundesrepublik (Federal Republic). This helped us to develop our knowledge of German culture and art.

The Ambassador's deputy was the Minister (Political) who supervized the political work of the Embassy and to whom, accordingly, my reports on internal affairs were submitted by the Counsellor Head of Chancery. When we arrived the Minister (Political) was Michael Williams. He was a shy and silent man who kept his opinions to himself and did not take many initiatives. It was said that when a German next to whom he was sitting at an official lunch asked Michael his opinion on various issues of the day Michael replied to every question that he could not comment on internal German political affairs. Eventually, the German gave up and there was silence for a few moments; so Michael felt he had to ask a question and said: 'Don't you think that is pretty view from that window?' The German is said to have responded: 'that is an internal political matter on which I cannot comment!'.

I used to read some five German newspapers every day including *Die Welt* and the *Frankfurter Algemeine Zeitung*. German papers tended to be regional, but the best had fair international coverage. I also had to look at the *Neue Zurcher Zeitung* because its Bonn correspondent known as *'humorloser Luchsinger'* (the humourless Luchsinger) was said to be close to Chancellor Adenauer, *'der alte'* (the old man), who still dominated the German scene. President Heuss, a Swabian with a regional accent, was much respected, but he was a constitutional figurehead. Von Brentano, the Foreign Minister, was a chain-smoking apparatchik.

Many of the civil servants and members of the Bundestag (Parliament) with whom we came in contact had had a Nazi past. Some had difficulty in concealing their sympathies and we heard a good deal about the iniquities of the Treaty of Versailles which was alleged by some to account for the rise of Nazism. We were, however, also able to meet younger Germans, especially outside the Civil Service, who were sincerely anti-Nazi. We did our best to make German friends and through entertaining them to know them better. Towards the end of our stay we felt a developing rapport.

We were particularly sensitive to any signs of resurgent German nationalism and anti-semitism. I recall a series of incidents involving desecration of Jewish graves and the daubing of swastika symbols. I drafted a despatch reviewing the evidence. We could not ignore these manifestations but should not get them out of perspective. We were also rightly concerned during our time in Bonn by the attempts of Germans expelled from East Prussia and other areas taken over by Poland to reassert German claims for the return of German lands. The irredentism of the former Sudeten Germans was also worrying. Inevitably, I compared German and Japanese attitudes. The Japanese have sometimes been described, not always fairly, as the Prussians of the Far East. Both Germany and Japan achieved economic growth and renewal under strict regulation and by achieving concensus in economic management. German and Japanese officials usually had a similar legal training and tended to be meticulous if not pedantic in matters of detail. Officials in both countries liked to be referred to by the titles of their offices. Germans and Japanese are said to have similar senses of (or lack of) humour.

But there were real differences. German officials were on the whole more forthcoming and somewhat more flexible than their

Japanese opposite numbers. Germany was and remains a federal
state with significant differences in culture and traditions betwen
the Länder. German Catholics and Protestants during our time
in Germany rarely intermarried and each area was proud (or jealous) of its religious heritage. While there are, of course, significant differences between regions in Japan for historical and
geographical reasons Japan, despite its division into prefectures,
is not in any sense a federal state and, despite pressures for more
devolution to the prefectures (*chiho bunken*), government in Japan
is far more centralized than in Germany.

Germany lying in the centre of Europe and with land frontiers
to many other European countries was much more international
even in the 1950s than Japan. The most outward looking Länder
were the old Hanseatic cities of Hamburg and Bremen, but even
Bavaria was becoming increasingly aware of being part of Europe. When we were in Bonn the European movement had not
been going for long, but there was no doubt of its appeal to Germans who were still recovering from the war. Unfortunately, Britain was not a founder member of the Treaty of Rome and we
maintained the view that Britain was separate. We continued to
think, at least partially mistakenly, of the special relationship
with the USA and of the British Commonwealth as enabling us
to act as a bridge between Europe and North America and Europe and the rest of the world.

The Germans at this time had not yet come to terms fully with
their past, but there was a growing acceptance among the post-
war generation that there must be no repetition of German im-
perialism and that, even if none of the new politicians or officials
had any personal responsibility for the holocaust and German
behaviour in occupied countries, Germany had to take steps to
atone for the past. The Japanese, on the other hand, have never
seemed to recognize fully the crimes committed by members of
the Japanese imperial forces or the need to take steps to atone for
what was done by their forces. It is sometimes suggested that this
difference arises from the sense of guilt which comes from Christian beliefs. Perhaps, but I suspect that it has more to do with the
difference between the new leaders in Germany and the pre-war

retread Japanese politicians and officials who controlled the levers of power in post-war Japan.

In neither Germany nor Japan were invitations to visit German or Japanese homes readily forthcoming. But when you got to know them German families even of the older and more formal generation were on the whole more willing than their Japanese counterparts to invite foreigners to visit them at home. Germans did not feel that they had to live grandly or entertain lavishly whereas so many Japanese in the past at least were somewhat ashamed of their cramped quarters and felt that it would not be seemly to entertain foreign guests in the simple fashion which many British at least would welcome.

Another of my tasks was to liaise with the Auswaertiges Amt (the German Foreign Office) and other European missions, especially the French and the Dutch, on questions relating to developing countries particularly in Asia. The Germans were then building up their missions abroad and generally welcomed the information we could pass on to them. In this context I came in contact with the Japanese Embassy in Bonn. The Ambassador and his number two were both called Takeuchi which was muddling for non-Japanese speakers who did not realize that the characters used for 'Take' were different.

As my brief also covered German relations with the developing world it fell to me to help to induct a couple of Nigerian novices into the intricacies of operating a Foreign Service. The first was quick and intelligent and in due course became Nigerian High Commissioner in London and Permanent Secretary in his Ministry until he was removed in one of Nigeria's coups. The other who had been brought up by missionaries can only be described as a pain. He seemed to learn nothing and tried my patience sorely.

After two-and-a-half years I was beginning to enjoy Bonn and felt that I had an increasing amount to contribute. But the Foreign Office decided that after six years away it was time for me to return to Japan. I was instructed to take up the post of First Secretary in Tokyo. At that time the Head of Chancery's post in Tokyo was filled by a non-Japanese speaking Counsellor. I was 36 and at that stage the average age of promotion to Counsellor was over 40. (I was, in fact, nearly 42 before I was promoted.) I would, therefore, be the number two in Chancery and fulfil the role of 'Japanese Secretary' as in the Embassy before the war.

We were allowed to travel out to Japan on a German passenger and cargo boat which after a very brief leave in Britain we boarded early in January 1961. I was glad to have this sea voyage so that I could once again revise my Japanese. It was also a good rest for Elizabeth, who was pregnant. She was looking forward to seeing Japan about which she had heard so much from me. We travelled overland to Genoa and joined the boat there. We went via the Suez canal to Aden, Colombo, Singapore and Hong Kong before calling in at Kobe on our way to our final destination of Yokohama. The voyage took some five-to-six weeks with short stops at the ports en route where passengers could disembark and enjoy the usual tourist attractions. The menus on our German ship were good, but we particualrly enjoyed the opportunity to sample occasionally the solid German fare available to the crews.

Life on board ship followed a regular routine. All passengers had to practise boat drill from time to time to ensure that we knew where to go and how to behave in an emergency, but that aside, we lived a life of leisure. We could read books on deck, play deck games and swim in the pool. We changed for dinner but only had to wear black tie on special occasions such as the night before arriving in a port where passengers were disembarking. As there were less than 100 passengers on board our ship the SS *Schwabenstein* we were not troubled on this voyage by the forced gaiety and party games of larger vessels. The Captain and senior officers joined the passengers for dinner and attempted to maintain a good social atmosphere. Every day there was a sweepstake on the distance which the ship would have covered between noon one day and noon the next. The unmarried pursued romantic attachments but most acquainanceships made on board rarely lasted long after disembarkation. There were days when the seas were rough and we were forced to remain inside but on the whole these were rare.

CHAPTER THREE

Japan in the 1960s

———————————— oOo ————————————

TOKYO: 1961-65

On our arrival in Tokyo at the end of February 1961, Elizabeth and I moved into Number 6 house in the Embassy compound which I had shared in my bachelor days. We were fortunate in being able to inherit a Japanese cook and an excellent maid/nanny. Our son, William, was born in June that year at the Seventh Day Adventist Hospital at Ogikubo. This was quite good medically but the atmosphere (not even tea was allowed) was depressing. It was a long drive out along a road where there were still trams and where there was much construction work going on. I was also put off by the fact that the putrifying corpse of a dog, which had been run over, was left for days in the humid rainy season on the narrow side road leading to the hospital. I was worried by the fact that Elizabeth had to go back into hospital with post-natal bleeding. Fortunately, however, she soon recovered. But it was a very hot summer. We had no air-conditioning in the house and our bedroom was very noisy from the road in front of the Embassy on which trams still ran.

In 1962 we were able to take a house in Minamihara outside Karuizawa. Minamihara was a settlement on the outskirts of Karuizawa which had been developed before the war by a number of Japanese intellectuals. The house which we rented had very basic equipment. The bath was a tiny wooden one heated by chopped wood. It was not easy to get it to light. Mrs Seki, the owner, was a formidable and old-fashioned elderly Japanese who firmly told Elizabeth that third-class futon (mattresses) were quite good enough for domestic servants! Elizabeth and William shared the house with Bridget Meese and her daughter Carolyn. Bridget was married to an old RAF and SOAS friend Reggie Meese. We were fortunate in being able to get a house in Karuizawa again in the summers of 1963 (we had home leave that spring) and of 1964. In April that year our daughter Rosemary was born.

We took the house for the months of July and August. Elizabeth stayed up with the children. I managed to get a week or so of local leave in Karuizawa each summer and used to go up by train at week-ends, arriving late on a Friday evening and returning late on a Sunday. It was good to get out of the oppressive Tokyo heat and away from the sound of the pile-drivers which worked all night outside the Embassy compound, building one of the 'high speed' roads needed for the Tokyo Olympics in 1964. But I had a constant struggle to buy reserved seats on the trains which were run by the Japanese National Railways. There was no competition and insufficient trains at weekends when Japanese began to flock to Karuizawa for golf, the increasingly popular sport among businessmen. Karuizawa had been opened by Christian missionaries in the late nineteenth century as a refuge from the heat of the Kanto plain. In the early 1960s it was still fairly unspoilt and the main street in the 'machi' (town) was quiet except for a few weeks in August around the O-Bon festival in the middle of that month. It was a good place for country walks.

Elizabeth was determined to learn some spoken Japanese. She had no intention of leaving all the talking to me and needed to speak Japanese if only to communicate with our domestic staff who spoke practically no English. Fortunately she has a good ear and was soon able to keep her end up in normal conversations. We concentrated in our entertaining on Japanese guests many of whom were not fluent in English. So her knowledge of Japanese was very useful.

There was a small commissariat in the Embassy from which we could purchase a very limited range of imported foods such as New Zealand butter. (As Head of Chancery from 1963-5 I was responsible for overseeing the Commissariat. I then discovered discrepancies in the accounts and the stocks held and had to close the commissary down in its then form.) We imported our own wines and spirits but for the rest depended on the Japanese market. Costs other than for imported goods were low especially at the then prevailing exchange rate. It was still possible, for instance, to get a book of 11 tram tickets for 100 yen (about 20p), but the tramways were being removed and replaced by new underground lines, although in the early 1960s the only line in use was the pre-war Ginza line.

Japanese domestic staff were becoming increasingly hard to find, but the houses in the Embassy compound were old-fashioned and had been built for the days when domestic servants, for whom each house had special quarters at the back, were plentiful. Apart from old-fashioned plumbing, the kitchen was antiquated and distant from the dining-room. The door furniture was of brass which needed constant polishing and the heating, which was inadequate, was either provided by open fires or by a boiler fed by coal. The resulting 'central heating' was little more than background warming. Because of the thickness of the concrete walls the houses got very cold in winter and uncomfortably hot in summer. It took a major struggle with the Ministry of Works to achieve any progress over modernizing the houses in the compound.

In the Embassy one of my priorities was to study internal politics. The Embassy's political contacts were not good at that time and we did our best to develop relations with a wide range of politicians and trade unionists. This brought me into contact with some politicians who were later to play important roles in the Japanese Government, including Fukuda Takeo who eventually became Prime Minister in the 1970s. I also attempted to cultivate officials in the opposition Japan Socialist Party (JSP) and in large Japanese Labour Unions, including the public sector unions such as the communications workers and the teachers union. A good relationship developed with Wada Haruo, the leader of the seamen's union. I also tried hard, not entirely succesfully, to establish a relationship with Iwai, the Secretary General of Sohyo, the main left wing group of unions.

The Japanese political structure was a rigid one. The Liberal Democratic Party (LDP) was divided into factions which owed loyalty to particular political bosses who managed the funds collected from business. Personalities mattered far more than ideology. To many observers it seemed that Japanese politics was almost as corrupt and lacking in political principle as it had been in the 1920s. However, some changes were being forced on the conservative politicians. The beginnings of a Japanese welfare state were being established in response to popular pressures, although initially the arrangements seeemed minimal. The LDP was thus not totally immune to popular pressures even if there was no likelihood of their being turned out of power by the opposition parties who lacked credibility.

On the left, the Japan Socialist Party (JSP) was still bedevilled by Marxist ideology and intent primarily on opposing the US-Japan Security Treaty which had been renewed in 1960 after a bitter struggle. There were frequent left wing demonstrations which could become violent. During the 1960s extremist students in various factions of Zengakuren (the Students Federation) took over the universities and treated with contumely their teachers, many of whom were Marxists. Their behaviour had many similarities with that of the Chinese communists in the Cultural Revolution. Many observers felt that if the communists had ever managed to come to power in Japan they would have been even more ruthless in suppressing opposition than the Chinese.

I occasionally listened to discussions in the Diet but opposition speeches were even more boring than those of members of the government and interpellations in the Diet which took the place of debates in the British parliament continued to be of little general interest. I also had frequent meetings with the Gaimusho. The British Government had at last begun to recognize the growing importance of Japan and the need to develop contacts over a wide range of topics. During these years we began regular exchanges of information. We gave the Ministry copies of selected despatches and memoranda in Foreign Office print and in return received some pieces of political analysis from the Gaimusho. We gave more than we received but a dialogue had been started. On one occasion, I recall that we introduced Denis Healey, then an opposition spokesman, to Gaimusho officials. His wit puzzled the serious officials of the Gaimusho, especially when he said of a famous Conservative politician that he was so crooked that if he swallowed a nail he would shit a corkscrew.

When Sir Alec Douglas Home was Foreign Secretary arrangements were made for bilateral discussions at Ministerial level. Mr Ohira Masayoshi was the Japanese Foreign Minister at the time and Mr Ohno Katsumi was the Japanee Ambassador in London. Sir Alec invited them to Scotland for some shooting. The Gaimusho were much exercised about what clothing they should wear for shooting. Having suggested initially that it really did not matter and finding that this did not satisfy the officials concerned, I suggested that perhaps they would like to wear plus-fours. I had great difficulty in explaining what these were. I had visions of the Japanese Foreign Ministry trying to explain to a Japanese tailor how to make plus-fours. I rather suspect that the Japanese visitors did wear plus-fours for the shoot, but I never heard for certain and do not know whether they managed to shoot any pheasant or grouse.

One serious foreign policy issue in 1963/4 was caused by 'confrontation' with Indonesia under President Sukarno. The Vice Minister in the Gaimusho at the time was Oda Takio who had been Minister in the Japanese Embassy in London and later Ambassador in Djakarta. He was thought to be close to Sukarno and it was suspected that owing to his influence the Japanese Government favoured the Indonesians in the conflict. There were anti-

British demonstrations by Indonesian students and we did not think that the Japanese police did enough to protect the Embassy whose entrance we had at one point to bar. We probably exaggerated Oda's influence and his sympathies, but the incident was not helpful for Anglo-Japanese relations and exchanges. It also demonstrated to us that, as we were to experience later, such as over the Falklands crisis, the Japanese were concerned more with their commercial interests than with the principles which were at stake.

We kept in particularly close touch with the American Embassy and with the old Commnwealth missions in Tokyo. We were left in no doubt that the Japanese attached the greatest importance to their relations with the United States. We were treated politely but Anglo-Japanese relations were not a high priority for Japan. The Japanese could not fail to note that anti-Japanese feelings continued to fester longer in Britain and Holland than in other European countries, North America and Australia. The Japanese were, however, beginning to realize that a closer relationship with Europe could help to reduce their almost total dependence on the United States, and the importance of the trilateral relationship was increasingly recognized, but there was much to be done on both the Japanese and European sides to develop the relationship which even today often seems to lack adequate substance.

The revised Anglo-Japanese Treaty of Commerce and Navigation was concluded in 1962. The text had been negotiated in English, but the treaty had to be in both English and Japanese with the two texts being equally authentic. This meant that the Japanese text had to be very carefully checked for any possible discrepancies or mistranslations. The Board of Trade had asked Professor Frank Daniels, Professor of Japanese at the School of Oriental and African Studies, to confirm the text on their behalf. Being a conscientious and competent scholar Daniels came up with a small number of queries and suggestions. It fell to me to discuss these with the appropriate official in the Gaimusho. A matter which should have been easy to settle proved extremely difficult. Iguchi Takeo, the official concerned, was proud of his English and strongly objected to each and every query or suggestion. He was a most obstinate young official. He also annoyed me by being rude to the Japanese assistant I took with me for these talks. In the end we persuaded Professor Daniels on most points and the text was accepted. So far as I know, no-one has since ever referred to the text in support of any dispute under the terms of the Treaty.

Arising out of discussions on the Treaty it was agreed that we should attempt to negotiate a Consular Convention. We were particularly concerned to ensure that arrests of British subjects were reported immediately to our consuls who should have speedy access to those arrested so that suitable arrangements could be made for their defence. Adrian Russell, the experienced home civil servant who was responsible in the Foreign Office for Consular conventions, came out on a number of occasions for the negotiations. He was an eccentric bachelor whose socks were invariably in holes. This did not seem to embarrass him at all when he had to take off his shoes to attend a Japanese dinner. A Convention was concluded without too much difficulty and has been helpful to our consuls.

Another problem which led to some complex negotiations was over permission for an additional British doctor to practise in Japan. A small number of foreign doctors had obtained permission to practise in Japan during the Occupation when Japanese medical examinations had been set for them in English. After the occupation was over the Japan Medical Association (JMA) insisted that foreign doctors should pass their examinations in Japanese. Apart from a couple of American Seventh Day Adventist missionary doctors no foreign doctor had sufficient knowledge of Japanese to qualify. The size of the British community was increasing and demands for the services of English-speaking doctors were growing. Eventually, after a series of talks which I conducted with Yamazaki Toshio, the then head of the British Commonwealth Section in the Gaimusho and eventually Japanese Ambassador in London, we reached an agreement allowing one extra British doctor to qualify through examinations in English on the understanding that he would not treat Japanese patients. At the same time the Japanese obtained permission for a

Japanese doctor to treat Japanese patients in London. The Japanese Medical Association and the British Medical Association were almost equally obstinate and narrow-minded over these negotiations. But our agreement opened the way for other British doctors to practise in Japan and the establishment in London of various Japanese medical clinics.

In 1961, Her Royal Highness Princess Alexandra of Kent accepted an invitation to pay an official visit to Japan. Her visit was the first Royal visit to Japan since the war and was intended to help reestablish closer relations with the Japanese Imperial family. I was made responsible for arranging her programme with the Gaimusho and the Kunaicho (Imperial Household Office). The Kunaicho appointed Kikkawa Shigekuni, a Vice-Grand Master of Ceremonies to represent them. Kikkawa was a brother of the Kikkawa whom I had visited outside Iwakuni in 1946 (see page 37). We became good friends. We met regularly for tea and cake at no 6 house in the Embassy. We were very meticulous and thorough over all the details. Even Sir Philip Hay, the Princess's comptroller, when he came on a reconnaisance visit, seemed satisfied. He came with a Group Captain Stack of the Queen's flight. Inevitably this was termed the Haystack visit.

My wife and I did a preliminary reconnaissance of the places to be visited including various sights in Kyoto and the Omiya Palace where she was to stay on her visit. (We tried, for instance, to ensure that the Princess would not have to make do with tiny Japanese towels when she had a bath at the Palace.) I came to realize that in some protocol matters such as whether the royal personage got on or off a boat first or last it did not really matter so long as firm and consistent decisions were made.

The Japanese were determined to do everything possible to make the Princess welcome. She was received by the Emperor and Empress who entertained her to lunch, but the main member of the Imperial Family who looked after her was Her Imperial Highness Princess Chichibu, daughter of a former Japanese Ambassador in London. (Her autobiography has been translated into English and was published by Global Oriental under the title *The Silver Drum* in 1996). Princess Chichibu was active in support of the Japan Red Cross; so naturally there was a visit to the Japan Red Cross Hospital in Tokyo.

The Japanese press soon realized that the young princess was not only beautiful but also charming and totally unstuffy. Her popularity soared and our greatest problem on her tour was the crowd of photographers who followed her everywhere. First, she went by the old imperial train to Toba (near Ise) where she visited the Mikimoto 'Pearl Island' where pearls are cultivated on the sea bed and collected by women divers. The pearls are then extracted and graded for stringing or prepared for brooches, earrings and cuff links. From there she went on to Nara where I feared that at Horyuji the photographers would prevent her from seeing anything. Sir Philip Hay got quite irate and threatened that if the photographers were not kept at bay he would cancel the rest of the visit. Fortunately, it all worked out well in the end and the Princess had an excellent time in Kyoto. She clearly greatly enjoyed her visit as did we all who fell for her charm and good looks.

Rather to my surprise, my wife and I, rather than the Ambassador Sir Oscar and Lady Morland, accompanied her throughout her tour outside Tokyo. Perhaps it was thought that as we were a little nearer to her in age than the Morlands it would be more relaxing for her.

It was not easy for me to get away on visits outside Tokyo, not least because we were beginning a family. However, the Princess's visit enabled us to visit Kyoto and Nara twice and after her visit was over we managed a trip to Kyushu as far as Kagoshima. I also visited my old haunts in Yonago and Matsue in the Sanin district where I was astonished to find that the Tokoen had been redeveloped into a large rather brash hot spring inn. I made one trip to Hokkaido where in addition to visiting Hakodate and Sapporo I went on to Otaru where I called on Taketsuru, who had studied whisky distilling in Scotland, married a Scottish lady and before the war had founded Nikka whisky. From Sapporo I took the train to Kushiro and later to Nemuro on the north-east coast of the island. Kushiro was a major fishing port. Nemuro was the nearest place from which one could view the Soviet occupied islands. It seemed particularly remote and bleak. At this period internal air travel was undeveloped and expensive. So I travelled by train. The journey to Hokkaido took the best part of 24 hours including the ferry from Aomori to Hakodate. There were very few Western-style hotels and I invariably stayed in Japanese inns.

After home leave in 1963 the Counsellor Head of Chancery was transferred and I was appointed Head of Chancery in his place but I remained a First Secretary. As Head of Chancery I was the Ambassador's chief-of-staff and responsible for the efficient running of the Embassy. This involved among many other duties supervision of the registry and the cipher room. We had a small diplomatic wireless staff and were, therefore, not dependent on Japanese communications. We had telex but, of course, there were no faxes and we almost never attempted to communicate with London by telephone. Every day we sent and received a significant number of telegrams. There was constant pressure from London to reduce the number of telegrams sent and received by diplomatic posts and to reduce their length. One of my jobs as Head of Chancery was to vet all telegraphic traffic originating in the Embassy and to question any unnecessary telegrams or ones that were too long. This led to quite a lot of friction especially with the service attachés.

The Head of Chancery was also responsible for the accounts. These were done by a junior officer who was not a trained accountant and I used to worry a good deal about the dangers of fraud and peculation of government funds as I knew that I would be held personally responsible for any losses. We had to arrange snap checks of cash and bank balances and ensure that all items of expenditure were properly authorized and accounted for. Preparing the monthly accounts for despatch to London was a time-consuming process. However careful we were we seemed always to receive some three months later a series of petty questions which had to be researched and answered.

Another of the Head of Chancery's duties was supervision of the administration and the public works section attached to the Embassy. Finding appropriate accommodation and negotiating leases was a major problem. I fought hard with the authorities for improvements to the Embassy premises. I won one battle in 1965 when individual office air-conditioners were finally installed. These had been refused on the grounds that although the Tokyo summer was undoubtedly unpleasant it only lasted at most for three months and the Treasury insisted that it was not necessary to have air-conditioning for such a short time. I did not succeed in getting the office to provide air-conditioners for bedrooms. The provision of these remained for another decade or more the responsibility of individual officers.

Among the most tricky problems for the Head of Chancery were staff morale, security and efficiency. This was the height of the cold war and our mission was a target for the large Soviet and satellite country missions in Tokyo. We had to beware, therefore, not only of the hazards of deviant heterosexual and of homosexual behaviour but also of electronic evesdropping. Vetting of staff had become a high priority. The junior staff of secretaries, registry and cipher staff needed to be looked after and jollied along. We did all we could by inviting junior staff to our parties and watching for signs of discontent or mental illness.

As I had passed the advanced examination in Japanese and was the senior Japanese speaking secretary in the Embassy I was responsible for language training. Each year, we received two or three language students from London. In our view the most effective language training was done in Japan, but this was expensive and the Foreign Office had begun to insist that language students should first do a course of study in Britain before coming out for their second year as language students. At one stage students were sent to SOAS, at another to Sheffield. Neither course proved ideal. The students did not get enough oral practice and the universities tended to be rather too academic in their approach, while teaching was not sufficiently intensive for our purposes. We did what we could in correspondence to improve these arrangements.

At first, students in Japan had been housed in Tokyo where individual teachers had visited them for so many hours tuition each week. This, too, was not very satisfactory. The teachers varied in their abilities and in their relationships with their students.

There was also the danger that in Tokyo the students might be called in too frequently to help out in the Embassy or might spend too much time with members of the foreign expatriate communities in Tokyo and Yokohama. So we decided to set up a small school in Kamakura which was only an hour away by train and where we hoped that the students would live in an almost exclusively Japanese atmosphere. Having a school, even if there were never more than a four or at most five students studying there at any one time, meant that it was easier to standardize the teaching and keep an eye on progress. The students were supposed to be able to pass the intermediate examination which required them to know the characters taught in primary school by the time they came out to Japan. The aim was that they should pass the higher standard examination (see page 73) at the end of their year at Kamakura. The advanced examination could only be taken after a further year in Japan working in the Embassy. Not all students in fact went on to take the advanced examination. Language allowances varied depending on the level passed and could only be granted after the Civil Service Commission in London had confirmed the marks of the candidates. Such allowances were subject to UK tax and were not generous.

The early 1960s were the days of Prime Minister Ikeda Hayato's 'Double the Income' policies. Japan was achieving very high rates of growth and there were huge developments and building projects. The Shinkansen, the new broad-gauge railway line (sometimes called the 'bullet train') between Tokyo and Osaka via Nagoya and Kyoto, was completed in time for the Tokyo Olympics in 1964. The time taken to Osaka was halved. The first motorway from Nagoya to Kobe (the Meishin expressway) was also opened in time for the Olympics. At the same time a system of high-speed toll roads was opened in Tokyo although there were initially only a very limited number of sections completed. Soon these so-called expressways were to become slow and expensive roads as traffic grew faster than the road system. With these new roads and railways Japanese factories were expanded. The area between Tokyo and Osaka almost seemed to become one factory after another. As environmental protection laws were either non-existent or not enforced in those days pollution grew worse every year.

Japan still faced a balance of trade deficit and Japanese trade policies remained highly protectionist. Japanese efforts to develop basic industries and exports were impressive and there were increasing fears in Britain about Japanese competition based on low wages and 'sweated labour'. Japan's economic potential was beginning to be recognized (for instance by Norman Macrae who began his series of special supplements on Japan in *The Economist* in the early 1960s). I was not at this time involved in commercial work and did not have contacts with the Ministry of International Trade and Industry (MITI).

Employment patterns were changing, but the Japanese salary worker was still generally poor and housing very cramped. Because Japanese houses were so cramped and salaries generally low invitations to visit Japanese at home were very rare. Japan had not yet quite reached the era of 'the three Cs' i.e. car, cooler and colour television in every household, but the aspiration was there. Golf was increasingly becoming the preoccupation of the politician and the company executive and golf membership was a highly expensive perk to which only a few could aspire.

The Tokyo Olympics helped to push Japan into the media. The British Embassy was closely involved with the British team. Richard Ellingworth, with whom I had shared a house in my bachelor days, was appointed Olympic attaché and did all he could for the British teams and the visiting media. The Japanese worked hard to make the games a success. Fine new stadia and gymnasia were built and the Olympic village which housed the athletes was generally praised. Few could fault the Japanese arrangements.

The British Ambassador for my first two years was Sir Oscar Morland. He had come from Djakarta to succeed Sir Daniel Lascelles who had stayed less than two years. I never knew Lascelles, but I gathered that he had been very much a square peg in a round hole. A bachelor who had never been in Japan before, he was said to have preferred bicycling in the country to ambassadorial life. Oscar had been in the Japan consular service before the war and his wife Alice was the daughter of a pre-war Ambassador. Oscar was competent in Japanese but was reluctant to speak it unless he had to. Strangely for a diplomat he was shy and diffident on meeting people. There was, of course, a hard core to his personality and he could be firm if not obstinate. He was also astute in his judgements, but he lacked charisma and push. The Embassy under Oscar was regarded as competent but not inspiring. I got on reasonably well with Oscar and with Alice although some of the Embassy wives regarded her as rather old-fashioned and a bit of a dragon on matters of dress and protocol. In those days, Embassy wives did not have separate jobs and were expected to support their husbands in their representational duties including entertaining at home and attending Embassy functions, where their task was to support the Ambassador and his lady.

Tony Rundall (or to give him his proper title Sir Francis Rundall) and his wife Mary who came out to Tokyo in 1963 were quite different although diplomatic staff today would have found their attitudes rather old fashioned. He had been an inspector and Chief Clerk (i.e. the senior officer in the Foreign Office responsible for personnel and administration). Accordingly, he and Mary took a close personal interest in all their staff and families. Tony was new to Japan and found the Japanese difficult to fathom. He was, however, very serious minded and extremely conscientious. He worked hard on his contacts especially with the Gaimusho, but his inability to speak or read Japanese (the Rundalls tried hard but without any real success to learn a little Japanese) meant that in any contacts with politicians he had to work through an interpreter. In the office he was meticulous and fussy and unfortunately for him (and for those around him) he suffered from a stomach disorder probably of a nervous origin. This made him rather tetchy from time to time. Attending a dinner party at the Rundalls was often an ordeal as they took their entertaining so seriously. We would be given instructions not only about whom we were to talk to before dinner but also after dinner. This might include instructions about changing places at a given signal. Once I recall being interrupted in an interesting conversation with a Japanese guest by a call from Mary Rundall to come over and talk to the Finnish Ambassador who was a fat, somnolent, porcine individual who only wanted to be left in peace to doze before the fire. This said, I found Tony a competent and conscientious, if uninspired, Ambassador. He and Mary were both good and kind people.

The role of a British Ambassador in the 1960s was very different from what it had been before the war. At that time Britain was a major power in the Far East and Japan posed a serious threat to our interests. Relations with Japan were accordingly politically important and there were frequent contacts with Japanese Ministers. The Ambassador was, of course, constrained by his instructions which could be given to him quickly by telegraph. These did not leave him much discretion, but through his high level contacts he had some influence.

By the 1960s Britain was withdrawing from East of Suez. The British economy faced serious problems and the sterling area was ceasing to be relevant. British Ambassadors had to adapt to the new situation. This meant becoming increasingly involved in economic and commercial issues and defending as well as promoting publicly the British position. A new breed of British Ambassadors was needed. Oscar Morland was too negative a personality to fill this role effectively. Tony Rundall tried hard to adapt to the requirements of the 1960s. He understood the changes taking place, but he did not find his new role an easy one.

The 1970s and 1980s were to bring further changes. Ambassadors in the 1960s began to receive more ministerial and business visitors, but the numbers were a mere trickle in comparison with the flood which was to come later. There were also the added complications resulting from direct contacts between Ministers at international conferences and direct telephone conversations.

When in 1965 the time came to return to London we were sad to say goodbye to so many good friends we had made. My attitude towards Japan was more objective and mature than it had been. I did not have rose-tinted spectacles but could see better both the good and the bad aspects of modern Japan. At our farewell parties we thought that it would be many years before we returned.

INTERLUDE: LONDON 1965-66

We had a bad journey back to London in the summer of 1965. William was just four and Rosemary 15 months. The BOAC (British Overseas Airways Corporation, popularly known as 'Better on a camel') aircraft were still using the southern route stopping at Hong Kong, Bangkok, Bombay, Bahrein and Rome. Just after leaving Bombay the pressurization failed. The children were naturally frightened by the masks which appeared. The aircraft descended quickly and after some time ditching fuel was diverted to Karachi where we landed in the middle of the night. Eventually, after some hours delay, we were put on a Pan American flight to Beirut. We had to change there onto another flight to Rome and then to Paris where we were told that there would be a considerable further delay. After a lot of pleading we got seats on an old Air France plane, a Caravelle, to Heathrow. We were exhausted as were the children. William had hardly slept on the flight but had fallen asleep in my arms as we arrived. I was not best pleased by the generally unhelpful attitude of the airport staff at Heathrow.

Our first task was to find somewhere to live as we had neither a house nor a flat in London. Eventually, after some weeks with my parents-in-law, we bought a small modern house in Maida Vale for just under £17,000 using almost all our capital. The house in a close had a combined dining/sitting-room, kitchen and cloaks on the ground floor plus a tiny patio. There were two bathrooms and four bedrooms plus a small study and playroom on the two upper floors. So it was a good family house. I could and often did walk to the Foreign Office. The distance was just over three miles.

In the early autumn of 1965 I took up my appoinment as assistant head of West and Central African Department. The department was *inter alia* responsible in the Foreign Office for South Africa and the foreign policy aspects of Rhodesia. I began to study the South African situation and the problems caused by apartheid. The head of my department gave a lunch for Helen Suzman, the Progressive Party member of the South African Party, to which I was invited. I was impressed by her courage and determination. Unfortunately, before I could do much in relation to South African issues, I found myself almost entirely involved with Rhodesian problems following the illegal declaration that autumn of Rhodesian independence. As the Commonwealth Office had a Rhodesia Department and other government departments in Whitehall were involved, including the Department of Economic Affairs where George Brown was the Minister and determined to take the lead, policy coordination was, to say the least, difficult. Although I was still only a senior First Secretary, equivalent to a Principal in the Home Civil service at that time, I frequently had to represent the Foreign Office on interdepartmental committttees. One of these was chaired by the second Permanent Secretary in the Department of Economic Affairs. Most of the others attending these meetings were in at least one or two ranks higher than I was. One day, I was summoned by Michael Rose, the Assistant Under-Secretary for African affairs, and told that the chairman had complained about the way in which as a junior official I had argued the Foreign Office's viewpoint against his views as chairman. I am glad to say that Michael Rose supported my position and told me to continue to argue the case effectively although perhaps I should do so more tactfully in future.

Harold Wilson as Prime Minister had the unfortunate habit of making snap policy decisions without considering the implications. One of these was to impose oil sanctions before he had even read the paper drafted by officials pointing out that oil sanctions would in practice be unenforceable. I regarded this as 'instant misgovernment' which I found as distasteful as instant coffee.

In those days the Foreign Office was not fully centrally-heated and we depended on coal fires for heating our offices on the second floor overlooking Downing Street. As we had to work until very late as well as on Saturdays and Sundays during the crisis I often wore my overcoat in the office that winter. My life was further complicated by the unfortunate habit of the head of department of not telling me what he was up to and then going off on leave. This led to some embarrassing moments, including an interview with Michael Stewart, then Foregn Secretary, when as a result of not being kept adequately informed I could not brief him properly.

Because promotions were so delayed at that time the Foreign Office introduced so-called notional promotion. At the age of 41 I was promoted to 'notional counsellor'. As this carried no increase in pay or responsibility it was pretty meaningless, but I suppose it was thought to constitute a boost to morale.

I had little contact with Japan during these months in London although on one occasion I was called to interpret at a Buckingham Palace luncheon for Prince and Princess Hitachi. He was the Emperor's younger son and hence younger brother of the Crown Prince. The Prince and Princess were on their honeymoon trip. He and the Duke of Edinburgh were interested in ornithology; I had some difficulty with the vocabulary. During the lunch I sat behind the Prince. When Prince Hitachi told the Queen that he had just been visiting Waterloo where Nelson had defeated Napoleon I substituted Wellington for Nelson and a gaffe was avoided. When the fruit came round Prince Hitachi took grapes but was not sure how to eat them and asked me what he should do. I told him he could eat them in any way he liked. Princess Alexandra who was sitting on the Prince's right and who recognized me from her visit to Japan heard this exchange and to my embarrasment forced me to interpret it to her. Fortunately, she agreed with the advice I had given the Prince.

I looked forward to getting out of West and Central African Department, but I was astonished when, in the spring of 1966, I was told that I would be going back to Tokyo that summer as Commercial Counsellor. In fact, the job covered both commercial and economic work. I was in two minds about this appointment at first. I had thought hitherto that political work was the most important in the service and wondered whether I was being sidelined. If I went back to Japan so soon would I not be written off as a Japanologist lacking in a broader experience? Perhaps the rumour would be that I was becoming slit-eyed! Moreover, I had not previously been involved in commercial work and such courses as were available for newly-appointed commercial officers dealt primarily with details about practical issues such as bills of lading, in which I would not need to be involved, and did not deal with the main issues on which exporters wanted the help and advice of commercial officers working in our missions abroad. I soon realized that this appointment was a significant challenge and threw myself with enthusiasm into the necessary briefing calls which I made in the six weeks or so available before I had to leave for Tokyo. In the event, I found the post of Commercial Counsellor in Tokyo one of the most interesting and stimulating in my career. I soon recognized the vital importance of commercial and economic work and greatly enjoyed the post.

We decided on this occasion, because of the difficulty of finding suitable Japanese domestic staff, to take a nanny with us. She was quite a pretty girl and on the ship which took us to Japan she enjoyed herself with the ship's officers. At one point we wondered whether she would be available to work for us in Tokyo.

TOKYO: 1966-70

On arrival in Tokyo we were assigned to Number 4 house, one of the counsellors' houses in the compound which my predecessor as Commercial Counsellor had occupied. Like Number 6 house where we had lived earlier it was near the main road and noisy. It was also large and not easy to run. We had only been in Tokyo a month when the male Japanese cook whom we had inherited told us that he was leaving. He had been filched by the American Minister for the new US Ambassador. I protested unsuccessfully against such undiplomatic behaviour. Some diplomats think it worse to go off with a colleague's cook than to make off with his wife. I do not agree, but I still resent the way it was done without any attempt to speak directly to me or give me a chance to dissuade our cook from leaving. Fortunately, after a brief interval, we found a good successor.

Tony Rundall, who was still Ambassador, made it clear that he had asked for me to return in this post. It was now more than ever obvious to all observers that the Japanese economy had begun to take off. There was a huge potential market in Japan. Despite the obstacles erected by the Japanese authorities to protect nascent industries and to limit Japan's then serious imbalance in the current account there were growing opportunities for British exports. British firms needed all possible help in overcoming Japanese barriers and in penetrating this distant and difficult market. The Japanese had not yet begun to complain about the lack of effort by foreign exporters – a moan which became a refrain in the 70s and 80s. In my view, it was not generally applicable to the United Kingdom which from the mid-60s made major efforts to penetrate the Japanese market.

Tony Rundall took all his responsibilities very seriously. Shortly after I returned to Tokyo in 1966 we received instructions from London about the forthcoming visit to Tokyo of Robert Maxwell, then a Member of Parliament, who liked to use his former army rank of Captain (hence he was called 'Cap'n Bob'). Maxwell was coming out to Japan to promote the sales of Chambers Encyclopedia to which he had purchased the rights. We were to give him every possible assistance as otherwise he would make trouble. He demanded a meeting with the Japanese Prime Minister, then Sato Eisaku, and a reception, hosted by the Ambassador, to enable him to meet Japanese book dealers. I thought both demands excessive, but Tony decided to try to comply with them. Rather to my surprise Sato agreed to receive Maxwell. Tony and I accompanied him on the call. Sato, who was a consummate politician, saw the political advantage to Maxwell and accordingly graciously accepted a set of Chambers Encyclopedia, but I thought we were unwise to use up good will in this way. I recall going with Maxwell afterwards to call at Maruzen, one of the leading Japanese book dealers. Maxwell boasted to me in the car about his ability in foreign languages. So I gave him a few simple tips about the pronunciation of Japanese words. He said 'yes, of course', but continued to mispronounce Japanese names. He had no idea how to behave to Japanese. I was horrified to learn that at a dinner given for him by Tsukasa, then President of Maruzen, he had treated Mrs Tsukasa as if she was a geisha. I met Cap'n Bob a few times after I retired and always disliked his arrogance.

Tony Rundall wanted me to revitalize the commercial department. My predecessor was a conscientious commercial officer, but his ideas of organization were peculiar. All incoming papers were shown to him before being registered and he would mark on each which member of his staff was to deal with the paper in question. No-one quite knew whether they were to specialize in trade promotion or in economic relations work. As the volume of paper was increasing very fast the system was leading to delays and inefficiencies.

My first task was to reorganize the department into economic and trade promotion sections under two first secretaries with clear lines of responsibility. Of course, frequently the work of the two sections overlapped. For instance, a visiting British businessman would encounter a non-tariff barrier or a patent problem and the staff of the economic section would become involved in trying to solve the businessman's problem.

I divided my time between the two types of work depending on visitors and the pressure of events. We took over temporary offices which had been put up on what had been the Embassy tennis court. These were a great deal better than the old offices in the chancery building which were cramped and which, because of security considerations in the confidential offices, were not 'visitor friendly', but as the new offices were of a flimsy contruction they felt distinctly unsafe in the minor earthquakes which regularly strike Tokyo. We also needed more staff, UK-based and local, to cope with our increasing work-load. Tony Rundall gave us all support possible and as a former Chief Clerk he knew his way round the Whitehall machine. I was fortunate in having some very able assistants. John Whitehead (later Sir John and Ambassador in Tokyo) was First Secretary (economic) while David Wright (later Sir David and also Ambassador in Tokyo) was Third/Second secretary (economic). Alan Harvey was First Secretary (Commercial) and responsible for trade promotion work.

□

Our main task, apart from economic reporting, was to liaise with the Japanese authorities, primarily with the Ministry of International Trade and Industry (MITI), but also with the Gaimusho and other Japanese ministries involved with trade issues. We had to negotiate over the quotas, tariffs and other restrictions which the Japanese placed on our exports as well as on the quotas and other export restraint arrangements which limited Japanese exports to the United Kingdom.

We had frequent visits from Board of Trade officials concerned with these issues and with GATT problems. Negotiations were generally very time-consuming and frustrating. The Japanese officials with whom we dealt fought every inch of the way as if making a concession of however small a nature impugned their virility. Talks would often go on late into the night and up to and beyond deadlines. We frequently felt very exasperated, but we had to continue to deal with the Japanese officials concerned and could not afford a bust up. So we had to do our best to persuade our visitors to treat Japanese negotiating methods as ploys in a silly game and not part of a trade war.

In the 1960s, although we were trying to expand our exports to Japan over a wide range of capital goods as well as consumer items, some of our best exports of consumer items were subject to various restrictions in the Japanese market. The primary obstacle at that stage for exports of Scotch whisky was the limited quota and we spent much time and effort trying to get this expanded. Of course, when eventually the quota was abolished, the industry found, as we knew they would, that there were other obstacles, in particular the discriminatory tax regime against Scotch whisky. The purpose of these restrictions was to protect the Japanese whisky distillers especially Suntory and to a lesser extent Nikka. There was no possible excuse on agricultural or employment grounds. We suspected (and I have no reason to suppose that our suspicions were unjustified) that Suntory in particular was a major contributor to the funds of the Liberal Democratic Party (LDP) and that officials of the Ministry of Finance (MOF) were in the pocket of the LDP.

Another major British export to Japan was woollen cloth. In this case there was an indigenous wool cloth industry to protect, but British woollen cloth from Bradford and Huddersfield was of higher quality and there was a strong demand for our cloth by

Japanese tailors. Once again it was uphill work getting the quota increased. Among other British products subject to quota, tariff and other non-tariff barriers were biscuits, chocolate and sugar confectionery. Here the Japanese excuse, other than protection of indigenous Japanese industries in these products, was the desire to protect the sugar industry of the Ryukyu islands. Japanese manufacturers of these products had high costs and their products were of fairly low quality. Japanese manufacturers would have benefited from some more foreign competition, but we were hardly in a position to put these arguments effectively in view of our own protectionist policies over textiles, pottery and other products.

The Japanese for their part were mainly concerned to get the restrictions lifted or expanded on Japanese exports to Britain imposed under the two exchanges of notes appended to the Treaty of Commerce and Navigation which had been signed in November 1962. Under the first exchange of notes the Japanese government had agreed to 'exercise voluntary export control' on the export to the United Kingdom of a list of 14 products. The first 12 of these items were textiles and included cotton yarn, woven and knitted fabrics as well as lace and netting. Item 13 covered radio and television apparatus and parts including semi-conductors and transistors, while item 14 covered domestic pottery and ceramic toys. Under the second exchange of notes the United Kingdom government were authorized to restrict the import of Japanese products subject to quotas which were to be increased annually and to cease by specified dates. The items covered included binoculars and microscopes, cigarette lighters, toys and games, fishing tackle (excluding fishing reels), sewing machines and cutlery. All items were to be liberalized by 1968 and most by earlier dates.

The greatest problems occurred over pottery, cutlery and electrical goods, but British manufacturers complained bitterly over alleged unfair competition as a result of sweated labour and low wages in textile factories in Osaka, in Japanese workshops in Tsubame (the main Japanese cutlery manufacturing centre) and in potteries around Nagoya. In addition to the tough arguments we had with the Japanese officials concerned we had to look after British visitors from the industries affected and arrange meetings for them with their opposite numbers in Japanese industry. The fact that many of these contacts were productive of understandings shows that not everyone on the two sides was always unreasonable.

We also had to be mindful of the first protocol under which if products were being imported into the territory of the other contracting party 'in such increased quantities and under such conditions as to cause or threaten serious injury to producers' in the territory of the other party, the government concerned could restrict imports of such products after giving notice and holding consultations. The government of the country whose products were thus restricted could take compensating action. In practice, every effort was made by both governments to avoid taking action under this protocol, but there were frequent pressures in Britain for the provisions to be used. One of the most contentious cases we had to deal with concerned fishing reels (specifically not covered by the second protocol) made by a manufacturer in Plymouth which was a marginal constituency. Eventually, after a good deal of brinkmanship on both sides the case was solved.

We had to deal with a number of complaints about infringement of copyright and copying of designs. Some cases were blatant enough to justify a tough stance. Others were sometimes the result of a failure of British producers to register patents and trade marks. One particularly blatant action was taken by a Japanese importer who registered Earl Grey as a trade mark when it has traditionally been simply a description of a type of tea. We were justifiably annoyed and I called in the Japanese businessman involved who was a major importer of British goods and reprimanded him for his behaviour. I do not think he cared about the damage done to Japan's reputation for honourable trading or for the limits which his action imposed on sales by other importers of Earl Grey. The Japanese Patent Agency was also open to criticism for dilatoriness even if it was difficult to prove that they favoured Japanese manufacturers deliberately.

I got on pretty well with our various visitors from the Board of Trade. The Under Secretary, Cyril Sanders, was an astute and affable man approaching retirement. He had a gammy leg and smoked a smelly pipe. Married to another civil servant, he looked generally as if he had slept in his clothes.

Trade negotiations were tough, but even tougher were negotiations under the UK-Japan Civil Aviation Agreement. Both sides were determined to protect their national airlines and enforce the best possible bargain for them. Negotiations were often acrimonious and long drawn out. They were so exhausting that one leader on the British side had a nervous breakdown. I came to the view then, which I have not changed since, that the Japanese Ministry of Transport, especially the Civil Aviation Bureau, was staffed by blinkered officials who had never learnt that competition is a necessity for efficiency. In view of their attitude it did not surprise me that Japan Air Lines never managed to take the leading role in civil aviation in Asia which Japan's industrial success would have justified. Unfortunately, British Airways had been slow to develop the polar route and in the absence of competition their service was at that time generally poor and flights were often delayed.

Shipping presented few problems. The conference system worked reasonably well except for problems with the Americans whose shipping policies have always been particuarly protectionist. British and Japanese shipping lines had good contacts and friendly relations were established under the leadership of Ariyoshi, then President, later Chairman of NYK line, who was the 'Grand Old Man' of Japanese shipping.

Shipbuilding was more of a problem. The Japanese were increasingly winning orders at the expense of European yards especially for vast oil tankers and bulk carriers. British shippers including BP were among firms ordering ships from Japanese yards in the late 1960s. The British shipbuilders complained of unfair competition but a high-level mission from the industry, including trade union representatives, had to admit that Japanese success was due to better building methods, efficient planning and high productivity. The Japanese yards, who knew that they had a competitive lead with which our yards were unlikely ever to catch up, were helpful in receiving the mission and demonstrating the methods of ship-building which they had developed

The British steel industry also complained about Japanese competition. A mission from British Steel led by Monty Finneston, who later became Chairman of British Steel, was given a very friendly welcome by Inayama, who later became Chairman of Keidanren (The Japanese Federation of Economic Organizations) and of Japan Steel. The British had to recognize the superiority of Japanese technology in steel production and had much to learn from Japan.

The attitude at this time of British Leyland towards the growing Japanese car industry was condescending. Lord Stokes, then Chairman of British Leyland, took the view that the Japanese companies had started on the basis of British models and it would take a long time for the Japanese industry to catch up. We did our best to convince him that he was wrong but failed even to persuade him that the company needed a full-time representative in Tokyo so that they could be properly informed of what was happening in Japanese industry. Fortunately, companies such as Lucas and GKN were more perceptive and began to look at the possibilities of some local manufacture.

The local representative of Jaguar at that time was an enterprising Chinese of nationalist persuasion by the name of Sung. His main problem was to get an adequate supply of cars. His Japanese clients were glad to have left-hand drive cars as this suited owners who almost always had their own drivers. He often had to import second-hand Jaguars from the USA to meet demand. I did what I could to help him even writing his telexes for him to Jaguar as his written English was not good. But Jaguar in those days regarded the Japanese market as a very low priority despite our representations. Unfortunately, it also has to be said that the quality of Jaguar cars, especially their engineering, left much to be desired.

Shell had been in Japan since the end of the nineteenth century and had a joint venture with Showa. The Japanese authorities were determined to do all they could to develop major Japanese oil companies and to control the operations in Japan of the international majors. This led to a good deal of friction between Shell, Showa and MITI who wanted their own men in positions of authority in Showa. One problem was that the board of Showa conducted its meetings, as it was a Japanese company, in Japanese and the Shell representatives did not speak Japanese. I found myself frequently having to help and advise on the best way forward for Shell. For most of my time as Commercial Counsellor the Shell manager was Neville Fakes, an able and likeable Australian. He was assisted by John Raisman, later head of Shell (UK). while his finance director was Jim Glendinning, who became secretary to the Japan Society in London after his retirement from Shell and London Transport. BP was not involved in Japan except as a seller of crude and in ordering mammoth tankers from Japanese yards. So we did not have to do much for them although we maintained good relations with Lyn Gardner the BP representative in Japan.

Unilever had established a joint venture with Hohnen Oil. This JV did not work well or easily and Unilever only really succeeded in the market after they had bought out the Hohnen shareholding and established Nippon Lever. There was little we could do to help them. ICI had been in Japan before the war and were interested both in licensing technology and in joint ventures. At this stage they had made only limited progress in the Japanese market. Both the ICI and the Unilever managers were important members of the British business community in Tokyo.

British pharmaceutical companies had begun to look hard at the Japanese market. The main companies involved, other than ICI, were Glaxo, Wellcome (who were established in Osaka) and Beechams. Fisons and Boots were also members of missions from the association of the British pharmaceutical industry. These visits and the problems the companies faced in Japan brought us up against the protectionist and blinkered bureaucrats in the Ministry of Health and Welfare as well as with the highly conservative Japanese Medical Association and its autocratic boss Dr Takemi. The Japanese Medical Association were just as difficult about foreign competition as the Japanese Lawyers Association (Nichibenren) proved to be in later years when British lawyers wanted to practise law in Japan.

In those days there was no representative of the Treasury or the Bank of England in the Embassy and the commercial department was also responsible for financial relations with Japan. During my four years as Commercial Counsellor the only British Banks with branches in Japan were the Hong Kong and Shanghai Bank and the Standard Chartered who had had offices in Japan before the war. The Mercantile Bank had an office in Nagoya but was absorbed by the Hong Kong and Shanghai bank. Their operations were subject to strict limits and they encountered difficulties with Japanese banking unions who organized strikes and other forms of disruption. The managers of the two banks tended to be of the old colonial type although there were exceptions, such as Neville Mills. The manager of the Hong Kong bank only moved his residence from Yokohama to Tokyo in the 1960s. However, towards the end of my time as Commercial Counsellor, we were receiving increasing numbers of visits from British financial houses, including the big four banks and the merchant banks. The possibilities of equity investment in Japan were also being explored and it was clear to us that we needed a financial expert on the staff. In due course, after I had left Japan in 1970, a financial counsellor from the Bank of England was appointed to the Embassy.

I used to call fairly regularly on officials in the Ministry of Finance (MOF) including Kashiwagi, the first Vice Minister for International Affairs in the ministry, later President and then Chairman of the Bank of Tokyo. We had occasional visits from a dour and silent Under Secretary from the UK Treasury, Raymond Bell. When I took him on calls I usually had to do the talking on our side. I once persuaded John Pilcher, who took over as Ambassador from Tony Rundall in 1967, that he should give a lunch for Raymond Bell to meet a group of MOF officials. Rather to the Ambassador's surprise the lunch went well as the Permanent Vice Minister in MOF who attended was interested in some of the cultural topics dear to John Pilcher's heart. However, relations between him and Raymond Bell which had been distant from the beginning, if only because of Bell's taciturn disposition, cooled even further after the meal. John Pilcher told Raymond that I was making him go to the Ministry of Agriculture that afternoon to talk about biscuits. He said the word 'biscuits' with much feeling suggesting that it was a bit much to expect an Ambassador to deal with such things as biscuits. Raymond Bell simply commented: 'Well, Ambassador, that is what you are paid for!' I feared that John would burst and I never dared bring Raymond to see him again.

In the late 1960s, MOF and MITI enjoyed great prestige and extensive power. Bureaucrats could and did summon the heads of the biggest Japanese companies and gave them 'administrative advice' (*gyosei shido*) about the running of their companies and industries. Normally, this advice was accepted as, especially in the early post-war years, the two Ministries were able through their controls on credits, raw materials and foreign exchange to make life difficult if not impossible for firms which rejected 'administrative guidance'. Occasionally, however, industries managed successfully to reject the guidance they were given. The most striking example was the Japanese motor car industry which refused to amalgamate into three companies as MITI wished it to do. Honda, which was advised not to start manufacturing cars in addition to motor cycles, ignored the advice and went on to become one of Japan's leading motor car manufacturers. Chalmers Johnson (e.g. in *MITI and the Japanese miracle: the growth of industrial policy*, 1982) has carefully analyzed the way in which MITI steered Japanese growth in the 1960s and 1970s.

MOF and MITI were able to strengthen their influence on Japanese institutions through the system of '*ama-kudari*' (literally 'descent from heaven') under which senior bureaucrats in their early fifties retired from government service and after nominal periods working for some semi-governmental institution took up senior posts in the industries with which they had worked in government. Some ex-bureaucrats in those days even went on to become Presidents or Chairmen of private companies and the system was generally accepted as normal although it aroused some resentment.

116

One advantage of this system was that it helped private companies to understand the workings of government and find their way to the officials who made the decisions. The ex-officials could also influence governmental decisions in ways which might benefit their new employers. The companies, by paying good salaries to former Japanese civil servants, made up for some of the meagreness of public sector salaries. The system meant that some of Japan's best brains were not wasted when they retired from the civil service, but were used productively.

The main disadvantage of the system was that it encouraged a corrupt relationship between the public and private sectors. In recent years, the system has been increasingly criticized in the media and in the Diet and further restrictions are being placed on civil servants moving into the private sector. This should lead to the age of retirement for senior civil servants being raised, but this will affect promotion prospects and the attractiveness of a career in the civil service.

MOF and MITI officials, most of whom had studied either law or economics at Tokyo University, were certainly able and intelligent but they were not entrepreneurs and had no direct commercial experience. They also tended to become blinkered as a result of their devotion to the interests of the industries they promoted. Some became arrogant and intolerant of opposition. This exacerbated the trade frictions which arose especially in the 1970s and 1980s.

□

There was just as large a job to be done on the trade promotion front. Perhaps the biggest task was an educational one. British exporters had many misconceptions and prejudices about the Japanese market. They knew little about the structure and complexities of the market and needed a great deal of help with information and contacts. We did our best to produce market information and to arrange programmes for visitors. When we could we accompanied them on calls and used our good offices with Japanese firms as well as government departments.

For every market the Board of Trade produced 'Hints to Exporters to ———'. The notes for Japan needed revision and updating, but we soon concluded that they were inadequate and produced a series of papers about aspects of the Japanese market to supplement the hints to exporters. Eventually, these papers were put together and printed as Board of Trade pamphlets for exporters to Japan.

We worked closely with the small British Chamber of Commerce in Tokyo and I attended almost all meetings of the chamber, for whom we produced papers and helped with the secretariat. But the British business community in Tokyo, with some honourable exceptions, was not of a very high calibre at this time. The trading companies had tended to put more effort into the Hong Kong market and the average British manager knew no Japanese. Indeed, in those days one could count the number of British businessmen with a good knowledge of Japanese on the fingers of two hands. One of these was Lew Radbourne of Dodwells who had learnt Japanese after the war and been with the Occupation forces. An outstanding businessman, although unfortunately he did not speak Japanese, was Duncan Fraser of Rolls Royce. He had served in the South African Air Force during the war and was dynamic and friendly. Fortunately, in 1969 he became Chairman of the Chamber and deservedly was awarded the CBE for his services to British business in Japan.

Without enthusiasm and support in London it would not, of course, have been possible to galvanize British business to tackle the Japanese market. Indeed, pressure to expand our work still further was coming from London. This was led by the British National Export Council (BNEC) through its Asia Committee. The chairman of the Asia Committee was Michael Montague, the young chairman of Valor. He had been critical of the Embassy and we regarded it as a high priority to get him on our side. The way to do this was to be more enthusiastic and more full of ideas than his committee. I think that in the end we pulled this off. We also needed the support of Fairs and Promotions Branch of the Board of Trade. This was forthcoming but we had to educate them, too, about the Japanese market and cut through a lot of red tape.

Our main instruments of trade promotion were:-

1. The contacts which we developed in Japan and the knowledge which we obtained about the Japanese market and the complicated channels of distribution in Japan. Staff of the commercial department, myself included, arranged a series of calls on agents and trading companies which we regarded at this stage as top priorities. The British visitors we liked were those who had done their homework and knew exactly what they were looking for. The worst type of visitors were those who knew nothing about the market and had done no homework. Sometimes, one's heart would sink when a visitor called and said 'Tell me about Japan'. I also wanted to explode when they would say that they had a representative in Hong Kong and he could cover the Japanese market. I used to point out that Hong Kong was as far from Tokyo as Cairo was from London and just as different.

2. Japanese trade fairs where we helped groups of British companies to participate. Where there were no appropriate trade fairs we helped to organize separate sample shows and presentations in hotels.

3. British trade missions. Chambers of Commerce in Britain and industry associations were persuaded with generous help from the Board of Trade and encouragement from BNEC to visit Japan. We organized briefings and individual programmes where requested. I usually also gave a cocktail party/reception for the mission members to meet Japanese and British businessmen. John Pilcher, the Ambassador, was always generous with his time and enjoyed telling the mission about Japan. As he was a good raconteur and actor they were often spellbound. To my fury, John often made them late for my reception and if I telephoned he would just lift and put down the receiver. It was a good Hugh Cortazzi tease! Some missions were easier to handle than others. Chambers of Commerce missions were more difficult than industry missions as the groups were so disparate. There were also inevitably some free loaders such as importers who should not have been allowed to benefit from Board of Trade subsidies. Some of the organizers of Chambers of Commerce missions were self-important busybodies who did not make up for these

traits by efficient organization. One or two members of these missions seemed more intent on finding fault with the arrangements we made for them than with developing sales of their products. I remember being incensed at one briefing for a Scottish mission to whom I had given an account of the progress of the Japanese economy when I was asked why I had not told them about Japanese strikes. They were unwilling to recognize that Britain had a lot to learn from Japan.

4. Store promotions. In 1966 the Mitsukoshi Department Store at Nihonbashi in Tokyo organized a French promotion featuring Napoleon. I called on the head of promotions at Mitsukoshi and urged the store to organize a British store promotion. I pointed out that there was a wider range of consumer goods available from Britain than from France and in any case we had beaten Napoleon. What about taking Wellington as a theme? They replied that very few Japanese had heard of Wellington. In the end, it was agreed that they would do a promotion of British goods in the autumn of 1967 with an exhibition of Nelson memorabilia. Nelson, they pointed out, was revered in Japan by the Japanese Imperial Navy and at the Naval Academy at Etajima, used by the Maritime Self-Defence Force, a lock of Nelson's hair was preserved as an inspiration to students at the academy. The promotion was a great success. The Mitsukoshi invited the Admiral from Portsmouth and the commander of HMS *Victory* to attend the promotion as their guests. In the brochure produced by Mitsukoshi to mark the occasion there was one unfortunate misprint. The Admiral was said to have been proud to 'fry his flag' in HMS *Victory*. I thought it funny, but the Royal Naval association members in Tokyo did not share my amusement. The main result of the promotion was a signifiant increase in sales of British consumer goods and other Japanese stores were induced to imitate Mitsukoshi. The success was also a major source of inspiration for the 'British Week' which it was decided would be held in Tokyo two years later in 1969. Mitsukoshi have held British promotions every other year since 1967 with occasional extra promotions.

□

British Week in Tokyo had two main objectives. Firstly, it was designed to promote the sale of British goods in Japan. Secondly, it aimed to atttract the attention of Britsh industry to the potential of the Japanese market. Norman Macrae had helped this process by his pieces in *The Economist* on the Rising Sun and the Risen Sun. But there was still a great deal of ignorance in Britain about Japan and its economy.

We wanted British Week in Tokyo to be the biggest ever. We first had to persuade the Board of Trade, who had organized British Weeks elsewhere, that the project was feasible and worthwhile. They soon became enthusiastic about the project and we were fortunate in having Ben Thorne, who had had much experience in Hong Kong, appointed as an additional First Secretary (commercial) in Tokyo and head of the British Week office.

The first priority was to convince all the department stores who normally only competed against one another to cooperate in holding simultaneous promotions of British goods. We had to induce them to send buying missions to Britain and to receive British salesmen in Tokyo. They had to be persuaded to agree to the sort of exhibitions and centre-pieces which could be offered and organized from Britain. The Palace was approached and it was agreed that Her Royal Highness the Princess Margaret, accompanied by the Earl of Snowdon, would come to Japan to open the week and to visit the stores participating. As British royalty in those days had a significant cachet in Japan the Princess's visit provided a valuable inducement to the stores to cooperate. The preparation of her programme was a major task. HRH Prince William of Gloucester, who had become a temporary member of the diplomatic service, had been attached by John Pilcher to the commercial department (it had not been easy to find him appropriate work). I decided that he should organize his cousin's programme. This decision caused some problems as he needed close supervision. (There were a number of stories current in Tokyo about Princess Margaret's sayings during her visit. At the dance which John Pilcher gave for her she is alleged to have been told by one imperial prince to whom she had commented on what a nice ball it was that he preferred his 'balls on ice'. It was reported to us that on another visit to Japan when she was on her way to Nikko she had seen a rather tatty reproduction in wood of the QEII. When told that it was a 'love hotel' she commanded the car to stop so that she could take a photograph. She is alleged to have commented that she had seen various things named after her sister, but this was the first time she had ever seen a brothel named after her.)

We also had to cope with other VIPs, including the then Lord Mayor of London who was outstandingly pompous and was anxious to parade in Tokyo in his fancy dress. It was far from easy to explain his role in Tokyo. He regarded the Governor of Tokyo as his opposite number, but there was no comparison between the ceremonial head of the square mile, however financially important, and the governor of a huge metropolis such as Tokyo.

In addition to promoting British consumer goods, we were also determined to let the Japanese know that we had advanced technology products and capital goods which Japan should use. As a preliminary, we organized a conference in Kyoto supported by British electronic manufacturers and Sir Robert Watson Watt, the inventor of radar, was wheeled out for the occasion. Unforunately, he was no longer fully with it and the conference had not been an easy occasion. However, it was a useful preliminary to the exhibition of British Scientific and Medical Instruments which we organized in the Science Museum in Tokyo to coincide with British Week. The exhibition was valuable, but Japanese research and development was leaving us behind and we had more to learn than to sell at this stage.

In order to make British Week a resounding success with the media we also organized a British exhibition which covered aspects of Anglo-Japanese relations since first contacts in 1600. This was held in the Budokan, the hall of martial arts in the Kita no Maru section behind the Imperial Palace and near to the Science Museum. It attracted significant crowds as free rides in double-decker buses were provided for visitors. I remember one occasion when we persuaded Princess Chichibu and some other members of the Imperial family to ride on a double-decker; they seemed to enjoy the novel experience.

We all felt rather flat when the razzmatazz of British Week was all over. The main result of all our efforts was that we were able to record a significant increase in British exports in 1969 and for the first time that year our exports to Japan and our imports from Japan were in balance. The figure of £100 million of exports seems puny in comparison with what has been achieved since, but sterling has since depreciated significantly and this was, we all knew, only a beginning for our exporters.

Our next priority was EXPO 70 in Osaka. This was not supposed to be a commercial affair and we were limited in what we could sell at the British pavilion but we all worked to try to ensure that our pavilion showed the best of what Britain could do and produce. We were fortunate in having Sir John Figgess, who had been Information Counsellor in the Embassy and who had an excellent knowledge of Japan and Japanese and with whom I had worked for some years in the Embassy, as the British Commissioner General. Unfortunately, Robert John, the Consul General in Osaka, who was a difficult man, did not hit it off with John Pilcher.

I always got on well with John Pilcher and developed an affection for him and for his 'larger than life' wife Delia. They were invariably kind and considerate and adored entertaining which they did well. John liked to use his Japanese which he had learnt in Kyoto before the war and caused amusement with his Kyoto accent. He was knowledgeable about Japan and could be most amusing as a raconteur even if one sometimes had to hear his stories too many times. I always thought it a pity that he never wrote his autobiography, but although conscientious he was not a workaholic. He would have been the first to admit that he did not really understand the modern diplomatic service with its emphasis on trade and economic issues, but he always gave me every support. In return we tried our best to assist him. I remember one Sunday evening, John Pilcher had been to the airport to meet George Brown who was visiting Japan in his capacity as Foreign Secretary. John rang to ask us to join them for dinner to help out with George. I soon realized that George, who was as usual drinking too much, had been trying to bully John. The conversation at dinner became quite heated when he attacked the public schools and the mentality of members of the diplomatic service. But James Murray, then head of Far Eastern Department, gave as good as he got and George, to be fair, did not seem to resent this. I could not help feeling sorry for his plain homey wife.

We did not have much opportunity to travel although I often had to visit Osaka and Nagoya. We did, however, manage to make a few trips, e.g. to Shikoku. We took houses in Karuizawa in the summers of 1967 and 1969. In October 1967 on the evening on which I was giving a party for the British model/actress 'Twiggy' our third child and second daughter Charlotte was born in the Seibo Hospital in Tokyo. We were delighted to have a second daughter but resisted the temptation to call her 'Twiggy'.

Our first nanny had left to get married and after our home leave in 1968 we took out an older woman. She proved even more tiresome than her young predecessor and we were glad to see her go when she resigned in the autumn of 1969 and went home by the Trans-Siberian railway. There was no British school in Japan at that time, but we had been fortunate during my time as Head of Chancery in being able to send William to the Cours St Louis, a small school run by nuns. Here he had a splendid teacher in Sister Mary with whom we have kept in touch. Later, after our return to Japan in 1966, William went to St Mary's, a boys' school run by Canadian Catholics, which gave him a reasonable grounding. Rosemary had to go to a kindergarten belonging to the order of the Sacred Heart where teaching was not very good.

In 1970, it was time for a change and John Pilcher, through whose good offices I had received in 1969 the CMG, told me that the office proposed to send me to St Antony's at Oxford for a sabbatical year. As I feared that I should then have to do a study of some aspect of Japan and greatly wanted a change I persuaded John to ask that this posting be altered. Instead, I was sent for a year to the Royal College of Defence Studies, formerly the Imperial Defence College.

I had developed a desultory interest in oriental antiques in my bachelor days. Elizabeth and I pursued this interest while we were in Tokyo, but we had only limited funds and were never major collectors. Three areas particularly interested us. These were antique maps of Japan, Yokohama-e (prints), especially those depicting English men and women in the Treaty Ports, and pottery, especially Mingei pottery. We had been introduced to Hamada Shoji by John Pilcher, who knew him from before the war, and to Shimaoka Tatsuzo through the good offices of John Figgess. Both in due course were given the honorific title of 'Living National Treasure'. We also met and entertained Bernard Leach in Tokyo. In these years we began a small collection of pots and Shimaoka Tatsuzo in due course became a good friend. Our collection of antique maps was the basis of a book I produced over ten years later. We enjoyed Kabuki and Bunraku but did not go to performances as often as we should have liked, mainly because of office and family commitments.

I did my best to find the time to read some novels in Japanese. I remember being particularly impressed by Endo Shusaku's *Chinmoku (Silence)*. I was introduced to *Ningen no Unmei (The Fate of Humanity)* by Serizawa Kojiro and managed in the following years to read all 14 volumes. I also read works by Shiroyama Saburo, Inoue Hiroshi, Inoue Yasushi and other writers, but I craved for something lighter and with more humour. This led me to the works of Genji Keita. I found his 'salaryman' short stories a fascinating commentary on contemporary Japanese life among 'white collar' workers. None of his stories had been translated into English and I decided, partly as a way of keeping up my Japanese, to translate some of his stories. I began the task on our way home from Japan by boat in 1970. Of course the task proved more difficult than I had thought. The dialogue was deceptively easy but it was very difficult to make it sound natural in English. Eventually I translated two volumes of his short stories, which were published by *The Japan Times*.

CHAPTER FOUR

The 1970s: London and Washington

———————————— oOo ————————————

LONDON: 1971

O n our return from Tokyo we reoccupied our house in Maida
Vale which had been let furnished while we were in Japan.
Our son William was now nine and we did not know when we
might be sent abroad again. So we decided rather reluctantly that
he should go to prep boarding school. He had been put down
soon after he was born for the Dragon School at Oxford and he
accordingly went there in the autumn of 1970. He soon settled
down and the school proved a good preparation for Westminster
to which he went when he was 13. Rosemary went to a London
day school (Norland Place) and Charlotte to a kindergarten (the
Jumbo).

The Royal College of Defence Studies (RCDS), formerly the
Imperial Defence College, where I began my course in January
1971, was conveniently located at Seaford House, an elegant
building in Belgrave Square. The college had been established
to give senior officers in the three armed services a chance to
broaden their perspectives and to enable them to understand bet-

ter the political, economic and social issues facing us in the modern world. There were some 70 students on each course which lasted one year. Over half of the students were from the army, navy and air force. They were of the rank of brigadier in the army and their equivalents in the other services. There were also a few civil servants of assistant secretary rank and on my course three counsellors from the Diplomatic Service (the Foreign Service had become the Diplomatic Service following the merger between the Foreign Office and the Commonwealth Relations Office). In addition, there were service students from the USA (plus a representative from the State Department) as well as from Commonwealth and NATO countries. I recommended (and in due course this recommendation was accepted) that the Japanese Government be offered a place on the course for a Japanese diplomat or senior officer from the Japanese Self Defence forces.

The College Commandant in my year was a civilian scholar of war studies, Alistair Buchan, who had been chosen personally by Denis Healey, then Minister of Defence. I found him lacking in humour and almost all of us thought his approach too theoretical. He was assisted by Major General Clutterbuck, Rear Admiral Morton, Air Vice Marshal Clementi and John Addis, a senior Diplomatic Service Officer who later became Ambassador to China. I gave them all nick-names based on characters in 'Alice in Wonderland'. I found that the contacts and informal discussions we had among ourselves were more interesting and valuable than the series of lectures and seminars on world affairs organized by the management of the college. The visits which we made to service facilities and to Brussels and Berlin were also useful to me in widening my perspective. There was one three-week overseas tour and I joined a group which visited Singapore, Indonesia, Australia and New Zealand.

Alistair Buchan, much to the irritation of many of the students, demanded that each of us produce a mini-thesis. I chose to investigate ways in which cultural activities could be used to further British commercial interests. My paper on this subject exceeded the prescribed length and did not find favour with Alistair who had wanted something more theoretical. The practical suggestions which I made in it were in due course reflected in the more commercial approach later adopted by the British Council, but I doubt very much whether my mini-thesis on the subject was in any way instrumental in causing this changed approach. I had little to do with Japan during the course although I was summoned to undertake some interpreting duties.

In September 1971 the Japanese Emperor (the Showa Emperor, Hirohito) and Empress were due to make a state visit. I had to return from New Zealand a day early in order to be ready to interpret for the Queen at Victoria Station on the arrival of the Emperor, but for almost all the rest of the visit I was definitely the number two interpreter as the main duties were undertaken by the Japanese official attached to the Emperor's suite. I was relieved as the interpreter to the Emperor needed to be both an experienced interpreter, which I was not, and accustomed to his method of speaking. At the Buckingham Palace banquet, the Lord Mayor's banquet and the lunch at Hampton Court given by the Foreign Secretary I interpreted largely for Mr Fukuda Takeo, then Japanese Foreign Minister, whom I had got to know in Tokyo in the early 1960s when I was a First Secretary in the British Embassy. At the Lord Mayor's banquet with trumpeters standing behind us I had to interpret a long and rather complicated discussion, largely about the current dispute between the United States and Japan about Japanese textile exports to the USA, between Mr Fukuda and Mr (later Sir) Edward Heath, the British Prime Minister. At the end of the conversation, Mr Heath said that he would like the contents of the conversation recorded for the Foreign Secretary who was meeting Mr Fukuda the following day. Could I do a summary or (and I thought this a kind offer) should he do it himself? I naturally replied that I would do my best. As I had not been able to make any notes and had been concentrating on interpreting I decided that the only way to cope was to go straight home and write out what I could remember. I think I made a fair summary by the time I got to bed at about 3.00 am.

I was not involved in the planning of the State Visit, but I had the impression that the Emperor, nervous and looking older and frailer than his 70 years, was pleased to have been received with all the pomp which attends a State Visit in Britain. I do not think that any of the British dignitaries whom he met found it at all easy to converse with him. The Japanese officials who accompanied the Emperor and Empress were understandably nervous about possible demonstrations of anti-Japanese feeling especially by former POWs. In fact, the visit passed largely without incident although the tree which the Emperor planted at Kew to mark his visit was uprooted by protesters and a new one had to be planted.

I had no idea what was in store for me after my course. I was accordingly pleased when I was promoted and posted to the British Embassy in Washington as Minister (Commercial). This was probably a more interesting post than that of an Ambassador in a small mission which might have been the alternative.

WASHINGTON: 1972-75

I had never been in Washington before but appreciated the importance of close and friendly relations between London and Washington. 'The special relationship' was regarded by all of us as something we had to cultivate. On almost every issue of importance the views of the US administration were sought and if not always heeded in detail these had a significant influence on British policies. The British Embassy in Washington was accordingly large and covered almost every aspect of the work of Whitehall.

The Ambassador's deputy was the Minister for political affairs, who was equivalent in rank to a Deputy Under Secretary in the Foreign and Commonwealth Office. The Chancery, headed by another officer with the rank of Minister, was considerably larger than in any of our other missions and included a number of counsellors who specialized in particular areas. The Minister (Financial) Derek Mitchell, later succeeded by Antony Rawlinson, was a very senior Treasury official who dealt not only with the US Treasury and Federal Reserve, but also with the International Monetary Fund and the World Bank. The Embassy's defence staff was headed by an officer of three-star rank.

As Minister (Commercial), I was responsible for commercial issues but not for trade promotion, which was organized from the Consulate General in New York by the Consul General, John Ford, who was my equivalent in rank. We had, of course, to work closely together and I needed to visit New York fairly frequently to liaise with him. The central focus of my work was on bilateral and multilateral trade matters, but I was also responsible for civil aviation, shipping and energy. On the trade side there was a counsellor from the Department of Trade. There were also counsellors for civil aviation and energy.

In trade relations my main dealings were with the office of the Special Trade Representative (STR). For most of my time the STR was William ('Bill') Eberle who had cabinet rank and with whom I established a good and friendly relationship. But I also had to deal with officials from the State Department, the Department of Commerce, the Departments of Agriculture and Transportation and the US Treasury. I dealt with other governmental organizattions such as the Fair Trade Commission and Department of Justice on anti-trust matters involving British firms, the Federal Maritime Commission on shipping as well as various civil aviation bodies on civil aviation issues. I tried in addition to develop appropriate contacts on Capitol Hill with senators, congressmen and their staffs and got to know many of the trade lawyers and lobbyists who earned vast fees for their efforts to promote the interests of their clients by their contacts with the administration and on Capitol Hill.

In trade, we were anxious to keep the US administration to liberal trading policies. This brought me in contact with my colleagues from EEC countries and the European Commission with whom we had regular meetings. I also had dealings with the Japanese Embassy. The Japanese had a particularly difficult job because the American authorities seemed to me so often very insensitive to Japanese concerns and ignorant of modern Japan.

In civil aviation we had to pursue particular UK interests, for instance in obtaining landing rights for Concorde and for the Laker Sky Train. Both proved difficult and highly contentious. The main issues which we had to tackle over Concorde were fears over noise and the environmental impact of a supersonic airliner. The Laker Sky Train raised complicated competition issues and rights under the US-UK Civil Aviation Agreement. In the end, we managed to get agreements allowing both Concorde and the Laker Sky Train to operate to the USA.

I made many good friends in the administration. I found that as senior officials could rarely spare more than half an hour at most in their offices the best way to get them to relax and speak frankly was to take them out to lunch on their own. I usually then had at least an hour and rarely returned without something of interest to record. In the British Embassy I gather that they called me 'the luncher'!

The majority of the young Nixon whiz-kids who lunched on a glass of milk and a banana rarely accepted invitations. They were not an attractive bunch. Their ambition was as patent as was their lack of honesty. There were, of course, exceptions. I developed a good working relationship with Bob Hormats who was Dr Kissinger's deputy for economic affairs in the office of the National Security Adviser in the White House. I had considerable sympathy with US civil servants who could not aspire to even an Assistant Secretary's post as these posts were normally filled by political appointees.

It did not surprise me that the best and the brightest Americans went into the private sector. The Department of Commerce had only a limited role in trade matters and its officials were often frustrated by their lack of influence. The State Department had a somewhat larger role but it was not held in much esteem by the Washington political establishment at that time.

US anti-trust legislation was upheld by both the Fair Trade Commission and the Department of Justice. It was often difficult to understand why the primary role in investigating a potential anti-trust issue was assumed by one and not the other organization. In such matters and in anti-dumping cases it was also tempting to suspect political influences in decision making. However, sometimes the decisions made did not reflect the wishes of particular American interests.

I learnt a good deal in my contacts with the office of the STR about the workings of the GATT. One of the leading counsel at the STR's office, John Jackson, was a top academic expert on the GATT and trade law. Sometimes, inevitably, protectionist interests had to be appeased and the politicians were not as convinced supporters of the GATT as were the trade lawyers. Nevertheless, on the whole, albeit with some backsliding, the administration generally supported the freer trade philosophy.

I thought that one of the administration's greatest trade mistakes was to ban the export of soya beans when a world shortage occurred. This was a major shock to the Japanese who depended greatly on supplies of soya beans from the USA. It provided the Japanese with a further excuse for their protectionist agricultural policies as they were able to argue that Japan could not rely on foreign supplies in a crisis. The US Department of Agriculture was unfortunately almost as parochial and protectionist as equivalent departments in other countries. Earl Butz, the US Secreatray for Agriculture, was a colourful man but no internationalist. His department rightly complained frequently about European agricultural policies, but would not admit that their policies, on for example sugar, were just as damaging and protectionist as elements of the Common Agricultural Policy (CAP).

I found it increasingly hard, as the facts of the Watergate scandal emerged, to maintain the neutral stand on internal political matters required of a foreign diplomat. Some of the Republicans we met were still enthusiastic supporters of President Nixon and reluctant to see how Nixon was undermining the prestige of the President's office. When Nixon, popularly known as 'Trickie Dickie' gave his broadcast about there being 'no whitewash in the White House' I was sickened by his obvious hypocrisy and felt real concern about the future of American democracy. I was greatly relieved to learn while we were on holiday in Italy in 1974 that Nixon had resigned.

Anyone who serves in Washington has to try to understand the almost invariably difficult relationship between the Administration and Congress. The President may propose but often it is Congress which disposes. If the President and the majorities on Capitol Hill are from different parties, the President's will is often frustrated. A British Prime Minister with a reasonable major-ity in the House of Commons generally has more actual power than a United States President.

In the Commercial Department we had a fair share of the vast numbers of ministers and senior officials visiting Washington. The Conservatives were in power during the first part of my stay and I recall in particular visits from Peter Walker and Michael Heseltine. During the subsequent Labour government I particu-larly remember having to take Peart, the Minister of Agriculture, to visit the prairie land of the mid-west. We travelled in a camper which enabled the Minister to sink beer all day. One of the most trying official visitors was Roy (later Sir Roy) Denman, then a Deputy Secretary at the Department of Trade. He was happy to go on into the early hours (we had to put up many vistors) drink-ing my whisky and condemning the Foreign Office and all his colleagues.

I was fortunate in finding excuses to travel and visit our Con-sulates throughout the United States. Some visits were arranged to enable me to give speeches on Britain and on trade issues. Others were fixed so that I could meet senior local business lea-ders and thus assist the Consuls General in their work. We also managed to travel fairly widely on local leave. We greatly enjoyed our trips with the children to the National Parks in the western states of the USA.

I was appalled to find on visiting Richmond Virginia and being taken to lunch at the club there that it did not admit Jews or coloured people as members or indeed as guests. The Amer-icans claimed to be shocked by British class consciousness, but in those days there was a good deal more racial discrimination in the USA than in Britain.

I got on well with Lord Cromer who was Ambassador for the first part of my stay and with Sir Peter Ramsbotham who was there for the second part of my posting. Lord Cromer was very much the patrician type of Ambassador but he established good contacts with the administration and was widely respected. Peter Ramsbotham was a conscientious professional diplomat. He was very shabbily treated by David Owen who, as Foreign Secretary, replaced him in 1976 by Peter Jay and shifted Ramsbotham to the governorship of Bermuda, having, it appeared, allowed some malicious and untrue stories to circulate about Peter Ramsbotham's alleged old-fashioned ways.

On our arrival we were put into a rented house which was dirty and very vulgar. Fortunately, we soon moved to a new house which had been bought for my predecessor as Minister (Commercial) in Bethesda, Maryland. This was a comfortable house which was quite good for entertaining although it was rather a way from the centre of Washington. It was not very suitable for putting up visitors which we had to do quite often as there were no guest rooms with en suite bathrooms. The heating and air-conditioning were quite efficient although on one ocasuion we were without either for some days as a result of a hurricane. The garden contained a number of dogwood trees and was quite spacious. As the Washington summers can be very hot we purchased a small overground pool which helped to keep the children happy and even provided me with adequate space to do small circuits using the breast stroke.

Domestic staff were a problem. We took out a nanny for the two girls, who went to a private school, the Sheridan in Washington DC, which had some good teachers and was sensibly run. We had a large Jamaican woman for a time as a resident maid, but she was lazy and incompetent. In her place we had a Portuguese cleaner and hired waiters to help out at parties. But the bulk of the cooking and housework fell to Elizabeth, who found herself very busy.

William came out to us for the holidays and was thus able to see a good deal of the United States. We also took all three children to Mexico one winter holiday, when we visited not only Mexico City and places nearby but also the Yucatan peninsula to see the Mayan ruins.

My years in Washington were on the whole happy ones and I was sorry to leave in the summer of 1975 when I was told that I was wanted back in London. My new job, however, meant promotion as I was to take over from Michael Wilford as Deputy Under Secretary in charge of Asian affairs and a collection of other subjects including information work. Michael was being sent to Tokyo as Ambassador. I was 51 and I realized that I needed to broaden my experience. When I called on Jim (later Lord) Callaghan who was then Foreign Secretary he told me that he had wanted me to go straight to Tokyo as the post should be held by a Japanese speaker, but he had accepted the recommendation of the board that I needed some London experience first.

LONDON: 1975-80

As Deputy Under Secretary of State (DUS) I had a wide area of responsibility and had to concentrate on issues of particular political difficulty where Ministers were involved and where there were potential parliamentary problems. The following are a few of the many topics in which I became involved in the almost five years during which I held this post.

Hong Kong

While the Labour Party was still in power (until 1979) I spent a great deal of time on Hong Kong issues. The Minister of State responsible to the Secretary of State on Hong Kong matters was Lord Goronwy Roberts. The Labour Government were more interested in improving social conditions in Hong Kong than in extending democratic rights. Sir Murray (later Lord) Maclehose, the Governor, was happy to oblige. He and the Chinese business leaders were opposed to moves for greater democracy and the government did not insist. I thought at the time that this was a pity and still think so, but such views were strongly resisted by the Hong Kong establishment, including top Chinese and British businessmen who seemed to regard me as a dangerous liberal. The establishment wanted to be left in peace to get on with the serious matter of making their millions without interference from liberal minded representatives in the Legislative Council. They stressed that Hong Kong was not a 'normal' colony preparing for self-government and independence. One day, Hong Kong would revert to China and in the meantime British diplomats and politicians should keep 'their dirty, cotton-picking fingers' (to use an Americanism) off Hong Kong. The China hands in the Foreign and Commonwealth Office supported the position taken by the Governor and the establishment. I was one of a small minority who felt that the people of Hong Kong should have a greater say in how they were governed. If the minority view had prevailed or if Ministers had been willing to give more attention to Hong Kong issues the difficulties which the last Governor of the colony, Chris Patten, had over his limited democratic reforms would have been at least mitigated.

Among the many other issues in Hong Kong was that of corruption. Murray Maclehose took a very firm line on this and the anti-corruption commission which he established was instrumental in ensuring that Hong Kong became one of the least corrupt societies in Asia. We supported him fully on this. Unfortunately, it was an important factor in the police mutiny. When reports of the mutiny reached London we had to work hard to get David Owen, Foreign Secretrary at the time, to give the Governor the necessary backing to settle the mutiny without bloodshed. Unfortunately the Commission against corruption sometimes had to take steps which seemed to many to infringe the rights of those accused, but I think that on the whole the Commission did not act unreasonably.

One issue which presented difficulties was the continued existence of the death penalty in the colony. The Governor was pressed hard by parts of the Chinese establishment to enforce it. He resisted these pressures. Another problem was that in Hong Kong homosexual activity was a criminal offence. The Chinese establishment, ignoring Chinese history, were very much opposed to any relaxation of the law despite the fact that homosexuals were reputed to be active in the police force and that the ban increased the dangers of blackmail.

Murray Maclehose was concerned about the future of the leases in the new territories. He argued that unless an agreement could be reached with the Chinese about the future of the New Territories after the British lease expired in 1997 it would not be possible to negotiate viable leases on properties in the New Territories. The general view was that while we had a legal right to retain Hong Kong island after 1997 the island was dependent on the mainland for water and power and our control of the island could only continue as long as the Chinese Government considered it to be in China's interest. There was validity in these arguments but it could also be argued that we did not have to take the initiative with the Chinese and could let them be the demandeurs. The Sinologists in the office agreed with the Governor and as my time in the office was drawing to a close preliminary soundings with the Chinese began. I was not a Sinologist and was not in a position to stop these soundings although I was far from convinced that the time was ripe. I left London before the negotiations got properly under way.

I was interested to read in the London *Economist* dated 17 May 1997 that a Chinese Communist Party 'stalwart' had claimed that Britain might never have had to hand back Hong Kong. 'Only when, with a humiliating and legalistic insistence, Britain pushed China into a corner during crucial negotiations in the early 1980s, did China feel compelled to insist on Hong Kong's full return on 1 July 1997. Before that, says Mr Huang, "we had no plan to recover Hong Kong".' Mr Huang apparently claimed that Chinese leaders were originally contemplating an arrangement similar to that made with Portugal in 1979 over Macao. According to Mr Huang China had no policy towards the 1997 date until the British first took the initiative during the Governor's visit to Peking in 1979. Mr Huang's account, however, makes it clear that there was never any chance of the Chinese recognizing British sovereignty over Hong Kong.

China

While I was serving in London China was emerging from its Maoist straightjacket. I visited China a number of times. On the first occasion, in December 1975, I went with Sir Kenneth (later Lord) Keith, then Chairman of Rolls Royce, who were aiming to sell aero-engines to China. The Chinese were highly suspicious and inward-looking. COCOM rules about exports to Communist countries also acted as a serious constraint. The negotiations were difficult but it looked as though agreement could be reached if we could overcome a COCOM problem. This could only be solved by the Secretary of State for Trade who happened to be Peter Shore. At one point, I encouraged Kenneth Keith to telephone Peter Shore in the early hours of the morning in Britain to get final approval.

I also visited China with Anthony Crosland when he was Secretary of State for Foreign Affairs. He was a clever man but his mind and health were by then deteriorating and he had an unattractive habit of sneering at his civil servants in front of foreigners. I shall never forget one dinner at the Chinese Embassy when Crosland seemed to be in a particularly unattractive sneering mood. On another occasion, I accompanied the then Chief of the Defence Staff, Marshal of the Royal Air Force Sir Neil (later Lord) Cameron. He was a loose canon and not inclined to listen to political advice. Towards the end, I had got so used to hearing him say to the Chinese that 'we are two people with a common enemy whose capital is Moscow' that I did not pay much attention to his remarks. However, when he repeated these words in Peking (Beijing) the British press picked this up; there were questions in Parliament and all hell let loose. I think I was exonerated as the CDS was known to be politically rather naœve and unlikely to listen to political advice.

In 1979 Hua Kuo Feng had taken over the Chinese leadership and he was invited to pay an official visit to London. At the beginning of the talks at No 10 Mrs Thatcher, then Prime Minister, made the cardinal and uncharacteristic error of asking Hua to give her his views on the international situation. He launched forth from his brief and I could see that Mrs T was thoroughly bored. She kept trying to interrupt but Hua put her off saying 'let me finish'. I feared some explosion but this was prevented by a little note from Peter Carrington to the Prime Minister which I read over his shoulder. It simply said: 'Margaret, you are talking too much!' Even she saw that this was an amusing tease.

Japan

In the office I kept a close watch on relations with Japan. Kato Tadao, was the Japanese Ambassador for the most of my time in London. I had known him since he had been appointed to Singapore in 1952. We had met again when he was First Secretary in London in 1954 and again in Tokyo when he was Director General of the Economic Affairs Bureau of the Gaimusho and I was Commercial Counsellor. We got on well. Together we promoted the plan for a major Japanese exhibition which eventually took place at the Royal Academy in 1981/2 under the title of 'The Great Japan Exhibition' and was devoted to works of art from the Edo period.

When the Queen had made her return state visit to Japan after the Emperor's visit to Britain in 1971 she had invited the then Crown Prince and Princess (Prince Akihito and Princesss Michiko, now the Japanese Emperor and Empress) to visit Britain and stay at Windsor during Ascot week. This was duly fixed for the summer of 1976. I recommended (and this was accepted) that they should also be asked to pay an official visit to Britain as guests of the Government. Rather to the annoyance of Protocol Department, I was determined to deal personally with certain aspects of the visit and took part in the planning. I also decided that I would accompany them on all their visits outside London. In Scotland, after visiting Edinburgh and St Andrews, they stayed with the Earl and Countess of Mansfield at Scone Palace and saw some fine Scottish countryside. They then flew to Cardiff where they stayed with the Lord Lieutenant and had very busy programmes. I shall not forget accompanying the Crown Prince down the deepest coal mine in Wales. He did his stuff valiantly but I feared that Tad Kato might expire from the heat; he was a big man and fond of good food. That evening a medieval banquet was given for them at Cardiff castle with Lord Goronwy Roberts as host. The Crown Princess, who was wearing a superb kimono, clearly did not dare to eat from the bread plates on which the food was served as it was soaked in gravy which might stain her kimono. It was frankly not the most sensible invitation, but this had been fixed by the Welsh Office.

The Crown Prince and Princess stayed in London at Claridges. It was a very hot summer but Claridges then had no airconditioning and seemed to the Japanese visitors a very old-fashioned hotel.

The Crown Prince was most anxious to see a rabbit in the wild. Fortunately, we managed to find one for him to see in Hyde Park. I made one bloomer by drawing his attention to white convolvulus in the East End of London when we were going to see a sewage works. He and I wondered whether this was not a white *asagao* (morning glory). Mercifully, someone warned us against the convolvulus weed.

When travelling with the Crown Prince and his chamberlain Yagi-san I used to keep up a commentary on where we were and chat generally until I saw His Imperial Highness's head beginning to nod. Then even I kept quiet. The Crown Princess who had studied English literature greatly enjoyed visits to Stoke Poges and Tintern Abbey. On their departure she kindly gave me a book about Basho knowing my interest in haiku. On the way to the airport, I gathered from Elizabeth who accompanied her and Mrs Kato, she sang various songs. I have no doubt that Their Highnesses both greatly enjoyed their visit and believe that this helped when discussions began while I was Ambassador in Tokyo about Prince Hiro, now Crown Prince, going to Oxford to study.

Much of my involvement with Japan as Deputy Under Secretary was caused by economic issues. The biggest problem was over cars where the Society of Motor Manufacturers and Traders (SMMT) were urging restrictions on imports of Japanese cars into the United Kingdom. A great deal of pressure was put on the Japanese government and eventually a so-called 'voluntary restraint arrangement' (VRA) was agreed between the two industries whereby Japanese cars would not take more than a specified proportion of the UK market (eventually set at 10.2%). This led to many telegrams from the Board of Trade to our Embassy. I recall having to discuss this issue on the telephone late one evening with Sir Leo Pliatsky, Permanent Secretary at the Board of Trade, who was in the middle of a meeting with his senior officials. He was dissatisfied with the action being taken in Tokyo and did not think that our ambassador was being firm enough. Leo Pliatsky was an odd character in many ways and obviously not good at delegating.

Japanese investment in manufacturing facilities was developing quite rapidly during the late 1970s. The Labour Government's
attitude towards such Japanese investment was ambivalent, not
least because of the old-fashioned protectionist attitude of many
trade unionists who accused the Japanese of continuing practices
which had either disappeared or were fast disappearing from Japanese industry. While many investment projects, for example, in
Wales, received a warm welcome, others such as a proposed investment by Hitachi in a television factory in the north-east were
bitterly opposed by the unions concerned. As a result, Hitachi
were forced into a joint venture with GEC to manufacture television sets in Hirwaun in Wales, while Toshiba had to start with a
joint venture with Rank in Plymouth. Both joint ventures were
unsuccessful and Hitachi and Toshiba only made a success of
their investments when they took sole control. When the Conservatives came to power a more forthcoming attitude was shown
towards Japanese investment, but it was not until the early 1980s
that the advantages of Japanese investment to the UK economy
were fully recognized and the promotion of inward investment
from Japan rightly became a particularly high priority for the
British Embassy in Tokyo.

Vietnam

After the Conservatives came to power in 1979 the biggest issue
which fell to me to deal with was that of refugees from Vietnam.
When the refugees began to pour out of Vietnam and were
picked up by British ships, decisions had to be made about where
they were to be landed. The Hong Kong authorities refused permission to land and so did other countries in Asia including Japan. British shippers began to threaten that, unless some solution
was found enabling them to land the refugees they had picked up
at sea, British masters would no longer pick up refugees in difficulties at sea despite their obligations under the Safety of Life at
Sea Convention. Mrs Thatcher was adamant that no refugees
should be admitted to the UK and refused to accept that there
was a real moral issue at stake. I remember attending one meeting
at No 10 after a public holiday when I had been the duty Deputy

Secretary at the FCO and the problem had reached a crisis. The only Foreign Office Minister I had been able to contact was Douglas Hurd, then a Minister of State. He and I were called to an ad hoc meeting by Mrs Thatcher. Others present at this meeting were Lord Carrington, the Foreign Secretary, Willie Whitelaw, Home Secretary, the Attorney General, and Sir Robert (later Lord) Armstrong, the Cabinet Secretary. I was frankly appalled at the way Mrs Thatcher ranted at her ministers as if they were errant school boys and would not listen to the arguments.

I did my best to keep the issue before ministers. It was, I thought, a moral one which overrode any questions of short-term political advantage. One day, Peter Carrington told me that he had not overlooked my representations and said I must leave it to him. By this time the Hong Kong government had had to accept large numbers of refugees who were housed in abominably cramped prison-like temporary quarters. Peter Carrington decided to visit Hong Kong and see the situation for himself both there and in Thailand. He deliberately took with him a crowd of journalists whose reports, as he knew they would, made shameful reading. Mrs Thatcher then decided that we should call an urgent international conference to deal with the Vietnamese refugee crisis. I naturally sought instructions on how many refugees Britain was prepared to accept. I was told not to bother about this but get the conference called first. Peter Carrington then persuaded Margaret Thatcher that if the conference were to be successful we had to show that we were prepared to cooperate. It was accordingly decided that Britain would accept some refugees and a quota of 10,000 was set. This certainly helped our position at the conference and was a step towards recognizing our moral obligations.

The Vietnamese refugee crisis was the only occasion when I ever summoned a foreign diplomat out of hours. I got the Vietnamese chargé d'affaires in one evening at 11.00 pm as he had not been available to see me at an earlier hour. I protested to him in vigorous terms against the policies of his government which had led to the refugee exodus.

Latin American Issues

For about two years I also had oversight of our relations with Latin American states. The Minister of State responsible under David Owen for this area was Ted Rowlands. He was another Welshman, affable and loquacious, who greatly enjoyed his gin-and-tonic. (On a Concorde flight to New York I recall the stewardess recognizing us from a previous flight and exclaiming 'You were the two who talked from London to New York without stopping!')

One issue which took up a huge amount of time was the British colony of Belize where we had to maintain a garrison to guard the colony against threats from Guatemala. Belize sought independence but could not achieve this because of the refusal of Guatemala to recognize the colony as an independent country. There was a highly complicated frontier dispute involving some small islands in the south of Belize which were claimed by Guatemala. I remember once going with Ted Rowlands to Guatemala city in a vain attempt to find a *modus vivendi*. Guatemala city was a lawless place and we had to go round with an armed escort of thugs from the Guatemalan army. We had earlier visited the Mayan ruins at Tikal in a ropey DC3 of the Guatemalan air force and accompanied by our guards as the area was alleged to be infested wth bandits.

I also recall going with Ted Rowlands to Panama. We were travelling from Mexico City in a crowded aircraft belonging to a central American airline and were in economy seats as there were no first-class seats. Ted Rowland, his private secretary and I were sitting three together on one side of the aircraft. I got up at one point and my trousers split down the backside. As we were to go straight to the Presidential Palace on arrival there would be no time to get my luggage and change. While Ted and his private secretary were discussing how to deal with this situation, for example, I should never turn my back towards the President even when withdrawing, or I should wear my raincoat throughout the interview, I told them that there was no need to fuss. I took out my emergency sewing kit and occupied the tiny loo while I sewed up my trousers. Everyone on the plane thought I must be suffering from Montezuma's revenge! The audience went off alright, but I did not think much of Panama or Panama City.

The other main problem which I had to deal with while Ted Rowlands was the Minister was that of the Falkland Islands. The government were unwilling to accept that if the Falklands were to be defended we needed an airfield, a base and a substantial garrison as well as a naval patrol. Judith Hart, the Minister for Overseas Development, refused to put up any money from the aid budget for an airfield (she preferred to pour money into projects of questionable developmental value in Indira Gandhi's India). The Ministry of Defence for their part said that they had neither the funds nor the manpower available for a strong garrison. The Royal Navy were reluctantly prepared to leave a small ship in the area but were always seeking excuses to withdraw the ship. The only viable alternative was to try to negotiate a solution with the Argentine government. This would inevitably involve some concessions to the Argentines over sovereignty but the islanders and their lobby in the House of Commons were adamantly opposed to any concessions. The lobby had the support of a majority in the House of Commons where few members understood the issues. We were accordingly landed with the task of negotiating with the Argentine authorities without any room for manoeuvre.

On one occasion in, I think, 1978 I had to lead a negotiating team at a three-day conference in Rome on a brief which instructed us to maintain a dialogue but give nothing away. We managed to keep talking but it was tough work and I am not surprised that the Argentine officials and their leader, a deputy minister, felt frustrated. Ted Rowlands and the department began to explore the idea, later taken up by Nicholas Ridley, his Conservative successor in 1979, of conceding sovereignty but with a 50-year lease-back to Britain. When the Conservatives came to power in 1979 I was fortunately relieved from this aspect of work. In my view, the Falkland Islands War should never have occurred. The Government and the House of Commons should have accepted either the alternative of a fortress policy or have agreed to negotiate a compromise. Instead, when the naval patrol was withdrawn, the Argentines grabbed their chance and invaded the islands. Mrs Thatcher's response was the right one in the circumstances then prevailing, but the need to retake the islands need never have arisen if common sense and judgement had prevailed earlier under the Labour and later the Conservative administrations. Britain could have bought out all the islanders and set every one of them up as wealthy farmers in Britain for much less than the cost of the war. I much regretted that Lord Carrington felt obliged to resign when the Argentine forces successfully invaded the islands. In my view, the Minister who should have resigned was John Nott, the Secretary of State for Defence.

OTHER ASIA/PACIFIC ISSUES

Brunei

Brunei was not a British dependency but we had a defence agreement with the Sultan and a battalion of British Gurkhas was stationed in Brunei under the agreement. The Malaysian Government were unhappy about this arrangement. The real power in Brunei in those days was Sir Omar, the Sultan's uncle, and Ministers were anxious to keep him on side, but this complicated relations with the Malaysians. Donald Murray (later Sir Donald and Ambassador to Sweden), the Assistant Under Secretary for Asia, bore the brunt of the negotiations on this issue. Donald and I worked closely together for nearly four years. Fortunately, there was more than enough to keep both of us busy without crossing wires.

Afghanistan

Another serious issue after the Conservatives came to power was the Soviet invasion of Afghanistan in late 1979. The protest which I made at that time to the Minister in the Soviet Embassy was, I fear, 'water off a duck's back'. There was in practical terms nothing that we could do except protest.

The Banaban Islanders

An issue in which Lord Goronwy Roberts (and later Peter, (sub-sequently Lord), Blaker) was involved as Minister of State was that of compensation for the Banaban Islanders who had been dispossessed by the Japanese occupation of the Gilbert and Ellice Islands during the war. This was a highly complicated matter involving both the Australian and New Zealand governments. The islanders had also got Sir Bernard Braine MP (later Lord Braine) on their side and he injected a good deal of emotion into his espousal of the islanders' cause. We recognized this but Bernard Braine caused much irritation by his personal attacks on Ministers and civil servants. During the Labour Government we had just reached, after some very difficult negotiations, a preliminary agreement with the two Commonwealth governments, when our position was undermined by some intemperate remarks by David Owen, then Foreign Secretary, to Andrew Peacock, the then Australian Foreign Minister, who was on a visit to London and had only reluctantly agreed to the compromise solution recommended by Australian officials. David Owen had been sent all the papers but had not read them or given us any instructions. I was angry at being publicly disowned at the lunch given by Owen for Peacock. When I explained to Lord Goronwy what had happened he was justifiably annoyed but he was not the resigning type and we had to spend three months resurrecting the compromise.

The Remaining British Colonial Possessions

My area of responsibility included all the last remaining British overseas possessions except Gibraltar. Our aim was to bring as many of these as possible to independence sooner rather than later. There were some difficult constitutional issues and not a little concern about how viable in economic and political terms some of the remaining British colonies in the Caribbean were. By the time I left London in 1980, apart from the Falklands, Belize, Bermuda, Hong Kong and Gibraltar the only remaining British possessions were very small, such as Tristan da Cunha and St He-

lena in the south Atlantic, or unsuited at that stage at least to independence, such as the British Virgin, the Cayman and the Turks
and Caicos islands. However small these possessions were, they
still caused us many problems. The Turks and Caicos had a reputation for corruption and smuggling. St Helena had to rely on
passing ships for supplies as it had no airfield and no appropriate
land on which to build one. Unfortunately, most shipping companies no longer operated liners but had gone over to container
ships and bulk carriers. So ships were few and far between. The
Home Office were difficult about giving permits to islanders
who wanted to come to Britain as domestic servants.

New Hebrides

One of the oddest places with which I was concerned and which I
visited was the New Hebrides. At that time we and the French
ruled the islands through a condominium. This meant that there
were competing administrations and police forces, British,
French and local. The opportunities for friction and misunder-
standing were legion. The negotiations for independence were
fraught by basic disagreements between the two governing
powers. The French with an eye on their other possessions in
the Pacific did not look kindly on local nationalists who they
thought were being encouraged by the British. Agreement was
eventually reached through long and patient four-sided negotiations (the third and fourth elements being the local quarrelsome
leaders) and independence was achieved without bloodshed.

☐

As Deputy Under Secretary with such a wide brief I travelled very
widely. In Asia I visited every country from Afghanistan to Korea
except for Burma, Indo-China (Vietnam, Cambodia and Laos)
and Taiwan. Burma had shut itself off from the rest of South East
Asia and its economy was stagnating. I could not visit Vietnam
while the refugee crisis was continuing and Cambodia was in the
midst of a civil war. As a senior official I could not visit Taiwan
without causing a strong protest from Beijing.

I went on more than one occasion to the Indian sub-continent. In 1976, having visited Bangladesh, I went on to Nepal. Here I was very sick and had to go into a missionary hospital in Kathmandu before being evacuated to Delhi where there was a small hospital in the High Commission compound.

I also made a couple of visits to Australia and New Zealand for consultations and managed to visit many of the Pacific islands. In 1978 I represented the government at the independence of Tuvalu (the former Ellice Islands) when Princess Margaret represented the Queen. Peacock, who liked to be with ladies such as the Princess, represented Australia. Unfortunately, on independence day, Princess Margaret was confined to bed with a fever. I picked up her germ and was one of the first out-patients in the small hospital set up in the capital with British aid money. To get to Tuvalu I had had to take a seat on a RNZAF aircraft. The return journey via Fiji to Auckland and thence across the Pacific to Los Angeles where I caught another plane to London was a very tiring one for someone with a feverish infection.

When the Conservatives came to power in 1979, I did my best to persuade ministers of the growing importance of ASEAN. Peter Blaker, then Minister of State, accepted this assessment and showed the importance which the new government attached to ASEAN by a series of visits, on some of which I joined him. One of these was to Thailand where we accompanied the King in helicopters to visit some of the land where attempts were being made to persuade farmers to grow crops other than the opium poppy. We later had dinner with the King and Queen. Although I had been warned in advance I still found it a strange experience to see the King's servants crawl in on their knees to wait on him and his guests at table.

On a separate visit to the Philippines where Bill Bentley (later Sir William and subsequently High Commissioner in Kuala Lumpur and Ambassador to Norway) was Ambassador I remember having an audience with President Marcos. While we were waiting our turn I was attacked by vicious mosquitos. When I asked why they did not use anti-mosquito sprays I was told that Madame Marcos disliked the smell. Neither she nor the President suffered from mosquito bites as they were so thickly covered in paint that mosquitos were put off or, if they did try to penetrate, they could not get through the layers.

I also tried to visit as many of the countries of Latin America as possible. Visits by senior officials were helpful to ambassadors who could use such visits to develop their own contacts. They were also useful in terms of staff morale. Officials in out-of-the-way posts often feel that they are forgotten by London, but I did not have the time or the opportunity to visit all our missions. Because of the Falkland Islands dispute I was prevented from visiting the Argentine. Chile was also out of bounds because of the appalling human rights record of General Pinochet's regime. I did manage a visit to Cuba. This involved a tiring journey via Brussels and Toronto. I did not find the experience of visiting Castro country at all exhilarating.

I made regular visits to Bonn, Paris, Washington and Ottawa at intervals for bilateral exchanges mainly, although not exclusively, on Asia.

□

As Deputy Under Secretary it fell to me on occasions to attend the Queen when foreign ambassadors presented credentials. The Queen was always very good with the Ambassadors and their staffs on these occasions. She spoke in French with some and was always well briefed. I remember on one occasion when I was in attendance, the Queen received a new Latin American ambassador in an upstairs reception room with a polished board floor. The Queen was worried that the ambassador might slip as one previous ambassador had done and come in on his bottom.

□

I was much concerned about the future of the Diplomatic Service and I served for a couple of years as Chairman of the Diplomatic Service Association. We had to combat the sillier proposals of the Central Policy Review Staff (CPRS) report which had been in part at least drafted by two ideologically-prejudiced females who did not understand properly the problems facing us. We felt that the report should be dismissed 'lock stock and Berrill' (Sir Kenneth Berrill was the head of the CPRS at that time). The report had been commissioned by the Labour Government, probably with the support of David Owen who in my view was one of Britain's worst foreign secretaries, not least because of his arrogant conceit, but also because of his unpredicatability. He was loathed by his drivers. He could not even be polite to messengers who were much relieved when Lord Carrington succeeded Owen as Foreign Secretary. He always had a smile and a polite greeting for them.

In my capacity as Chairman of the Diplomatic Service Association I spoke, as I had every right to do, to a number of Conservative politicians in an attempt to gain their support for the Service. They were only too glad to have ammunition with which to embarrass the Labour government. Unfortunately, however, Mrs Thatcher was strongly prejudiced against the Foreign Office and against most civil servants. So the Service has continued to have to cope with an increasing work load with reduced resources.

As Michael Wilford was only just two years older than I and he had not been appointed to succeed Murray Maclehose in Hong Kong as he had wanted, I doubted whether I would be able to go back to Tokyo as Ambassador as I had, for understandable reasons, hoped and expected. I explored the possibility of getting some other senior post in the Service but the Permanent Under Secretary, Sir Michael Palliser, thought that it would be a mistake not to make use of my knowledge and experience of Japan. Early in 1980, Michael Wilford agreed to take slightly early retirement so that I could be appointed Ambassador to Tokyo. In the birthday honours in 1980, prior to taking up my new appointment, I received a knighthood, being made a KCMG.

It was suggested to me that in the interim before going to Tokyo I should take up golf, which some diplomats regarded as a *sine qua non* for success in Japan. I was not convinced that, to be successful, an Ambassador in Tokyo needs to be a good golfer and I did not follow up this suggestion. I do not think that in the event I was any less successful as head of mission in Japan because I did not play golf. I had other hobbies and interests. Before leaving for Japan I did some intensive briefing. This included visits to major exporting companies and to Japanese investments in Britain as well as conversations with ministers and senior officials involved in one way or another with Japan.

Five years in London had been good from the point of view of the family, even if I had had to travel widely leaving Elizabeth on her own. It was certainly helpful to be at home while William was at Westminster, as the school is adapted more for weekly boarders than for boys who have to stay at school at weekends. Rosemary and later Charlotte went first to Sibton Park, a prep-boarding school near Folkestone, and later to Benenden. If we had known we would be in London for five years we might well have tried to keep Charlotte at least at St Paul's as a day girl. Benenden did not turn out to be a good choice for either girl as both reacted against what they considered the Sloane Ranger atmosphere and the rather old-fashioned attitudes of the staff. In 1976, we began a desultory look for a country cottage not too far from Benenden in south-east England. In 1979, we intensified our search and eventually decided on a house in East Sussex which has the strange name of Ballsocks (not Bullsocks, Bullcocks or Ballcocks!). This is a grade II listed Sussex farmhouse with the main framework dating back to the fifteenth century, a flower garden for Elizabeth and a vegetable patch for me. At first, I refused to look at the house when, after we had received the particulars, we were in the area, because I thought it more than we could afford. Elizabeth had a look at it from the outside and I was persuaded to go over it. We both decided that we should negotiate to buy it and we put all the resources we had into the purchase. We took possession early in 1980 and have never regretted the decision, although the garden is rather too large and the house, being old, requires a good deal of expenditure on maintenance.

We did not travel much within Britain during these five years but we did spend three very enjoyable holidays in Tuscany where we rented a 'casa colonica' (an Italian country farm house) near Siena.

CHAPTER FIVE

British Ambassador to Japan

———————————— oOo ————————————

TOKYO: 1980-84

ARRIVAL

It used to be common practice to send a new ambassador a despatch giving him his instructions for his mission. I do not recall receiving any such despatch. As I had been the responsible Deputy Under Secretary I would have approved my own instructions and it was probably assumed that I would know what I should be doing.

We left for Tokyo in September 1980, travelling via New Delhi, Bangkok, Hong Kong and Beijing. (We also visited Canton, Shanghai, Hangchow and Suchow in China.) On arrival in Tokyo in early October 1980, one of our first engagements was a reception for old friends from past periods in Japan. As soon as I had introduced myself to the Ministry of Foreign Affairs (the Gaimusho) I was officially permitted to carry out my duties as British Ambassador at Tokyo.

Early arrangements were made for me to present my credentials to the Emperor. This was a very formal occasion with no opportunity for informal conversation with His Majesty, in contrast to the way in which, after the formal presentation of credentials in London, the Queen invariably had informal chats with the ambassador and his spouse. I managed to persuade the Imperial Household to allow me to make the brief formal remarks permitted to me in Japanese and not in English through an interpreter. This was quite an achievement considering the conservative traditional character of the Imperial Household who at first said there were no precedents for doing so (I do not believe this was true).

Elizabeth was not permitted to attend the formal presentation and was introduced by a side door for the briefest of calls on the Empress who was fairly immobile though not yet senile. I also bowed to the Empress and we signed the books of other members of the Imperial Family. We naturally made an early visit to Princess Chichibu who was the honorary patron of the Japan-British Society in Tokyo and whom we had met many times before in Japan and London. Princess Chichibu was the widow of Prince Chichibu, the eldest of the Emperor's three brothers. She had been born in London and was the daughter of a Japanese Ambassador.

CALLS

Ambassadors are supposed to call on all the heads of diplomatic missions. As there were over one hundred missions, some of whom had their residences quite far out and driving in Tokyo traffic was very time consuming, this was a formidable task. We tried but after some fifty calls and over three months had passed we quietly gave up. Of course, we gave priority to the heads of missions of European Community and Commonwealth countries. Naturally, also, I made an early visit to my US colleague, Senator Mike Mansfield, whose favourite phrase was that 'the US-Japan relationship was the most important bilateral relationship in the world bar none'. He was already in his eighties and looked rather like a pickled walnut. He was certainly not senile and the Japanese authorities were glad to have someone with his authority and access in Washington as US Ambassador. He did his best to represent Japanese views to the US administration. We also called on the Soviet Ambassador and his wife in their forbidding fortress-like mansion in Roppongi. This was not a productive call even if it was a necessity.

New arrivals have a perfect excuse to pay courtesy calls and I took advantage of this to visit senior politicians, businessmen and officials. Many of these calls led to the development of further contacts which were useful in our main task of promoting British interests. I established a good relationship with two future Prime Ministers, Nakasone Yasuhiro and Takeshita Noboru, as well as with influential members of the LDP including Watanabe Michio and Koizumi Junichiro. I also called on members of the opposition parties, except the Communists.

Many contacts could be cultivated by judicious entertaining which we did whenever we could, but I maintained the habit of calling especially on senior Japanese business figures throughout my stay in Tokyo. Some calls were inevitably boring. Just occasionally there were amusing incidents. I remember once calling with the Commercial Counsellor on one old boy, chairman of an important company, who had become rather thin. When we left he got up to say goodbye and his trousers fell down revealing his long johns! I just managed to suppress an outburst of mirth.

Many industrial companies had their headquarters in the Marunouchi district which was barely 30 minutes walk away from the Embassy. I liked to take sharp walks when the weather was bright and cold and would often walk to the Marunouchi business district; however, it was not regarded as appropriate for an ambassador, or anyone senior for that matter, to call on a leading Japanese businessman without arriving in a suitably prestigious chauffeur-driven car so that he could be properly greeted. Accordingly, having walked to the area I sometimes asked my driver to pick me up just round the corner from the office which I was visiting.

REPRESENTATIONAL DUTIES
A good deal of time has to be spent by an ambassador on representing his country at functions. Much of this is boring, but

sometimes attendance at functions can be useful. It gives opportunities for widening contacts and following up on official calls. It would be pointless to list all the kinds of functions which we had to attend; these were not much different in Tokyo than in other capitals except for the large number of business-related receptions. These were held whenever major changes were made in boards of directors or to mark some significant anniversary. There were also many politically related receptions when Japanese politicians sought donations for their campaigns. Ambassadors were often asked to these occasions if only to demonstrate that the politician concerned was knowledgable on foreign policy issues. One useful feature of receptions in Tokyo was that you could come in by one door and after greeting your hosts leave by another. This made it possible on occasions for those with a car and driver to attend three receptions and a dinner on one evening if they had to.

Some occasions sponsored by the Imperial Household were peculiar to Japan. Apart from the New Year's Day ceremony, when I had to dress up in diplomatic uniform and Elizabeth had to wear a long dress with long sleeves, and annual garden parties, when the men wore morning coats, we were invited to duck netting parties at one of the imperial duck preserves. In addition to other Ambassadors and their spouses, there were usually some senior officials present together with some of the more junior members of the Imperial family. An excellent barbecue of duck (the duck we were given to eat was cultivated, as the wild ducks netted by members of the party were released again into the wild) was served together with specially selected imperial saké. Afterwards, princes, princesses and ambassadors could play ping-pong. Another perk for ambassadors was an invitation to one of the imperial stock-farms where those who wished could ride on horses belonging to the household, or on bicycles, before partaking of a barbecue of lamb in what was called Genghiz Khan-yaki style. Elizabeth once rode a huge horse at one of these parties. Never having ridden a horse I preferred to stick to a bicycle.

POLITICAL WORK

It is sometimes asked why an embassy has to spend time on political reporting. Surely the political situation is adequately covered in the media? Alas, this is not true. The only reliable coverage of events in Japan in the British media has been in the *Financial Times* and to some extent in *The Economist*. A good embassy can also add useful interpretations to routine reporting as a result of political and other contacts. A good understanding of the political situation is in any case essential for the economic and commercial work of the Embassy. Many businessmen come to see the ambassador to learn about the general scene and about the political background to their business operations. I gave, I hope, adequate attention and priority to this aspect of political work without getting it out of proportion.

The Japanese political scene had not changed much in essence during the 1970s when I had been away from Japan. The LDP was still dominant and remained a collection of factions loyal to faction bosses. The main changes resulted from the death or retirement of some factional leaders and the selection of replacements. But many of the personalities I had known earlier were still in positions of influence. Cabinets continued to be formed as a result of horse-trading between the leading figures and were designed to give members of the factions their turns to hold ministerial posts. Some ministerial jobs, which were more important than others, such as those of Minister of Finance and Chief Cabinet Secretary, tended to go to stronger personalities, but the three top party jobs, especially that of LDP Secretary-General, were especially sought after because of the party power which went with these positions. Many members of the LDP represented particular local or business interests. These were the so-called '*zokugiin*' who by their membership of party and parliamentary committees had close contacts with civil servants in the relevant ministries and were thus able to promote the interests of their backers. The 'iron triangle' of politicians, civil servants and business still held sway. Keidanren (The Federation of Economic Organizations) and top Japanese businessmen had a significant influence on policies. The civil service remained the key element in the efficient working of the Japanese Government. We needed good contacts with people in all three groups.

There had been little significant change in the composition of the opposition parties. The main opposition party remained the Japan Socialist Party (JSP) which was still dominated by Marxist ideologues and continued to focus on opposition to the US-Japan Security Treaty. There were elements in the party which wanted to modernize its image and policies but they were unable to prevail at this time. Komeito (The Clean Government Party), dependent on Sokagakkai, a mass so-called 'religious' organization with considerable funds and a dubious reputation, seemed to have reached its electoral ceiling. The Democratic Socialist Party (Minshato) remained feeble and ineffective. The Japan Communist Party (JCP) had limited support in some of the cities but its philosophy and policies had little appeal to the mass of the electorate. In view of their control on the levers of power we had to concentrate on contacts with the constituent parts of the 'iron triangle'.

Another important aspect of our work was political cooperation. Increasing importance was rightly attached to political exchanges with the Japanese Government. Ever since the early 1960s there was an agreement to hold regular exchanges at ministerial level, but, because neither side had given these adequate priority, and because of other more pressing commitments, there were times when there were no meetings at Foreign Secretary/ Foreign Minister-level. We did our best both in London and in Tokyo to press for the resumption of regular meetings and for the British Government to give priority to relations with a country as increasingly important as Japan. The Conservatives were quicker to recognize this than the Labour Party. Both Edward Heath and Mrs Thatcher had visited Japan and recognized that there were things we could learn from modern Japan. During my stay as Ambassador Lord Carrington, Foreign Secretary, came in April 1981, and Humphrey (later Lord) Atkins, the Lord Privy Seal, on another occasion. When senior ministers from the Foreign Office could not fit in a visit we had exchanges at the level of Permanent Under Secretary/Vice Minister. Gradually, the content of these exchanges improved and there was a greater meeting of minds on issues such as the UN. But sometimes the exchanges tended to be routine and rather boring. Peter Carrington did his best to enliven the proceedings, but even so one member of the Gaimusho team seemed to be permanently asleep. When Peter asked me who the sleeper was I teased him by scribbling that the man was not asleep just absorbing Peter's words of wisdom.

FALKLANDS WAR

Unfortunately, our efforts to develop political cooperation failed to ensure Japanese support in the Falkland Islands conflict. I did not think that the dispute should have been allowed to reach a point of armed conflict and, as I have said above, I blame the House of Commons and the blinkered Falklands lobby for this situation. However, when Argentine forces invaded the islands I had no doubt that the British Governmnet's response was right and justified and much as I disagreed with Mrs Thatcher's policies on many other issues I admired her forthright determination on this occasion. A senior Tory MP who was staying with me at the time, was at first inclined to think that we should have to appease the Argentines. I did my best to put fire into his belly and we pulled out every stop in an attempt to persuade the Japanese Government to give us their support at the UN and over sanctions against Argentina. Unfortunately, there was a strong pro-Argentine lobby in the Diet which was concerned about the possible effect on Japanese trade with Latin America and with the safety of communities of Japanese origin in Latin American countries. I am sure that Japanese fears on both scores were greatly exaggerated. We stressed the important principles which were at stake and reminded the Japanese authorities that they had a territorial dispute over the Northern islands occupied by the Soviet Union after the war. They had not yet signed a peace treaty with the Soviet Union and they wanted our support on the issue which involved an important point of principle, namely that disputes over the sovereignty of territories should not be preempted by illegal occupations. I called on a range of officials and parliamentarians and urged Kato Tadao, formerly Ambassador in London and Chairman of the Japan-British Society in Tokyo, to use his influence with the Gaimusho. We emphasized the help which the Americans through General Haigh were giving us and arranged for messages to be sent from Mrs Thatcher to Mr Suzuki Zenko, then Japanese Prime Minister, but he was a feeble politician who did not take a grip on this or other issues. In the end, the Japanese Government turned us down in a note which consisted of typically wishy-washy sentiments.

I was particularly aggravated by the way in which the final reply was delivered. Late one evening, when I had returned from the airport after seeing off Prince Philip, Duke of Edinburgh, and, not surprisingly, was very tired, I received a telephone call from the Gaimusho to say that Kato Yoshiya, the Director General of the European Affairs Bureau, had an important message to give me. It was clear that this was going to be negative and that it was too late to do anything more to get it changed. I replied that I would come down immediately to receive it, but was then told that as the message was being translated into English it was not ready. I said that I would receive it in Japanese, but this was not acceptable to the Gaimusho officials. Eventually, when at 1.00 am the English translation was still not ready, I insisted on going down to the Gaimusho and receiving it in Japanese. I had a frosty meeting with Kato and returned to the Embassy to send a brief 'Flash' telegram to London giving the gist of the message and saying that the full text of the note would follow.

The following day, at a reception I was giving, I was still smarting from what I considered the Gaimusho's silly behaviour over the note and spoke about this to a friendly journalist on the Asahi Newspaper, pointing out that the only justification for summoning an Ambassador in the middle of the night was if there was an emergency or a declaration of war. The journalist twice asked if he could use the story to which after consideration I said 'yes'. I felt that the Gaimusho needed a lesson in diplomatic courtesies. John Whitehead, the Minister, thought I had gone too far. The story duly appeared and led the Gaimusho to deny that there had been any discourtesy and to complain publicly about my leaking the facts to the press. There were no repercussions in London and I do not think my action did any harm to our interests, rather the contrary. The only pity was that Kato Yoshiya, the Director General in question, who was a sensitive man and who was basically friendly to us, no doubt felt hurt. One problem with him was that he seemed to have very little sense of humour. Sadly, he died shortly before he was to take up a senior ambassadorial post in Europe.

At this time, the Ambassador from Argentina in Tokyo had a Scottish name. My name of Italian origin sounded more appropriate for an Argentine diplomat than his own which might have been that of a British diplomat. Stories circulated that we had been wrongly introduced at receptions and that there had been some embarrassing diplomatic mix-ups as a result. Sadly, perhaps, there was no truth in these stories.

THE EUROPEAN COMMUNITY

An important part of our work which straddled political, economic and commercial issues was European cooperation. The ambassadors of the European Community (now the European Union) countries had meetings and lunches once a month and our staffs met also on a regular basis to discuss particular issues.

The European Commission was represented by Leslie (later Sir Leslie) Fielding as head of the European Community Delegation with the rank of ambassador. I had known Leslie from when he was a member of the British Diplomatic Service and we got on well. The European Community countries were represented in Tokyo by senior ambassadors and relations between us were always friendly and easy. We had especially close relations with our German, Italian, French, Belgian and Dutch colleagues. The French, Belgians and the Italians had, as we did, summer villas at Lake Chuzenji and this facilitated contacts. We had also known earlier the Dehennens, the Belgian Ambassador and his wife, as we had served together in Washington. Klaus Blech, the German Ambassador, and Boris Biancheri, the Italian Ambassador, were outstanding diplomats who went on to serve in other senior posts. The Dutch had long historical connections with Japan and the Kaufmanns and their successors, the Goodharts, were forthcoming and friendly. Whenever any of the Commissioners came out to Japan, we met for special briefings and we worked together on the development of a common commercial policy towards Japan. The Japanese at this stage used to claim that they did not know with whom they should be dealing on particular issues. The Dutch were especially interested in getting Japanese restrictions removed from flowering bulbs; was this a bilateral or a European issue? As we cooperated so closely, the Japanese began to realize that on commercial issues the community was trying to establish a common front and that as we kept one another closely informed of developments on our own special problems they could not hope to play one European country off against another. Still, there was quite a long way to go before we were always able to show a united front on trade relations. In trade promotion we were still very much competitors.

THE DIPLOMATIC CORPS

The diplomatic corps in Tokyo was huge and it was not possible in the time available to get to know more than a small proportion. We concentrated on developing friendly relations with the Americans, the Europeans and the Commonwealth Ambassadors. We also met quite often the Doyen, the Ambassador of the Ivory Coast, and his deputy, the Moroccan Ambassador, who had been in Japan for many years.

The cold war was still continuing and we were careful about our relations with Communist missions. China seemed to be changing and as the Chinese Ambassador had served previously in London we invited him to lunch. Unfortunately, he did not warn us that his second wife was a Muslim. This caused some problems for our cook as we had ordered a special pork dish!

One Communist diplomat whom I got to know was the Polish Ambassador Ruarz. It had come to our notice that he might wish to defect. I entertained him circumspectly and tried to draw him out. At one stage he let it be known that he would like me to meet him at a certain point one night. I went to the rendezvous with a colleague, but he did not appear. We later learnt that he had defected to the USA, but he wrote and thanked me for my friendly advice at a difficult time for him.

ECONOMIC AND COMMERCIAL WORK

The Japanese economy, which had emerged in better shape than many other developed economies from the two oil shocks in the 1970s, was booming. Japanese growth-rates continued to be higher than those of other developed countries. Japanese products were of high quality and Japanese exports were growing fast. There was great interest in and admiration for Japanese management methods. Japan was surely, some believed, destined to be number one and ready and able to dominate the world economy. A certain arrogance was creeping into Japanese attitudes towards foreign countries. In particular, there was much talk of the so-called 'British disease', by which was meant the effects on Britain of the welfare state mentality and our proneness to strikes. We stressed that there was no such thing as a 'British disease'. There were, of course, problems associated with the welfare state and with union activities, but Britain under Mrs Thatcher's government was tackling these issues with firmness and vigour. Throughout my time as Ambassador in Tokyo our relations were dominated by economic friction arising from the serious imbalance in trade in Japan's favour, the troubles experienced by British industries affected by Japanese exports, and by the continuing obstacles facing British exporters to Japan. The imbalance reflected the undervaluation of the yen, the efficiency of Japanese exporting firms and the difficulties our firms faced in the Japanese market.

I was disturbed by the repeated accusations by British politicians and industrialists against Japan of 'laser beam' marketing and of 'concentrated and torrential exporting' (*shuchu go-u teki yushutsu*). This led to increased demands for restrictions on Japanese exports, especially of motor cars and electronic goods. The Japanese authorities did not want to appear directly involved, but they were ready to promote where absolutely necessary inter-industry agreements which were euphemistically called 'voluntary restraint arrangements' (VRAs). Much time and effort had to be devoted to helping teams from the Society of Motor Manufacturers and Traders (SMMT) and from the British electronics industry. The leader for the latter was Lord Thorneycroft, who managed to establish a good relationship with his Japanese opposite number from the Sony corporation. The talks on motor cars were always more difficult.

Unfortunately, it was becoming increasingly obvious that the time bought by the VRAs was not being well spent. British motor manufacturers were very slow in improving their productivity and competitivity and were if anything falling further behind. This meant that the VRAs were constantly being extended. They were a nuisance to Japanese manufacturers but instead of increasing the quantity of their exports they were able to increase their margins. So, in fact, the VRAs damaged the interests of British consumers who had to pay higher prices than was necessary for Japanese cars and frequently could not buy the car they wanted. They also benefited the Japanese manufacturer's profits while engendering complacency in British industry. The political pressures were too great for us to do more than try to limit the damage and argue for a European-wide policy and our obligations under the GATT.

To defuse economic friction it seemed to us that we had firstly to step up still further our export efforts, particularly in the area of capital goods such as aircraft, and secondly to do more to promote Japanese investment in manufacturing in the United Kingdom which would help to replace jobs lost through Japanese competition, and to promote import substitution and the restructuring of British industry.

The Commercial Department worked hard on trade fairs, trade missions and store promotions. I went to as many exhibitions and promotions as possible and gave speeches in Japanese to demonstrate our determination to increase our exports and to counter the irritating Japanese refrain that foreign countries did not try hard enough. We were particularly annoyed by some Japanese politicians' comments that the only things Japan wanted from abroad were a few luxury consumer items. Mr Nakasone Yasuhiro, when he was Prime Minister, had himself photographed buying a foreign-made tie and boasted of his suit of English cloth. Mr Akazawa, the head of JETRO, eventually bought a Jaguar for his use but complained frequently of inadequate service from the agent.

We put a great deal of time and effort into promoting the BAe
(British Aerospace) 146 aeroplane and I felt at times that BAe 146
was written across my heart. We used every possible occasion in
and outside Tokyo to persuade the Japanese airlines and authorities that the aircraft was particularly suitable for conditions in Japan, requiring as it did only a short runway for take off and
landing. When Prince Philip, Duke of Edinburgh, came out for
a World Wild Life fund-raising exercise we persuaded BAe to
make a 146 available for the Prince to fly to Sapporo and Kushiro
in Hokkaido. I also pushed its merits hard at the Japanese airshow
in Nagoya. Rather to the annoyance of other foreign exhibitors,
who felt that as I was supposed to be speaking for the foreign
diplomatic corps I should have taken a neutral stance, I used my
speech to call on the Japanese to increase their imports of aerospace products especially the BAe 146! But sadly our efforts came
to nothing.

We gave as much priority as possible to other firms involved in
aerospace and other capital goods. One company with which we
worked closely was Rolls Royce, who had developed good working relations with Japanese firms especially Kawasaki Heavy Industries. The three service attachés knew that the promotion of
the sales of British military, naval and air equipment was their
main task, but owing to close Japanese ties with America and
US firms it was uphill work. We did our best to support their sales
efforts.

Hitherto, the main emphasis with department stores had been
in promoting British goods in Tokyo and Osaka stores. We continued to work closely with them throughout my time and successfully organized a series of British promotions. Mitsukoshi
continued to put on special promotions of British consumer
goods every other year and we also had promotions at Takashi-
maya and other stores in Tokyo. In Osaka Hankyu did British
promotions every year. Their Chairman, Mr Noda Ko, who was
particularly friendly to Britain, invariably invited us out to his
house near Takarazuka for a slap-up dinner after the official
opening of the Hankyu promotion. We first had cocktails in the
garden. As the promotion usually took place in November we

soon got cold. We then went into a dinner of lobster, accompanied by Chateau Yquem(!), followed by steak, accompanied by a superlative claret. Girls from the Takarazuka troupe were in attendance and asked to sing to us until Mr Noda showed us his film depicting him doing kendo (the art of the sword). Then it was time to go home. The pattern never changed.

We did all we could to arrange promotions of British goods in provincial stores. We had some success but the demand was limited and we were often stymied by the complicated nature of Japanese distribution channnels which meant that the prices of British goods when they reached the Japanese consumer were three or four times the retail price in the United Kingdom.

There was no longer a quota on Scotch whisky, but the alcohol duty discriminated against high value foreign products and the whisky distillers complained about parallel imports which they claimed were undermining their hold on the prestige end of the market and taking advantage of advertising campaigns by sole importers to whom the parallel importers made no contribution. I had to point out to the Distillers Company that they could not expect the Japanese Government to stop parallel imports and that they must deal with this problem at home or in other foreign markets from which the parallel imports were coming. This led Distillers to complain to the FCO that I was not supporting them. I was able to show that this was absolute rubbish. Sadly, this company was at that stage managed by people out of touch with the Japanese scene.

Although most other consumer goods did not face major obstacles, except for the complexities of Japanese distribution systems, cheese and butter were still subject to very restrictive quotas. Whenever we had a store promotion we had to request special quotas for small quantities of such products. The tariffs on biscuits, sugar confectionery and chocolate remained in our view unjustifiably high.

As we developed our exports we kept on coming across bureaucratic obstacles which were new to us. Many importers were at first frightened to report these obstacles for fear that the Japanese authorities who still had considerable powers, especially through 'administrative guidance', would make life difficult for them in other ways. We gradually overcame these fears and were able by hard slogging to get the obstacles mitigated if not withdrawn. The Japanese reputation in trade remained one of never making concessions until they had to and then giving too little and too late. In fact, of course, freeing trade was very much in the Japanese national interest and the Japanese government could have gained immense credit if they had been bold and taken on the various protectionist lobbies in Japan, but the officials and their friends in the Diet prevented such a sensible policy from being adopted.

In the course of discussions on VRAs and on Japanese obstacles to imports, I had many talks with Mr Amaya Naohiro, the International Vice-Minister in MITI. I came to have great respect for him. He was courageous and a thinker. I consider that the Japanese motor car industry did him a great injustice when, after he had reached a very difficult understanding with the Americans on cars, they termed him, if I remember correctly, 'the whore of the Americans'.

An increasing amount of time had to be spent on financial services. This was an area where British firms had considerable advantage and the invisible balance, because of the contribution of the city of London, was in our favour. The big banks had all by now established branches in Tokyo and the merchant banks were following suit, at first with representative offices, and then with branches. There was growing interest in investment in Japanese equities and British stockbrokers showed interest in obtaining seats on the Tokyo Stock Exchange, which was very much of a closed shop. This was an issue which came to a head later in the 1980s. The biggest problems were those caused by the restrictive and opaque rules imposed by the MOF and by their use of 'administrative guidance'. The MOF line was that whatever had not been permitted was forbidden. We did what we could to help British financial institutions develop their business in Japan.

It struck me then that the merchant banks were sending a higher calibre of staff to Tokyo than the big four clearing banks. I remember the Vice Chairman of one of the big four British banks coming to see me (I had altered my programme to accommodate him) with his local manager, a nice enough fellow but hardly bright. The Vice-Chairman in the presence of his manager asked me to tell him about Japan. I also recall speaking with another high level director of a British clearing bank and pointing out that the heads of Japanese banks in London were very senior people; indeed, some were members of the main board. Why did they not appoint someone of similar calibre? The trouble was that at that stage the big four did not have many people with the right qualifications and did not give high enough priority to their operations in Japan.

We noticed that those who had already carved out niches for themselves were not keen on welcoming newcomers or in any way challenging MOF. They feared that their little corner might be upset or invaded. This was particularly true of the insurance companies who, despite prodding from us, in those days liked to keep a low profile. The heads of the main British shipping companies were regular callers at the Embassy. On the whole they remained satisfied. While I was Ambassador in Tokyo, I was very glad to be able to hand to Ariyoshi Yoshiya, the 'Grand Old Man' of Japanese shipping, the insignia of an honorary KBE.

British Airways, not yet privatised, had been slow in developing the route to Japan, but they were increasingly irritated by the restrictive attitude of the Civil Aviation Bureau, who did all they could to prevent new and competitive fares being introduced. The Minister of Transport changed at each cabinet reshuffle on the 'Buggins turn' principle. They were almost completely under the thumb of their senior officials. When I called on each new Minister I expressed my regret that the Ministry did not seem to believe in the merits of competition and free markets. Such comments merely raised an embarrassed smile.

INWARD INVESTMENT INTO THE UK

Our efforts to expand our exports had some successes, but it was uphill work and we decided, with the agreement of London, to put a high priority on the promotion of inward investment. We organized missions and seminars and invited companies which had been successful investors to speak. We also did our best to help the representatives of the different regions when they came to Tokyo. Some such as the Telford Development Corporation had already established an office of their own in Japan. But as the Scottish and the Welsh Offices in Britain competed for inward investment from Japan we increasingly felt that the taxpayer might be paying too high a price for sometimes quite small initial investments. It seemed to us that the regional efforts should be properly coordinated at the centre. Officials agreed in principle but the Scottish and Welsh Ministers were unwilling to cede authority to the centre and competition between the regions for Japanese investment continued.

Our main target companies were those involved in electronics and motor cars. We had already managed to attract most of the major Japanese electronic manufacturers of televison and audio equipment. We now looked for investment in semi-conductors and were successful in getting NEC to invest at Livingston in Scotland. This decision owed much to Mr Kobayashi Koji, Chairman of the company. The investment was huge and the Queen agreed to open the factory in 1983. We also sought investment from manufacturers of tapes and office equipment. Maxell and Ricoh both chose to invest in Telford. Sharp and Brother went to Wrexham in North Wales. Yuasa batteries eventually went to South Wales. We widened our net to cover machine tool manufacturers such as Yamazaki (Mazak) and chemical companies.

The Rank Toshiba JV at Plymouth was wound up and Toshiba eventually turned the investment round and began manufacturing a wider range of products. The GEC/Hitachi JV at Hirwaun had even greater problems. I had got to know Misu, the chairman of the Hitachi side of the business. One day, I saw him at a cocktail party and asked him how they were getting on. When he replied despondently I urged him to come and see me. He then poured out a tale of woe about the lack of support for the JV from GEC and complained that Arnold Weinstock, GEC's Managing Director, had never once been near Hirwaun. Hitachi label TV sets and GEC label TV sets made by the factory were essentially the same products but because of Hitachi's record and reputation Hitachi label models sold for a higher price than GEC label sets. I duly reported this conversation to London. Unfortunately, an official in the Department of Trade and Industry in London passed a copy straight to GEC and Arnold Weinstock was furious. Thereafter, he always thought I was in the pockets of the Japanese. Weinstock had never liked anything to do with Japan since the problems which had occurred at the first Japanese atomic power station of the Calder Hall type at Tokai Miura. This had been built by English Electric just before it had been taken over by GEC. Eventually, the JV had to be broken up and Hitachi started again from scratch at Hirwaun. In due course, they made a success of the plant which began to manufacture a wider range of products. I recall that GEC continued to oppose Japanese investment which might in any way compete with their products, such as elevators.

The British government wanted to preserve what little there was of the British computer industry. This was concentrated in ICL which was too small and did not have sufficiently advanced technology to compete in world markets. ICL did, however, have a relationship with Fujitsu in Japan, one of the most important Japanese computer manufacturers. It became an important priority to develop this relationship and we did our best to cement contacts with Fujitsu. The Minister concerned in the Department of Industry was then Kenneth Baker who visited us more than once. Fujitsu's top man in relation to ICL was Yoshikawa, a genial tough Managing Director who loved parties, especially where there was plenty to drink and he could enjoy himself thumping on Japanese drums. I can remember a number of occasions when, with Kenneth Baker, we enjoyed his hospitality. Eventually, Fujitsu bought a majority of ICL's shares and ICL's fortunes began to improve.

In cars our targets, in order of priority (dictated by the interest being shown by the companies), were Nissan, Honda and Toyota. By the time I arrived in Tokyo Nissan had expressed interest in the possibility of investing in Britain, but no decision had been made. Accordingly, one of my first calls was on Ishihara, then President of Nissan. I wanted to get some form of commitment by Nissan to go ahead with the project. In January 1981 Ishihara agreed to a letter which might be interpreted as one of intent to make a major investment but which was not a firm commitment. It was nevertheless an important step forward.

Over the next three years investigations were carried out by Nissan and negotiations conducted with central and local authorities in the United Kingdom. I was as closely involved in these as I could be in view of my other commitments. I had many talks with Ishihara and did my best to speak to Kawamata, the Chairman, who from the beginning was very reluctant to endorse the proposal. He was close to the Nissan union who were opposed to the investment. Among many lunches and dinners which I gave in support of our discussions with Nissan I gave a lunch for the union representatives and tried to explain the backgound to them, pointing out that in the long run investment in Britain would help to preserve the profitability of Nissan and consequently the jobs of members of the union. I am not sure how far my efforts were successful with the union. Kawamata was obstinate and grand. Fortunately, Mrs Thatcher became interested in persuading Nissan to invest and agreed to meet Kawamata, who was charmed and flattered by her. Ever after I used to feel that Kawamata only believed in talking to God and Mrs Thatcher. When we encountered major problems over the financing of the investment Mrs Thatcher instructed that the possibility of lease-based finance should be investigated. She was convinced that a deal should be made with Nissan.

The Department of Industry nominated a senior team to undertake the Nissan negotiations. Robin Mountfield, the Under Secretary involved, was a frequent visitor and became a good friend. He feared at times, understandably I think, that we might be 'paying' too much for a Nissan investment. Other officials, too, had their doubts. I was, however, convinced that if we could once win this investment it would open doors to many others. I felt sure that it could transform the British car industry and lead eventually to significant improvements in British productivity, competitivity and quality control. Finally, and it must be said due to a considerable degree to Mrs Thatcher's backing, a deal was concluded in early 1984. I was sad that I had to leave Tokyo before the deal was sealed but felt that all our efforts had been worth while. Unfortunately, Nissan failed to invite Patrick (then Lord) Jenkin, who had been Minister of Industry through much of the negotiations, and me to the opening of their factory in Sunderland.

We had many talks with Honda and did all we could to encourage their growing relationship with Austin-Rover. I also tried hard to persuade them to set up a motor-cycle plant in the United Kingdom if only because the British motor-cycle industry had been largely destroyed by Japanese competition. I failed in this, but the Austin-Rover connection deepened and led to much-needed improvements in Austin-Rover's productivity and quality control. I often hoped that Honda would one day purchase Austin-Rover, but they were coy about this and preferred to develop their own investment at Swindon. I think that they feared above all a political outcry if the sole remaining British manufacturer of motor cars in significant market numbers were purchased by a Japanese company. In my view, the Rover group, as it had then become, did not display sufficient diplomatic skills with Honda when eventually the firm was bought out by BMW.

Toyota had been slow in undertaking foreign investments and from our point of view it seemed unlikely that they would make any quick decision to invest in Britain. However, we did our best to keep in touch with them and offer help if and when they might decide to invest in Europe, if only to overcome European restrictions on imports of cars from Japan. Their distributors in Britain and some other foreign markets were the Inchcape Group. When the late Earl of Inchcape, then Chairman of Inchcape, came to Japan I invited him and the then Chairman of Toyota, Toyoda Eiji, to lunch. When I began to speak to Toyoda about investment in Britain Lord Inchcape intervened to say that he thought Toyota should do no such thing. The British did not work hard and were union dominated. I countered Inchcape's remarks. When Toyoda had left I upbraided Inchcape for his unhelpful attitude. I think he feared that Inchcape's valuable franchise for Toyota cars might be upset if Toyota invested in Britain. The success of the

Nissan investment in Sunderland was, I am sure, an important factor in the eventual decision of Toyota to make significant investments in Britain.

We did our best to promote Japanese purchases of components for motor vehicles if only to increase the local content of any Japanese motor-car plant which might be set up in Britain. Japanese quality standards were rightly very high and it was clearly going to be some time before our manufacturers could match them. We naturally expected and hoped that Japanese parts manufacturers would invest in Britain to supply Japanese motor manufacturers, as in due course they did, thus leading to improvements in productivity and quality in British parts manufacturers.

PUBLIC RELATIONS

An ambassador, as a representative of his sovereign or state and responsible for promoting his country's interests, must nowadays be ready to cooperate with the media. I had regular sessions with British press correspondents in Japan and tried to answer their questions as frankly as I could. Unfortunately, few British papers had full-time correspondents in Japan and the more popular papers, including *The Times*, tended to be primarily interested in stories which showed up the peculiarities of Japan or which were not flattering. The *Financial Times* correspondent during my stay was Jurek Martin who was later their chief correspondent in the USA. We got on well and while we did not always agree I thought his reporting was invariably stimulating and basically sound. *The Economist* had various correspondents while I was in Japan. One of these was Bill Emmott, who later became editor. They made some useful and provocative analyses of the Japanese scene. The BBC were well represented by William Horsley who had the advantage of having a good knowledge of Japanese. Unfortunately, with the exception of Horsley, British correspondents generally had to rely on local staff to scan the Japanese papers for them and to use interpreters when conducting interviews with Japanese who did not speak English. This limited their usefulness.

The British press correspondents found the Japanese *kisha kur-*

abu (Correspondents' Club) group system operating in Japanese ministries an obstacle to their access to information. In my view, these groups, from which foreign journalists were excluded, often led to a cosy relationship between the journalists in a particular group and the ministry or organization to which it was attached. Journalists, in return for confidences, were often persuaded to suppress or downplay scandals: they feared that if they played up a problem they might be excluded from valuable information in the future. I supported publicly the British journalists' objections to this system.

I considered that relations with the Japanese media were an even more important part of the Ambassador's job. Alan Pinnell, the First Secretary in charge of the information department, which rightly devoted the bulk of its time and resources to promoting British exports, encouraged responsible Japanese newspapers and journals to seek interviews. As I always spoke in Japanese with Japanese journalists we were generally able to strike up a rapport which it would have been much more difficult for a non-Japanese speaker to do. I also responded positively whenever possible to requests for articles. Some of the more routine ones were drafted for me, but I preferred, if at all possible, to write my own pieces and draft my own speeches. Through these interviews and articles I was, I think, able to help to promote our image and interests.

One article which I wrote for the Asahi was directly productive. I had learnt from my friend Dr Carmen Blacker, senior lecturer in Japanese in the Oriental Faculty at Cambridge University, that Japanese studies at Cambridge were in danger of extinction following the retirement of two members of the staff and a lack of funds. I felt that it would be a major blow to British relations with Japan if we could not maintain Japanese studies at one of our two oldest and most prestigious universities. I accordingly wrote first to friends in business and banking in Britain to seek British support, but I had no success. So I began investigating possibilities in Japan and the Asahi agreed to print a short article by me on this subject. This was brought to the attention of our friend Dr Hiraiwa Gaishi, President (later Chairman) of Tokyo Electric Power

Company, and very influential in Keidanren, the Japanese Federation of Economic Organisations, of which he became Chairman. Through his good offices Keidanren put up a sum of £800,000 to establish a chair of Japanese studies at Cambridge, thus ensuring their continuation. Japanese studies at Cambridge under Professor Richard Bowring, who was appointed to fill the chair in 1984, have since expanded considerably and attracted further funds from Japanese sources.

Television was just as important as the press. I found again that as a Japanese speaker I was much in demand for interviews, discussion groups and even chat shows. Usually there was a preliminary session at which the content of the broadcast would be discussed and one could prepare one's thoughts for the questions. Sometimes broadcasts were prerecorded; some went out live. I remember once being asked if I would appear on a breakfast show in Osaka. I duly arrived in plenty of time and was waiting to learn what the topics were when I was whisked into an elevator and taken up to the top of a TV tower to find a popular show in full swing. I was propelled in front of the cameras, introduced to the presenter and asked a series of personal questions. As it was just before Christmas I managed at least to give a good plug for Scotch whisky. I soon decided that one thing I would not do was look at recordings of TV shows/interviews on which I appeared. I always shuddered when I heard my plummy voice and English accent. I also disliked looking at my prominent chin and nose and noticing myself, as my wife always said, scowling at the camera. I did try hard to smile, but it usually looked like a smirk.

TOURING

I found that while Britain received a modicum of attention in the media in Tokyo and Osaka there was much less information about or interest in Britain in the remoter parts of Japan despite the fact that in many parts of Japan industries were developing fast and standards of living improving rapidly. I remember once when calling on the Mayor of Sendai to be surprised to see that instead of the Union Jack (crossed with the Japanese flag) being displayed on the table in the customary Japanese way we had the Stars and Stripes displayed to us. I did my best to stress that we were British and not American and I hope the distinction registered, but the mayor was not a very internationally-minded type. Perhaps there had been a linguistic muddle; America was usually referred to as *Beikoku* and Britain as *Eikoku*. I decided that this was the charitable interpretation of a minor incident which amused rather than irritated us. Elizabeth noted that more often than not the Union Jack was upside down.

I determined that we would pay official visits to all the Japanese prefectures (there are 47 of them, including the three metropolitan districts of Tokyo, Osaka and Kyoto and the island of Hokkaido). This was not easy. I could only get away on tour when there were no important visitors from Britain or other events requiring my presence in Tokyo. This meant unfortunately that many visits had to take place at the worst time of year in terms of the prevailing weather (e.g. in the heat of summer or the depths of winter or in the rainy season). It also meant that we had to pack far too much into each day when we were away travelling.

Before going on tour I tried to do my homework and in particular to find out about earlier British connections with the prefecture in question. I then wrote an article for the local newspaper. These articles and some other articles and speeches which I made were later collected and published by Chuokoronsha under the corny title of *Higashi no Shimaguni, Nishi no Shimaguni* (Eastern island country, Western island country).

I always offered to give local press and TV interviews. Usually these offers were taken up and I might be asked to give a speech in Japanese at some function. In practice, the local media were not very sophisticated. Interviews were rarely if ever controversial. They tended rather to be repetitive and boring. Local journalists often only seemed to be interested in our impressions of their prefecture. This question was often asked almost as soon as we had got off the plane. I remember on one occasion giving a press conference and finding that there was a dearth of questions. So I began asking the journalists questions. This led the chairman of the group to rebuke me, saying it was their job to ask the questions.

We always called on the Governor of the prefecture whose Tokyo office helped in the preparation of our programmes. A few of the governors were interesting personalities. One of them from Hokkaido was Yokomichi, a former socialist, who had always interesting things to say. Another who much impressed me was Hiramatsu of Oita prefecture, formerly a MITI official. I found Hosokawa Morihiro, then Governor of Kumamoto, outstanding. He was descended from the former daimyos of Kumamoto and we attended a tea ceremony in the Hosokawa style in his ancient and elegant tea house. Most of the other governors we met have since become blurred images in my memory. Many were formerly from the *Jijisho* (Self Government Ministry or Home Affairs Ministry) and although they had had to be popularly elected to become governor tended to be typical Japanese bureaucrats with few, if any, outside interests. One governor, however, was a keen violinist and when we went to dinner with him he and his wife played us some classical pieces – he on his fiddle and she playing the piano.

We also called on local mayors and chairmen of chambers of commerce as well as other appropriate dignitaries. We did our best to find out about local industrial development and possibilities for British exports. We usually tried to visit the main local department stores and look at the limited selection of British goods they were displaying. Some suggestions from us hopefully bore fruit in future purchases by them.

Many of these calls were distinctly hard work. Elizabeth knew that I was getting to rock bottom when I began to ask the mayor we were visiting about the development of the public drainage systems. One or two of those we called on seemed moribund: indeed, I remember one who found it difficult even to nod in assent and looked as though he had to be propped up. These visits could prove a strain on the bladder as we were always given tea or coffee, sometimes both. (I remember one day that I counted having drunk 14 cups of tea.) We rarely had time, let alone an opportunity, to go to the loo between calls. In the end I got used to asking for

the loo on arrival at an office before going into see the local dignitary. One could hardly go after making our call as this would
mean keeping the dignitary waiting for us at the elevator. On some
of these calls we would, to our embarrassment, find the staff waiting in line to bow and clap us in.

Looking back, as our hosts were almost invariably very hospitable, our visits seem to have consisted of a series of meals –
lunch at 11.30 am and dinner at 5.30 pm. The only advantage of
these timings was that we often got back to the hotel around 8.00
pm and were glad to be able to rest having been on the go for
about 12 hours with no time to put our feet up or change. The
meals varied from good, bad to indifferent, although there was
always too much food. We kept on urging, especially at lunch,
that the meal should be kept simple. We would have been quite
happy with *zaru-soba* (cold buck-wheat) or a *domburi* (bowl of rice
with a topping), but this was never allowed. I think that our
minders wanted the chance of a good blow-out at public expense.
On the whole, the Japanese-style meals were better than Western-
style which tended to be pretentious with too many sauces
thought to be French. Wines were sometimes imported, but often they were local Japanese varieties and pretty undrinkable. At
least with a Japanese meal there was almost invariably excellent
saké. In Kyushu one might be offered *shochu* (a white spirit often
made from sweet potatoes) which I never got to like, but one
could politely say that saké agreed better with one's digestion
than white spirit. Sometimes, we were faced with items which
required an effort to eat; for instance, in Oita, we were given tiny
live fish swimming in water and were expected to lift these out
with a sieve and swallow them down live after dipping them in
sauce.

We usually took one of the junior Japanese-speaking secretaries with us on these trips. It was good practice for them and
they were useful in looking after the presents we had to take with
us and in coping with the presents we brought back. We tended to
take Scotch whisky, little bits of Wedgwood and picture books
about Britain to give to our hosts. In return, we would be given
dolls in glass cases, lacquer boxes or pieces of pottery. Sadly, most

items were not to our taste which had become increasingly Japanese in that we preferred the *shibui* (restrained) and less showy colourful pieces thought by Japanese to be in Western taste. The problem was often how to transport large items back to Tokyo. There at least we could dispose of them without causing offence. Each Christmas we had a raffle for the domestic staff in the residence. They were apparently pleased to receive some of our cast-offs. I shall never forget the gardener's delight when he received a clock set in pearls which we thought a monstrosity.

On one visit to Hokkaido I wanted to visit Matsumae where the daimyo responsible for Ezo (Hokkaido) from the sixteenth to the nineteenth centuries had had his castle. The Seikan tunnel between Northern Honshu and Hokkaido which was then being built was to emerge near Matsumae. I was taken down to see the tunnel workings, but my wife and Phillida Seaward (later Purvis) who had come with us (she was working in the economic section of the Embassy and had been a Japanese language student) were not permitted to go with me as women were not allowed in the tunnel diggings for fear that this would arouse the jealousy of the *yama no kami* (the mountain god). The tunnel was many years late in being completed. It was a major engineering feat, being longer and deeper than the Channel Tunnel. I doubted whether it would ever be economic. This was a view which one MOF official endorsed. When I asked him what should be done with the tunnel, he replied that the best thing would be to bury it. I thought this rather extreme.

In some prefectures, such as Nagasaki, we were accompanied by police escorts. I found this rather a bore; I think they were merely using our visit as an opportunity to train for a real VIP visit. A visit to Kagoshima led me to study the life of Dr William Willis who was regarded as the founder of the school of Western medicine there, now Kagoshima Medical University. I had written about him in my article for the *Minami Nihon Shimbun*, the local paper, and met in Kagoshima doctors who had done research about him. I began to do some more research and in due course found that Professor Hagihara Nobutoshi, who was the expert in Japan on the life of Ernest Satow, had discovered a set of letters which Dr Willis had sent home. He allowed me to borrow them and I copied them after office hours on the Embassy copier. I found Dr Willis's story fascinating and eventually produced a book based on my research, entitled *Dr Willis in Japan, British Medical Pioneer 1862-1877*, which was published in London by Athlone in 1985.

William Adams (1564-1620), the British pilot on the Dutch ship *Liefde*, was reputed to have been the first Englishman in Japan when he came ashore from his damaged ship off the Usuki peninsula (now part of Oita prefecture) in 1600. He was probably buried either at Hirado where the British trading post (factory) had been from 1613-23 or near Yokosuka where, at Hemi, he had been granted an estate. We visited Hirado on one tour and had to go annually to Yokosuka for a ceremony with speeches at the Adams memorial there. This took place in spring-time, usually when the cherry blossoms were out, but the ceremony was often marred by rain. We were then entertained to lunch by the Mayor of Yokosuka which has a twinning relationship with Gillingham, Kent, where William Adams was born. Adams was also recorded as having worked at Ito, a hot spring resort in the Izu peninsula, where he apparently taught ship building. Ito was also determined to make use of our hero's reputation and organized every August a William Adams festival which included a procession, a Japanese dinner with dancing and fireworks. The fireworks were, I thought, the best part. In the procession the year we went to Ito, Richard Jones, a Japanese-speaking officer in the chancery, played the part of William Adams and, at the request of the local mayor, we followed in the Embassy Rolls with flag flying. This was armour-plated and, as the windows could not be opened, supposedly air-conditioned, but at the slow walking pace of the procession the air-conditioning would not work. After some time sweating it out we got out and walked too. The affair was jazzed up (or enlivened depending on your point of view) by dancing girls including some scantily dressed English chorus girls who were acting as Ito hostesses at the time. On future occasions I decided that attendance at the Ito festival might suitably be delegated to the Naval Attaché.

I wanted to learn more about how Japanese members of the Lower House got themselves elected in multi-member constituencies and in particular how they cultivated their *jiban* (electoral base). One member of the House of Representatives whom we got to know quite well was Tamazawa Tokuichiro whose constituency was in Iwate Prefecture on the Rikuchu coast. He and his wife invited us to do a tour of their constituency with them. I found this fascinating although it was somewhat embarrassing to discover that I was expected to make speeches supportng his candidature. I got round this by speaking about his interest in international affairs. Shortly after I retired Tamazawa lost his seat. I do not think this was in any way due to my visit! He was later reelected and became for a time Minister of State responsible for the Defence Agency. His constituency included a very beautiful part of the Japanese coast line. Unfortunately, it rained throughout most of our visit. We were impressed by the way in which Mrs Tamazawa gave active support to her husband, speaking whenever he was not available. When we moved from one part of the constituency to the next and made contact with the organizer of the local *jiban* this was termed '*baton-tachu*' as if we were in a relay race.

One element of our tours which we much enjoyed was the opportunity it gave us to visit regional potteries, to collect specimens of Japanese pots and meet Japanese potters. Most of the potters were interesting men although one or two had developed a certain arrogance due to their eminence. Japanese crafts generally, including textiles and folk toys, provided an extra interest to our travels.

CULTURAL WORK

We were fortunate in having a good British Council office in Tokyo. The head of the Council in Tokyo had the status of Cultural Counsellor on the diplomatic list and his deputy was also an Embassy First Secretary. The Council worked hard at developing English-language teaching and provided a good service of advice and help on British educational facilities. The British Council sholarship scheme ensured that a good number of Japanese scholars (I should have liked there to be more British Council scholarships for Japanese) had opportunities to study in Britain. It also meant that we had many good friends in influential positions throughout Japan. Meetings of former British Council scholars were held regularly and I did my best to meet as many as I could.

I found the *Mombusho* (the Japanese Ministry of Education) a conservative and on the whole illiberal bureaucratic organization, but the Mombusho scholarship scheme did help to ensure that British students of Japan had increasing opportunities for study and research in Japan. The JET (Japan English Teachers) scheme brought increasing numbers of young English people to Japan to teach in Japanese schools and help Japanese companies. Unfortunately, partly because of local opposition and bureaucracy, they were not always used properly. But many returned to Britain interested in expanding their knowledge of Japan and Japanese. While in Japan they clearly helped many Japanese to understand more about Britain. On our tours round Japan we always tried to meet the JET teachers and to encourage them in their work. Some, especially those in remote prefectures, however friendly and hospitable some of their Japanese hosts were, inevitably felt isolated and occasionally lonely.

The British Council also worked hard to promote Britain as a centre of art and culture. While I was Ambassador we had a stream of orchestras and soloists from Britain. We tried whenever we could to entertain and encourage British artists and musicians. We held receptions for British orchestras and conductors. Sometimes these were difficult occasions. For instance, the British orchestra whose Russian conductor was Gennadi Rozhdestvensky, arrived almost an hour late for a large buffet lunch which we gave for them and to which we had asked many Japanese guests. They had been kept rehearsing by the conductor who was 'too tired' to come to us. I determined after this that while I would do what I could for prominent British conductors and soloists, I was not going to be stood up in this way in future. One of the most amusing musical occasions we had was a dinner for the

British conductor Georg (later Sir Georg) Solti. He was a marvellous raconteur with a good sense of humour. We enjoyed giving lunch to Sir Michael Tippett, the composer, and on another occasion to Julian Bream, the guitarist. We had to produce lots of food for the Royal Ballet whose tour in Japan was the occasion for a visit by Her Royal Highness Princess Anne. Our dinner was, I think, a successful 'cultural' occasion.

The British Council organized exhibitions of British art with varying success. I remember on one occasion there were some photographs by Gilbert and George on display which included four-letter words, so we quickly moved Princess Chichibu on to look at other exhibits. One British artist for whom we gave a lunch was David Hockney. He asked if he might bring his camera and take a few pictures. We naturally agreed. In fact, he took hundreds of shots with a tiny camera. The result was his photo-montage 'Lunch at The British Embassy Tokyo'. We would have liked a copy even though it showed us with numerous chins and noses, but it was too expensive for us. However, a copy was eventually bought by HMG and sent out to the Embassy for display.

RELATIONS WITH THE IMPERIAL FAMILY

If only because Britain is a monarchy we attached much importance to developing our contacts with members of the Imperial Family. Apart from the Crown Prince and Princess, we entertained his younger brother Prince Hitachi and Princess Hitachi, as well as the then Emperor's younger brothers Princes Takamatsu and Mikasa and their wives. We attended the wedding of Prince Mikasa's eldest son, Prince Tomohito, popularly known as *hide denka* because of his beard, to the daughter of Mr and Mrs Takakichi Aso, but never hit it off with him. Our favourite was Princess Chichibu who was well loved by members of the British royal family and very active in Anglo-Japanese affairs.

When Prince Hiro, the elder son of the Crown Prince, was approaching graduation from the Gakushuin (the former Peers' college), I expressed the hope that like his uncle Prince Chichibu he might be sent to study in Britain. This idea jelled with the thinking in the Imperial household and we started to explore possibilities. His uncle Prince Chichibu had been at Magdalen as had Prince Tomohito. It seemed sensible for the Prince to go to a different college. We had just had a visit from Sir Rex Richards, then Vice-Chancellor of Oxford University and Warden of Merton College. I thought that, although I am neither an Oxford nor Cambridge man and am not, therefore, very *au fait* with conditions at either university, Merton might be a good place for the Prince. It is one of the oldest and smallest colleges in Oxford. Rex Richards welcomed the idea and in due course Prince Hiro was entered for Merton. As we know from the little book which the Prince wrote in Japanese about his experiences (*Thames to tomo ni*) he greatly enjoyed what was for him a unique experience.

OFFICIAL VISITORS

A modern Ambassador has a constant stream of official visitors who expect to be entertained and looked after. Indeed, at times, he and his wife feel that they are little more than hotel keepers. Our life was no different in this respect from that of other British Ambassadors, except that because Tokyo was so far away and different, and was being recognized as increasingly important, the number of visitors and the strain on Embassy resources grew. Visiting Ministers and their private secretaries naturally expected to stay at the official residence as did some senior officials.

A few of our VIP visitors went out of their way to show appreciation of our hospitality and to be pleasant. Two couples stand out in this way. They were Peter and Iona Carrington and the Weatherills. Lord Carringtom was Foreign Secretary up to the Falklands War. Bernard (Jack) Weatherill was the Speaker of the House of Commons. The Carringtons, who were in Tokyo when we should have been celebrating our silver wedding, were considerate and charming. After the dinner for some 30 Japanese which we had given for them they insisted on going into the kitchen to thank the domestic staff. Before the Weatherills came we were a little worried about them. Jack (later Lord) Weatherill, we were told, did not eat meat, while his wife was a Christian Scientist. We feared they might be difficult guests but they could not have been nicer. They behaved impeccably when we took them to Fukui prefecture to visit the constituency of Fukuda Hajime, the Japanese Speaker, who guided them to the great temple of Eiheiji and entertained them royally.

We were also a little apprehensive about Sir Keith Joseph in view of his Thatcherite reputation and the warning that he could only eat almost liquid foods. A further complication in his case was that he was moved from Trade to Education while he was on the aircraft to Japan. In fact, although we often feared from the ominous sounds from his bathroom that he might be choking, he was a gentlemanly guest. He was very serious and took all my off-the-cuff remarks as if they were important and not, as they sometimes were, light-hearted. Rather to my horror, he would write down some of what I said about Japan and education in a little notebook.

I had known Patrick Jenkin from the time of his first visit to Japan when I was Commercial Counsellor. As Secretary of State for Industry he was the Minister responsible for inward investment and we took him to Nissan and Honda. I recall that he was pleased with his *bon mot*: 'We have grown fonder with Honda but the kissing with Nissan is missing'. We had made good progress during his visit in talks with Honda but little with Nissan.

Kenneth Baker, then the Minister responsible for information technology, and Norman Lamont, then another junior minister, appeared to enjoy their visits. John Biffen, as Secretary of State for Trade, was rather an enigma. When I took him to call on the MITI Minister he left me to do the talking. On the night David Howell, then Secretary of State for Energy, arrived in Japan we were due to attend a performance of opera given by the Italian company from La Scala at the invitation of our Italian colleague. Fortunately, he kindly produced another ticket, and David, though tired by his journey, enjoyed the performance. I always endeavoured to travel with visiting Ministers in the back of the Rolls so that I could give them a last-minute briefing. I knew that the points I made just before a call were likely to be uppermost in the Minister's mind and were more effective than any amount of written briefing.

The then Secretary of State for Wales came on an inward investment mission with what I thought an unnecessarily large delegation, including a press officer. The latter got a flea in his ear from me when he telphoned in the middle of the night to ask me to wake the Secretary of State and tell him that the Prince of Wales had just announced his engagement. I told him to get his priorities right; his Secretary of State could send an appropriate message in the morning. I noted that the Permanent Secretary, who was a member of the Welsh delegation, was far from pleased when his Secretary of State began to criticize officials in front of Japanese guests at the dinner we gave for him. I teased the Secretary of State on his arrival by telling him that in view of the continuing controversy over whaling by Japanese vessels some Japanese might think that he was the Secretary of State for Whales, not Wales. He did not appreciate the tease.

We did not take to one particular senior Foreign Office Minister who was very conscious of his own importance. In this he received stout backing from his wife. We arranged a very full programme for him. (I always believed that if Ministers travelled at HMG's expense they should work hard on their visits.) The programme included at his request visits to Nara and Kyoto. During this part of his tour we visited the Sharp electronic experimental laboratories at Tenri, south of Nara. As the person concerned had been a Northern Ireland Minister the Japanese police were strict about his security and provided escorting cars. The road from Nara to Kyoto was even slower than usual and we arrived late in Kyoto for a dinner. The Minister was furious with me because the Japanese police had, in my view rightly, not used their sirens to clear a way for his car through the traffic. He then insisted on extra time to have a bath and change, making us even later for dinner. I did my best to make our excuses to our host.

The least attractive guest we had was a junior Education Minister. He was rude to the Japanese, refusing to eat a Japanese meal to which he had been invited, and he annoyed me at the dinner which I gave for him by running down Britain in front of Japanese guests. When he went to bed I reminded him of the tradition that when politicians go abroad they do not criticize their own country in public. He never asked to see my wife and never sent a letter of thanks for our hospitality. Nor did he leave a gratuity for the domestic staff.

We had to cope with numerous visits from MPs, including members invited to visit Japan with Sir Julian Ridsdale, the Chairman of the British-Japan Parliamentary group. Some of these MPs, such as Chris Patten, went on to important ministerial posts. We did our best to make MPs, including members of parliamentary committees, work hard when they sought our help. I did not see it as our job to entertain them on the Ginza as some expected.

□

Our most important and difficult visitor was Mrs Thatcher, who made an official visit to Japan on her way to Beijing and Hong Kong in the autumn of 1982. Fortunately, she was put up in the Japanese government guest house, but she had a number of meals at the residence and caused numerous problems, especially for me.

On her first evening when we had a 'briefing' dinner she spent much of the time insisting that we must find an appropriate Japanese proverb for her to use in her speech at the official dinner which the Japanese Prime Minister, Mr Suzuki Zenko, was giving for her. He was going to use the phrase 'where there is a will there is a way'. We tried all sorts of ideas on her, all of which were rejected with contumely. Eventually, the third butler came up with the phrase '*makanu tane wa haenu*' (If you don't sow the seeds they won't grow). We then had to teach her how to pronounce the words; this was not an easy task. Dennis Thatcher, who was enjoying a quiet drink but longing to get to bed, said to Elizabeth, 'It's always like this, but she'll make a good speech in the end.' She did.

A great fuss was made about the arrangements for the dinner for some 60 people at the residence. She had brought some regimental silver out to decorate the tables (this required a great deal of cleaning) and her own chocolates. The menu had to be approved by her. I knew that on other occasions the main course was going to be beef, but the alternative, suggested by our cook (I had returned from leave earlier than Elizabeth) of venison I had rejected, as Japanese guests do not really care for game, and she rejected the alternative I suggested of quail, saying she would only eat the stuffing. So it had to be beef once again.

The worst occasion was a Japanese dinner given for British businesmen on the Sunday night of her visit at the official guest house. She and Denis clearly hated the food and she was in a filthy mood, finding excuses to attack anyone who even mildly disagreed with her. She was particularly nasty to David Wilkinson, the British Airways representative in Tokyo (BA had not yet been privatized), implying that he was personally responsible for BA's failures. He was in fact a very good representative and I sprang to his defence. Eventually, the dinner was thankfully over. I was just about to go home when she summoned me and John Whitehead, the Minister, to come and have a drink in her sitting-room. We were joined by Robin Gray from the Department of Trade and her private secretaries, Robin Butler (later Sir Robin and Cabinet Secretary) and John Coles (later Sir John and Permanent Under secretay at the FCO). Mrs T. began to attack us, demanding to know why we did not take tougher action like the French did against imports of Japanese cars into Britain. We argued back pointing to the existing VRA and our obligations under the GATT. She went on and on arguing, but neither Robin Gray nor I were prepared to give in. Eventually at 1.00 am the private secretary sent me a note with the brief words 'leave it to me'. I went home and told my wife that I would probably have to resign the next day. In fact, of course, it all worked out quite satisfactorily in the end and she stuck to her brief.

She was much preoccupied while in Tokyo with what she should say to the Chinese about Hong Kong, and my colleague from Peking, Sir Percy Cradock, had come over and was staying with us. As is well known, Mrs Thatcher hardly needs any sleep. She certainly did not have much time for sleep while she was in Tokyo. For our part we said goodbye to her at the airport with a feeling of considerable relief. The visit had in fact gone well and all our planning had been worthwhile.

Mrs Thatcher had managed to put over her personality and make some valuable points about Britain on Japanese TV. 'That woman' as former Prime Minister Fukuda Takeo referred to her, came to be much admired in Japan as a unique phenomenon. She did not display much interest in things Japanese but she had as always absorbed the facts set out in her briefs prepared in White-hall and coordinated by the FCO. She was a glutton for statistics and in order to answer her endless questions I kept a statistical summary in my pocket so that I should not be caught out.

☐

Our two royal visitors were Princess Anne and Prince Philip. Princess Anne came to support the Royal Ballet and her tour was paid for by the FCO. I did my best to keep costs down. I queried with her comptroller, out on a reconnaissance visit, why she needed to bring a hairdresser when Mrs Thatcher had happily used a local hairdresser every morning (Mrs T. never had a hair out of place). The comptroller replied grandly: 'Prin-cess Anne is the Queen's only daughter; Mrs Thatcher is merely the Prime Minister.' I almost exploded.

The visit went reasonably well in the end, but I found talking to the Princess uphill work and Elizabeth did not find it much easier to discover things to discuss with Captain Mark Phillips. Neither of us are horsey people. We felt that they went through the programme as a duty to be performed and showed little en-thusiasm. When Princess Anne visited a children's nursery with Princess Chichibu she showed no real rapport with children although she was the President of the 'Save the Children Fund'.

I was apprehensive about the proposed visit by Prince Philip, who was coming on behalf of the World Wildlife Fund as it then was. We were told that the Japanese end of the Fund would make all the arrangements. Fortunately we did not rely on this informa-tion and took a grip on things early on. This was in any case ne-cessary as the Japanese authorities would be responsible for security and calls had to be made on the Emperor and Princess Chichibu. I also wanted (as previously noted) to make use of the visit to show off the BAe 146. The Japanese branch of Woof-woof, as the World Wildlife Fund was popularly called, were, to say the least, disorganized.

Two aspects of the visit irritated the Prince. The first was the rather obtrusive Japanese security arrangements. I could do nothing about this except try to distract his attention from them. The second was his impatience with Japanese photographers who, for instance, were not content with a single shot of him putting money in the Panda box at the zoo but wanted him to repeat the gesture time after time while they took new shots. When he asked why they could not be content with one shot when they had such good cameras, I replied that if they did Fuji films would not make half such a good profit. The Prince was, however, very good at giving off-the-cuff speeches and even listened patiently while a Japanese professor warbled on about the likely extinction of what sounded like 'the wrong taired lat' (he meant the long-tailed rat). In the house he was affable and friendly. One evening when I asked his aide if the Prince had ordered his breakfast, I heard a reply over my shoulder 'he has' from the Prince. He asked if he might join us for an informal drink not in the drawing-room but in our small sitting-room. My wife said: 'Of course, but I am afraid it's rather untidy'. On coming into the room he commented 'I see what you mean'. On the whole the visit went much better than I had feared.

THE TOKYO RESIDENCE

It would have been impossible to look after so many VIPs without a spacious residence and an efficient domestic staff. We also had a lot of entertaining to do. The vast majority of our guests were Japanese VIPs and British visitors. An important part of any ambassdor's duties is to facilitate contacts and this was the main purpose of the lunches, dinners and receptions we gave. Most of the criticism of diplomatic entertaining is based on ignorance of the aims and results of what we did. We did not go in for luxury parties with champagne flowing freely but Japanese have got used to lavishness in entertaining and we should have made a mistake if we had been mean over what we served.

We were fortunate in having a large residence built in earth-quake-proof Queen Anne or Georgian-style in the 1930s after the old residence became unsafe as a result of the 1923 earthquake. (For details see Dr J. Hoare's long essay on the history of the British Embassy, Tokyo in *Embassies of the East*, Japan Library, 1998). The dining-room could seat about 32 people to lunch or dinner and the double sitting-room overlooking the lawn provided adequate space for pre-meal drinks and coffee etc after the meal. The large ballroom opposite the sitting-room was used for larger dinners, for example, when Mrs Thatcher and Princess Anne were visiting, for buffet lunches and suppers and for receptions. It was also occasionally used for dances and concerts. In addition, the down-stairs accommodation included a small private sitting-room, a study and offices for our social secretary as well as loos. The kitchens behind the dining-room were large and behind these were living-quarters for domestic staff. There was also a wine cellar.

We had to deal with a number of problems. The kitchen equipment was out of date; when we arrived there were, for instance, no dish-washers and the old-fashioned knives had to be cleaned with corks. The fine panelling in the dining-room had been painted white on the orders of one of our predecessors; in Japan it is a sacrilege to paint over good wood. A hideous carpet in dog-sick brown and yellow had been commissioned from David Hicks for the ballroom. This had been removed by another of our predecessors, not only because of its colour and pattern but because it was of poor quality. Some of the carpets upstairs had been discoloured by one of our predecessors' dogs. The bath-rooms were old-fashioned and needed modernizing. Eventually, after some struggles, all these problems or deficiencies were remedied. But nothing could be done to make the residence easy to heat and cool (it had very thick walls and high ceilings) or easy to keep clean (the door furniture was all of brass which had to be polished).

We had what must seem to anyone living in England in the late twentieth century a huge domestic staff. There were three butlers (Adachi, Sugawawara and Aoyama) as well as three cooks (Negishi, Hatakeyama and Miyazaki) plus three maids to clean and help with serving. We also had a full-time gardener (Kishino) and two drivers (Kitsutaka and Ishikawa) to drive the Rolls and our own car which was used for guests and various errands. Fortunately, there had been a long-standing tradition of loyalty among the staff in the residence and there were practically no changes in the domestic staff except for one or two maids while we were in Tokyo. We were also fortunate in avoiding the sorts of quarrels between domestics which have plagued our colleagues elsewhere. Organizing and controlling the domestic staff and supervising the catering and the accounts was a major task. We were lucky to have throughout our time in Tokyo Yoshida Hiroko, daughter of a former Japanese Ambassador in various countries, as our very efficient social secretary. She also drafted the table plans and prepared the place-cards. Without her help we could not have coped. The domestic staff were paid by HMG and we were provided with *frais* to cover the expenses of entertaining and looking after visitors. These were adequate although by no means generous and we had to watch expenditure carefully. Whenever we received gifts of flowers one of the butlers would whisk these away to be refrigerated to use at our next lunch or dinner party.

We continued Embassy traditions such as giving a Christmas party for the children of Embassy staff, expatriate and Japanese. Presents had to be bought for all the children and an appropriate member of the UK staff played the part of Father Christmas under a huge Christmas tree. (I remember being horrified to find that a tree costing over £250 had been ordered one Christmas by the butlers without authorization.) I discovered that this tradition stemmed from the early 1890s when Mrs Fraser was in Tokyo as the wife of Hugh Fraser, then Minister and head of the then British Legation. This discovery led me to her book *A Diplomatist's Wife in Japan: Letters from Home to Home*, published in London in 1899. I selected and edited these letters, having done some research about Mary Fraser's life. My edition was published in 1982 by Weatherhill of Tokyo and New York in 1982 under the title *A Diplomat's Wife in Japan: Sketches at the turn of the Century* by Mary Crawford Fraser.

Every Christmas we also had separate parties for local staff and expatriate staff. The British staff used to do skits for the latter occasion guying members of the staff, naturally including the Ambassador. We instituted a party which we gave for our domestic staff. I did the drinks and we ordered *sushi* to be sent in. It was on these occasions that the raffle which I have already mentioned was held. At New Year we sent all the staff on holiday and fended for ourselves exploring, for instance, the eleven refrigerators in the kitchen quarters.

Our three children were able to join us for their holidays. The two girls' fares were met from public funds. William, who was at university, had only one free fare to cover the long vacation, but we were able to meet the costs of fares for his visits at Christmas and Easter. They had mixed feelings about staying in such a large residence with so many staff and I think that the girls in particular rather resented all the entertaining we had to do. William certainly enjoyed the luxury and was old enough to join us at some dinner parties. I remember he had to sit next to Mary Archer (wife of Jeffrey Archer, politician and writer) at one dinner we gave for the Vice-Chancellors of Oxford and Cambridge Universities. She resented having to sit next to him and they did not hit it off. Rosemary and Charlotte found it all a bit overwhelming after boarding school. Both William and Rosemary had friends from England out to stay and travelled around Japan on rail passes staying at youth hostels and cheap *minshuku* (similar to a B and B). They greatly enjoyed visits to Chuzenji where they could enjoy swimming in the lake and walking and where there were no domestic staff to inhibit them from going into the kitchen to make their own coffee as they liked it.

EMBASSY STAFF

Much too little has so far been said about the Embassy staff on whom we relied for so much. Of course there were some weak elements, but these were few and the work was generally performed willingly and efficiently. I must pay a handsome tribute to all the staff who worked with us in Tokyo. Some Ambassadors were inclined to refer to members of the staff as 'my staff'. I never did this consciously. They were members of a team of which I happened to be the temporary leader. I disliked being called 'Excellency' and requested that no-one should put HE on a memo or anything coming to me. I was doubtless a demanding Ambassador, but I hope that I was not as difficult and tiresome as Sir Harry Parkes who was head of mission in Tokyo from 1865-83. Perhaps I did not delegate enough and tried to keep tabs on too many details, but I am by nature an activist and work-aholic. My wife describes me as a maker of work and I suppose this is true.

Throughout my stay in Tokyo John Whitehead was my number two and Minister. I realized that being the number two is a difficult position to fill and tried to give John niches to carve out for himself. He is also an able activist and no doubt found his position trying from time to time. But his chance came a few years later when he became Ambassador in Tokyo and had nearly six years as head of mission.

I had two Counsellor Heads of Chancery. They were Mark Elliott and Andrew Bache, both of whom went on to become Ambassadors in important missions. I also had two Commercial Counsellors (Merrick Baker-Bates and Jim Hodge, who became Ambassador to Thailand in 1996) and two Economic Counsellors (Jenkin Thomas and David Wright. The latter became Ambassador in Tokyo in 1996). The consular and information sections were headed by First Secretaries. Both had important roles to fill. Consular work may seem routine, but if a mistake is made in dealing with problems encountered by British subjects it can have serious political repercussions. I took an active interest in the work of both sections.

The office of the Science and Technology Counsellor became of increasing importance while I was in Tokyo. I was fortunate in having Dr Graham Marshall and then Dr Clive Bradley as Science and Technology Counsellors. They did a good deal to educate British firms about Japanese research and development and promote British science and technology. In 1982-3 I tried hard to persuade London that we should conclude, as the Americans had done, a science and technology agreement with Japan, but the then Chief Scientific Officer in the Cabinet Office was opposed to the idea and, because of prejudice and obscurantism in Whitehall, it was many years before an agreement could be concluded.

I have referred to the service attachés in the context of arms sales, but they had other work to do including getting to know the Japanese Self-Defence Forces. Our three attachés were conscientious and competent. Captain Mike Forrest, the Naval Attaché, was a good Japanese speaker; he was the last Naval attaché who had studied Japanese as a language student. He and his wife accompanied us on a visit to Etajima, the naval academy in the Inland Sea where a lock of Nelson's hair has been preserved and is much revered. I had been invited by Admiral Maeda, the Chief of Staff to the Maritime Self-Defence Force (MSDF), to give a speech in Japanese to the cadets. I had the temerity to speak to them about the defeat of the Spanish Armada and lessons for modern navies. We went on to Iwakuni where there was an MSDF base and where Admiral Maeda entertained us to dinner. I told him that I had been there nearly forty tears earlier. The most important service VIP visitors we had were Admiral Sir Henry Leach, Chief of the Naval Staff, and General Sir John Stanier, Chief of the General Staff. Both proved interesting and pleasant guests.

The language school at Kamakura was maintained throughout my time in Tokyo. I tried to visit it at least once a year and to get to know the language students. HMG were making a big investment in their training and it was important that the language students should be carefully selected and correctly motivated. In addition to bearing the costs of tuition, HMG had to pay the students for two years when they were not available for normal diplomatic work. Although we lost some former language students who resigned to take up business appointments, a majority stayed on and ensured that the British Embassy in Tokyo had a greater proportion of language speakers than any other mission in Tokyo. This greatly improved our access and our understanding of Japanese developments.

I took an interest, as most of my predecessors had done, in the Asiatic Society of Japan, serving on its council and becoming chairman in 1982 and 1983. In view of our collection of old maps of Japan, at one point I rashly offered to give a lecture on the subject. This led me to pursue my researches not only into antique European maps but also ancient Japanese maps of the country. This in turn caused me to look at the way in which Japanese and foreign maps had influenced one another. In 1983 Weatherhill published my book on the subject entitled *Isles of Gold: Antique Maps of Japan*. This was copiously illustrated and beautifully produced by Weatherhill.

The Ambassador in Tokyo has the use of a villa on Lake Chuzenji which had first been leased in the late 1890s when Ernest Satow was Minister in Tokyo. It is a simple wooden house with some four bedrooms overlooking Lake Chuzenji in the Nikko National Park. The time taken to get there depended on the traffic. In the summer and autumn, and with the hordes of Japanese tourists visiting Nikko and the surrounding area in order to view the maples when they reached their best colours in late October, the journey could take many hours. We tended to go up to Chuzenji late in the evening and come down very early in the morning. We went there usually without any domestic staff, for rest and to recuperate from our visitors. In summer, it was possible to swim in the lake although it was very cold. In spring and autumn the walks were superb and the scenery breath-taking. One moment one could look out on a brilliant blue lake and the next moment the mists would be swirling down and Mt Nantai and even the lake would be invisible. We continued the practice of our predecessors in encouraging members of the UK staff to take breaks at the cottage and we established a roster for this purpose.

In May 1984, I would be sixty and due to retire from the diplomatic service. So in early 1984 we began to pack up and say our farewells. We had one final visit to make to Sapporo in Hokkaido to open the ice sculpture of Buckingham Palace made by members of the Ground Self-Defence Force for the Snow Festival. An Embassy team competed that year in producing a small sculpture. It was cold work as we soon discovered even when wearing all our winter woollies. (I had to buy a woman's peaked mock fur hat in a Sapporo store as I had nothing with me to cover my head.) It was snowing heavily in Honshu when we were due to leave Sapporo and we heard that the Tokyo airports were closed. We had to get back that night as we were due to have a farewell lunch with Princess Chichibu the following day. We thought of flying to Sendai and picking up the train there, but it was also closed. Finally, we got a plane to Nagoya and eventually caught the last train to Tokyo which was running very late because of snow. We finally got home about 2.00 am.

In December 1983 Nakasone Yasuhiro, who had taken over as Prime Minister in late 1982, had suffered a set-back in the elections, but he was very cheerful when I called to say farewell in February 1984. Nakasone noted that I was wearing a tie with the Union Jack and the Japanese flag crossed; this was the tie of the Japan-British Society in Tokyo. As he was going to Britain in the late spring he asked if I could get him a similar tie to wear in London. I naturally replied that I should be delighted to send him one. But Nakasone with an eye to a good PR gambit proposed that we exchange ties there and then. I was the gainer as his was a smart French silk tie; the tie I gave him was only polyester. The press were immediately informed and it made a good story for the Prime Minister.

□

Before leaving for London I wrote the traditional farewell despatch, except that in my case I wrote three despatches. The first was a survey entitled rather pompously, 'Japan, Yesterday, Today and Tomorrow', the second was on British policy towards Japan and the third was on the diplomatic service. The first two were in accordance with tradition marked 'Confidential' and the third was graded 'Restricted'. As a result, I suppose that they will not be released under the thirty-year rule until 2014. In my view, there is no real reason why they should not be published in full now. They would not do any damage to our relations with Japan and there is nothing embarrassing in them. Sir Nicholas Henderson's farewell despatches found their way quickly into the columns of *The Economist* and they were critical of British policies.

Mine were much tamer. However, even if permission were given to reproduce them, they would be too long for this memoir. Moreover, as they were written while the cold war was continuing and the bubble had yet to grow and burst they are out of date. But I think it is appropriate to summarize what I wrote in these despatches.

In my first despatch, after referring briefly to Japanese war crimes, I noted that Ministers tended only to focus on Japan when a problem arose. I stressed that Japan was a force of major importance and it behoved us to make greater efforts to get on with the Japanese.

After a very cursory review of Japan since the end of the war I focused on the advent to power of Nakasone Yasuhiro with his different style, which I thought had given an impetus to change. I noted the Japanese Government's efforts to remove trade barriers but pointed out that while the Japanese market was legally as open as that of other developed countries the self-sufficiency structure built up behind protectionist walls had barely begun to alter.

Looking to the future, I stressed that the Japanese were much more diverse than they and the world at large liked to think. I noted that manifestations of Japanese arrogance were matched by Japanese sensitivity and resentment of discrimination against themselves. Over the past 130 years the country and people of Japan had changed vastly, but the Japanese people, at heart at least, were less internationally-minded than the peoples of most other advanced countries.

I commented briefly on the Japanese consensus approach, on competition in Japanese society and the role of factions in Japanese politics.

I pointed out that Japan faced many of the same problems as other advanced countries. There was an ageing population at a time when urbanization and changed aspirations for leisure and comfort had led to a decline in the concept of the unitary family. This would mean that greater provision would have to be made for health and welfare. I thought that Japan could not avoid some increase in real unemployment.

I expressed concern about education in Japan. I noted the merits of the Japanese education system with its high standards of basic education and pointed out that with its emphasis on performance it was highly meritocratic. But there were serious weaknesses, not least the rigorous and highly competitive examination system which had led to what had come to be called Japan's 'examination hell' (*shiken jigoku*) and the development of parental pressures on their children to shine in school work, hence the emergence of the phenomenon of the so called 'education mother' (the *kyoiku mama*). But a more fundamental weakness of the system was the emphasis on conformity, which could lead to a decline in creativity and independent thought. This might not matter if Japan continued to produce the sort of dynamic leadership which still marked its top companies. I suspected that such leaders would be found among those who rebelled against the system and worked up through medium and small-scale industries.

I noted the decline in parental discipline and the end of the frugal life-style of the past. While drugs were fortunately not yet a major problem I had seen examples in Tokyo of way-out and bad behaviour among some sections of Japanese youth and thought that the problems of modern Japanese society were compounded by the general lack of a coherent philosophy of life and the breakdown in or lack of ethical teaching. This made me wonder about the strains in Japan's social system, although Japan was still one of the safest countries in the world in which to live. I thought that the Japanese would manage to deal with their social problems at least as well as other advanced countries.

Turning to the political scene, I commented on the long period of political stability in Japan. In my view, democratic institutions fostered by the Occupation had taken root and developed in their own Japanese way. In Japan it was democratic to seek a compromise and undemocratic to force through unwelcome bills by use of the government majority without at least taking some account of opposition views. It seemed to me that an important factor in the maintenance of political stability was the absence of any credible alternative to the LDP. The Japan Socialist Party (JSP), with its adherence to an outdated Marxist ideology, had

had difficulty in expanding its representation despite the LDP's tarnished image as a result of the exposure of corrupt political practices within the party. The lunatic fringes on the extreme right and extreme left remained a nuisance rather than a real threat. If the LDP failed to achieve working majorities in future, ways would be found for them to obtain support from the centre parties. I did not expect a left-wing government to emerge in Japan, but the pork-barrel tactics of politicians and the parochialism of the average Japanese electorate did not bode well for the future of Japanese politics.

Japan would, I thought, find it difficult to adapt to a lower rate of growth in the next few years. I drew attention to Japan's budgetary constraints and the problems associated with plans which had been prepared for the introduction of a consumption tax.

In commenting on Japan's external relations I stressed Japan's lack of raw materials and feelings of vulnerability. I did not think that the Japanese would for some years to come be in a position to play an active part in UN peace-keeping operations. Unfortunately relations with the European Community were unlikely to be central to Japanese foreign policy and I thought it improbable that the Japanese would be willing to sacrifice any important national interest to achieve solidarity with the Europeans.

I briefly reviewed Japan's relations with China, Korea and ASEAN countries, noting that ASEAN would continue to be a major factor in Japanese foreign policy. I referred to Japanese efforts to act as a bridge in North-South relations and increased Japanese aid to developing countries. Much Japanese aid would continue to go to Asia where it would be of particular benefit to Japanese interests. I thought that Japan would to try to be both an advanced country and the special friend of the developing world.

I did not think that Japan could do much about its relations with the Soviet Union. At that stage the Soviets seemed to be strengthening their position in the northern islands and this increased Japan's feeling of threat from the Soviet Union.

I stressed that the crucial relationship for Japan was that with the United States. On the whole, I was reasonably optimistic about the future of this relationship, but I was concerned by the

US belief that Japan had been having a free ride in defence. I noted the difficulties for Japan in responding adequately to this accusation. These were constitutional, psychological and fiscal. The Japanese also had to take account of neighbouring countries. I was concerned by the possibility that at some stage the US nuclear umbrella might become less credible. On the whole, however, I thought that the Japanese would get by without a major row with the Americans, but noted that expenditure on the Japanese Self-Defence Forces would make Japan a formidable military power by 1990 and that this could complicate relations with Japan's Asian neighbours.

I believed the future of Japan depended very much on whether they could manage smoothly their economic and trade relations with the US and also with Europe. I went on to discuss the implications of American pressure for agricultural liberalization on the LDP's farm vote and of American demands for a stronger yen. I thought that internationalization of the yen would come and that we would have to face increasing Japanese competition in financial services, although it would be some years before Tokyo could rival New York, London and Frankfurt as a major financial centre. I noted that pressure for increased imports into Japan raised problems not least because some two-thirds of Japanese growth came from exports. The Japanese Government faced a major task in educating Japanese industry and business on how to cope with Japan's external economic problems. I thought that changing attitudes of mind would not be easy. If the Japanese response was again too little and too late, the Japanese position and ours would become increasingly difficult and confrontation might become politically unavoidable. This could have serious implications for the free-trading system.

I concluded by saying that in viewing the next decade I was relatively optimistic about the Japanese ability to cope with most of the problems they faced at home. I stressed that Japan would be an increasingly important factor for us in Europe in the years to come. I also thought that Japan was likely to remain politically stable and prosperous. A question-mark lay over whether they could manage their external economic relations in such a way that the GATT system was maintained and anti-Japanese feelings and policies did not get the upper hand in other developed countries.

□

At the time I was writing this despatch I was concerned by pressures arising from the then economic recession which was mild as compared with that of 1994-98. My forecasts were not entirely right, not least because I did not foresee the ending of the cold war and the speed of growth in China. Nor did I anticipate the effects of the bubble and its bursting. With hindsight I might have put some of my points rather differently. However, most of the problems to which I drew attention remain even if progress has been made in a number of areas.

In my second despatch on policy towards Japan, I said that the broad outlines of British policy towards Japan should remain unchanged but some elements needed refining. I stressed our major interest in Japan remaining a responsible member of the group of advanced countries in alliance with the United States. Anything which undermined the credibility of the US defence commitment to Japan or which led to serious differences between Japan and the US was accordingly contrary to our interests. I expressed concern about the potential Soviet military threat to Japan. If there were a decrease in the credibility of the US defence commitment there could be pressures in Japan for an arms build-up. We and the Japanese needed to watch carefully developments in Korea and China. Our political interests and those of Japan in South East Asia and the Middle East largely coincided.

This led on to a discussion of the importance of political cooperation with Japan. I was glad that we had been at the forefront of European countries in this aspect of our relations. But we needed to reinvigorate Ministerial-level consultations and ensure that these did in fact take place every year. I urged that when any international problem affecting Japanese interests arose the Japanese should automatically be consulted. We could not and should not leave the process of consultation solely to the Americans. Although the European political cooperation framework was still weak we should do what we could to reinforce the EC-Japan dialogue, but at that stage priority should be given to the bilateral dialogue.

Turning to defence, I urged that we should keep our lines open to the Japanese Self-Defence Forces and the Japanese defence industry. I thought this was best done through inter-service and inter-industry links, but I noted that because of the Japanese ban on the export of defence equipment any improvements made in technology, licensed by us to Japanese makers, could not be released back to us. I considered, however, that the Japanese ban on exports of defence equipment would be eased and that the Japanese defence industry could become a formidable competitor in third markets. We should aim for more visits at Chiefs of Staff level and regular staff talks. In this context I regretted that after the then Naval Attaché left there would be no service attaché with a knowledge of Japanese. I had urged without success that this situation be rectified by reinstituting Japanese language training for selected service officers.

I noted that British understanding of modern Japan had risen in recent years but was still inadequate. We needed a relatively limited pool of people competent in the language and with an adequate understanding of Japanese society, culture and history to ensure that official and business contacts were developed and maintained in sufficient depth. This could not be done properly if, as at that time, the British business community in Japan consisted almost exclusively of people who did not speak or read Japanese. Business in Britain had to be persuaded to recognize its need for Japanese specialists. The universities in Britain should tailor their courses less academically and more practically. The right kind of students, properly motivated, should be encouraged to take up Japanese studies and ensured suitable jobs on graduation. (In these remarks I was anticipating the recommendations of Sir Peter Parker's report 'Speaking for the Future'.)

I said that we could learn from Japan, especially in management, labour relations, quality control and technology. We did not want a conformist Britain but we could benefit from less confrontation at all levels and should make a greater effort to achieve consensus.

Japanese understanding of modern Britain was also inadequate. I was shocked by the prejudices and misunderstandings about modern Britain which I had found in Japan and had tried hard to counter. I urged that more should be done in London to educate the Japanese press corps who tended to take their stories from the British press.

I emphasized the value of the British Council's work in Japan and of the JET (Japan English Teachers) scheme. I urged that the British Council's work in Japan should not be cut.

I left till last the most difficult aspect of our relations, namely economic and trade issues. If these were mishandled, no amount of work on political, defence or cultural cooperation could put matters right. The size of the problem was demonstrated by the huge trade imbalance of four to one in Japan's favour. The three main elements in our policy, namely promotion of exports to Japan, Japanese restraint on their exports to Britain and industrial cooperation (i.e. inward investment) should remain the same. Britain had to become more competitive. Sadly, my time in the diplomatic service had been marked by a decline in British competitiveness which had undermined our efforts in promoting British interests.

Japan was a particularly difficult market for small and medium-scale exporters. The market was distant and expensive to cultivate. It was not a market for the single-shot operation. We needed to be careful to ensure that help was given to companies who did their homework. With the larger companies we should urge them to improve their representation in Japan and increase their investment in the country. They needed expatriate staff with a good knowledge of Japanese language and culture. Their decisions must, however, be made on a commercial basis.

We should no longer bail out incompetent British companies who had failed to prepare themselves for Japanese competition. Why, I asked, had not British companies foreseen the demand for VTR or digital audio discs? It was sad that 'voluntary restraint arrangements' (VRAs) on Japanese exports to the British market had been necessary. This led me to reject the thesis of some trade unionists and city people at that time that the Japanese, because of their social system, were unbeatable. I also warned against the idea that Japanese competition was the main cause of British unemployment. As far as I could discover, unemployment due to Japanese competition perhaps amounted to some 100,000 jobs.

I pointed out that export restraint by the Japanese at that time covered nearly half of Japanese exports to Britain. The inter-industry arrangements involved had been unavoidable but they had been a restraint on competition and put up prices to the consumer. The Japanese did not like VRAs in principle but many Japanese firms had benefited by being able to increase their margins. The basic thesis was that the VRAs were temporary but many had continued for over twenty years. The VRA on cars had continued for eight years and there was no sign that it would be ended. In my view, if our aim was improved competitiveness, we should tell our companies and associations that we were only prepared to tolerate such cartel-like practices for a specific and limited period while they put their own houses in order.

This led on to the theme of inward investment. At that stage there were only some thirty Japanese companies with investments in manufacturing in the United Kingdom and it would be some time before those employed by Japanese companies reached the figure of 10,000. I particularly regretted that up to then no Japanese company had established facilities which included research and development (R & D); Japanese investment was almost entirely in secondary technology. I deplored the failure to coordinate our efforts effectively in order to promote inward investment and recommended more effective targeting. The taxpayer, I noted, not only had to pay for costly visits and presentations but might also end up paying over the odds for the resulting Japanese investment.

I was doubtful how far a stronger yen would benefit our exports. (In this I was clearly wrong.) Internal demand could not be greatly increased by government measures while attention was focused on the budget deficit. We needed to take account of our surplus on invisibles.

I rejected the idea that if the imbalance with Japan continued to grow we should follow the protectionist route pursued by the

French government. I urged that we should support European
Community action over trade with Japan. When the European
Community countries were united and had clear objectives they
could achieve more than the individual countries acting on their
own. Unfortunately, the decision-making machinery in the
Community was slow. We should go on trying to achieve a common European commercial policy towards Japan.

I concluded that the thrust of our policy should be to seek to
persuade the Japanese that it was in their interests as well as ours
to recognize and live up to their international responsibilities as a
powerful member of the group of seven. We must continue to try
to persuade the Japanese to be less inward and more outward-
looking. To be effective we had to be consistent and patient, however tiresome the Japanese might be at times. The Japanese
wanted to be liked and must never be talked down to. Businessmen had shown that when Japanese got to know and trust you
they could be reliable and good partners. A friendly relationship,
based on firm and consistent, sensitive and explicable policies
could reduce the threats to our interests and help us to benefit
from Japan's increasing power.

□

The FCO never told me to what extent my policy recommendations had been endorsed in Whitehall, but political cooperation
with Japan has intensified. British export promotion efforts were
redoubled and a larger dent in the Japanese surplus made than I
had thought likely in the 1980s. British firms greatly increased
their presence in Japan. Britain managed to secure a large share
of Japanese manufacturing investment in Europe and a number
of Japanese firms have invested in R & D in the United Kingdom. According to one estimate in 1996 the number of people
employed directly by Japanese-owned manufacturers in Britain
was over 100,000. Unfortunately, little progress seems to have
been made in coordinating the efforts of the Scots, the Welsh
and the English regions in their investment promotion efforts.
A common European Community commercial policy was de-

vised and VRAs, except in the case of motor cars where the arrangement will continue on a European basis until 1999, have been largely phased out.

My third despatch about the diplomatic service only dealt peripherally with specifically Japanese issues. I was concerned about Japanese language studies. We needed good Japanese speakers. Incentives should be improved for language students and the syllabuses for the examinations reformed. I said that our students suffered from the incompetence and inaccuracy of the specialist examiners employed by the Civil Service Commission and as a result of the bureaucracy of the system. Officers trained in the Japanese language needed to broaden their experience and should not serve solely in Japan as pre-war Japan Consular Service Officers had done, but they should not spend too many years away from Japan. I urged that officers serving in Japan should have annual leave at home.

We left for home at the end of February 1984, travelling via Hong Kong and India. We had hoped to go on from India to Kenya but I had to be hospitalized in Bombay and flew home direct from there, arriving at the end of March 1984. In the month or so before I officially retired from the Service I made various calls to report on my mission. Mr Norman (later Lord) Tebbit, Secretary of State for Trade and Industry, listened carefully when I spoke to him about Japan. I was dismayed to be told that Sir Geoffrey Howe, then Foreign Secretary, did not see retiring Ambassadors individually but only invited them some time later to an informal drinks party. After nearly 35 years' service, having attained Grade 1 in the Service and coming from a post in a country important to Britain and a capital which he would shortly be visiting, I thought this behaviour discourteous. I protested to the Permanent Under-Secreatry and the Principal Private Secretary to no avail and had to be content with an interview with the relevant Minister of State. I do not know whether Sir Geoffrey himself, or his private office, decided that he need not bother to see retiring Ambassadors, but it made a deplorable impression. Of course he was very busy but he only needed to spare me ten minutes.

CHAPTER SIX

A Different Perspective 1984-97

—————————— oOo ——————————

WORKING IN THE PRIVATE SECTOR

I was only 60 when in 1984, in accordance with the regulations, I retired from the Diplomatic Service. The advantage of retiring at 60 is that it gave me a chance to do something else. Inevitably and rightly, I became involved in business with a Japanese dimension. But before I could start any job I had to obtain permission from the committee set up under cabinet office auspices to vet ex-civil servants going to work in the private sector. The committee was a mixed one, partly political and partly business. At that stage, they were under pressure to be strict about the criteria for giving permission, although Ministers were free to join immediately on their retirement or resignation even private sector businesses with which they had dealings as a Minister. I found the procedure and the attitude of the committee tiresome. They insisted that I should wait six months before taking up an outside appointment and that this should date not from the date I left Tokyo when to all intents and purposes I ceased to work for HMG but from my formal retirement in May, 1984. I told them

207

that this put me at a disadvantage as compared with home civil servants and could not be justified. I stressed that I would be working for companies which were contributing to British exports visible and invisible. I also pointed out that I had not had any close dealings with the companies concerned, certainly not any relating to contracts.

The committee in due course agreed to my taking up appointments in November 1984. That summer I spent recuperating, gardening and doing a little writing. I also went to the Palace to receive the insignia of a GCMG (Knight Grand Cross of the Order of St Michael and St George) which had been gazetted in the New Year Honours on 1 January 1984.

I had some three years as a non-executive director of Austin-Rover Japan. I found that Japanese car dealers exhibited character traits and ways of doing business which were just as dubious as those in other countries. I became a non-executive director on the boards of Foreign and Colonial Pacific Investment Trust and GT Japan Investment Trust. Later I became a non-executive director of Thornton Pacific Investment Trust which was turned into a Luxembourg open-ended fund managed from Hong Kong. My wife and I were asked to become advisers to the Mitsukoshi Department Store which I had first got to know as Commercial Counsellor in Tokyo in the second half of the 1960s and which I had consistently encouraged to increase its import and promotion of British consumer goods. We were able to help them in Britain and with their regular British store promotions.

My main job was as a director of Hill Samuel and Co (later Hill Samuel Bank Ltd). I was given an office at the bank and part of the time of a secretary. This gave me a base in the city which was very useful. My role was to assist in establishing a Tokyo office for the bank and to help to secure business for the bank in relation to Japan. At the time of Big Bang in the City the bank expanded and bought Wood Mackenzie, the stock-broking firm. Hill Samuel saw itself as both a merchant bank and a securities company. But Hill Samuel was too small to prosper in the increasingly competitive environment in the City. It also lacked united management with a clear view of where the bank should be going.

Morale deteriorated and some of the best staff left. Internal communication was poor and team-work neglected. When eventually the bank was sold to TSB hopes were high. The bank was given a large infusion of capital and told to lend it at a good profit. This inevitably meant taking risks and Hill Samuel's loans, especially to property companies, led to large losses as the property boom bust. Changes had to be made but the new team brought in lacked a coherent strategy and fired many of the better people who had remained. Hill Samuel was set on a declining path and when Lloyds Bank and TSB merged no buyer could be found for Hill Samuel bank, not least because its human assets had been run down. The demise of the bank in 1996 was probably inevitable. It is sad to see an institution, which had once been a prosperous merchant bank and which, given the right management and direction, might have carved out a limited niche for itself, destroyed by trying to do things for which it was not properly equipped and by a lack of a coherent corporate philosophy.

From the begining I stressed that to win business in Japan it was essential to be 'patient, persistent and consistent'(PPC). Sadly, Hill Samuel as a whole, although not some of its staff who worked hard in Japan, failed on all three criteria. The bank wanted quick profits and results. As these were not available they changed their strategy and tactics without thinking through their objectives. The result was inevitable disappointment. In my final memorandum to the Chief Executive in December 1991 I wrote: 'We have so far failed to be consistent, constantly changing our objectives and products. We have also lacked persistence because we have not been willing to put in the resources needed to follow up the openings which have been made at a high level.'

At the end of 1991, when I retired from Hill Samuel, I became a senior adviser to NEC Corporation and a member of NEC's international advisory council. I also became a senior adviser to Daiichi Kangyo Bank Ltd (DKB). I later became a senior adviser to the Bank of Kyoto (from 1993) and to Matsuura Machinery Company (from 1996), a Fukui-based high-technology machine-tool company which in 1996 opened a plant near Leicester.

Japanese companies do not give much, if any, indication to a senior adviser like myself about what they expect from them. Apart from responding to a small number of specific requests for help in Britain, I concentrated on producing short accounts of developments in Europe, in particular in the European Union. I also tried to give advice about internationalization and localization. Both these aspects of management are difficult ones especially for Japanese companies. Inevitably, the responses will be different for each company.

I have also been employed since 1992 as an adviser to Wilde Sapte, a long-established firm of London solicitors, in relation to their marketing to Japanese clients. In 1993 I agreed to become an adviser to PIFC, a medium-sized employee benefits consultancy, specializing in providing services to Japanese and Korean companies operating in Britain.

VISITS TO JAPAN

In the first few years after my retirement from the diplomatic service I sometimes visited Japan three times a year, but in recent years I have normally made two visits (in the spring and the autumn).

On one occasion, on 25 February 1986, I was asked to give evidence in Japanese to the budget committee of the House of Councillors. In speaking to them I stressed the importance of Japan importing more manufactured goods and pursuing positive free-trade policies. I made a number of suggestions about Japanese investment abroad, about Japanese export policies and the removal of obstacles to imports. I also spoke briefly about invisible trade and replied to a number of interpellations which were on the whole friendly.

On my visits to Japan I have given talks in Japanese on a variety of themes political, economic and cultural. Japanese audiences are always polite but rarely responsive. Many of those who are regular attenders at lectures in Japan are old retired gentlemen. I always reckoned that there would be a few who would sleep peacefully through my talk. Accordingly, I often used to tell my audience at the beginning of my speech that I would not be at all offended if they were bored and went to sleep so long as they did not snore too loudly.

I was rather ashamed of my pronunciation on one occasion in Sapporo when I had been talking about the Japanese sense of humour. As there is no good translation of 'sense of humour' it is usual to refer to '*Nihon no umoru no sensu*'. One old boy obviously had not heard properly or did not understand, because at the end of my talk he asked if I could say a little more about *Nihon no umore no senso* i.e Japan's humour *war*! He was embarrassed by the giggles from other members of the audience.

LECTURING IN BRITAIN

During the years since my retirement, I have also been asked frequently to lecture about aspects of Japan to various audiences, including university audiences in Cambridge, London, Oxford, Essex, Sheffield and Stirling. In 1985 I was asked to give a talk to the Eastbourne Ashridge circle in a large theatre on the subject of 'British Ambassador to Japan'. Unfortunately, the only questions related to Japanese wartime behaviour and treatment of POWs. As an uncle and a cousin both suffered from Japanese brutality to prisoners employed on the building of the Burma-Siam railway and as I was involved in some war crimes investigations in Singapore after the end of the war I have much sympathy for those who suffered.

DEATH OF THE SHOWA EMPEROR

When the Emperor Showa died in early 1989 I wrote an article for *The Times* emphasizing his efforts to act constitutionally and his final decision to end the war. This decision, in my view, was his most significant contribution to history. I had been very critical of Edward Behr's book *Hirohito* depicting the Emperor Showa as a war criminal and I objected strongly to the BBC's decision to show the film based on this book at the time when the Emperor was clearly dying. Against this background, and after the Emperor's death, I was asked to join two BBC TV programmes where there was likely to be a hostile audience. One programme was the *Wogan Show* where I found myself up against Edward Behr and a hard-line representative of the ex-POWs who could neither forget, nor forgive. I managed to keep my temper and tried to take a dignified line. The second programme was a morning audience participation show. This ended in a shouting match as I tried to ensure that my points were at least heard.

HISTORY TEXTBOOKS

While I have always stressed the changes in Japan and the need for Britain to develop a good understanding with modern Japan I have been critical of attempts by some Japanese and some of their, in my view, unwise friends abroad to try to forget or conceal what happened in the past. I realize that in the textbook controversy some of the critics may have gone over the top, but I have never disguised my belief that, for instance, it was a serious mistake on the part of Japanese historians, under pressure from illiberal members of the LDP and their supporters in the conservative Japanese Ministry of Education, to try to deny or ignore the fact that a horrific massacre occurred in the rape of Nanking, whatever doubts there may be about the exact statistics of the number of deaths.

JAPANESE STUDIES IN BRITAIN

In these years my involvement with things Japanese has been constant and varied. I have done what I can to encourage Japanese Studies following the Parker report of 1986 'Speaking for the Future'. At Sir Peter Parker's request I served on the committee of the University Grants Committee set up to allocate funds made available, in response to the report, to various universities. This committee had a difficult task as each institution wanted a significant share in limited funds and there were political pressures, for example, to establish posts in Japanese at the Univesrsity of Wales. The decisions inevitably disappointed many institutions and there was a real danger of 'spreading the butter' too thinly and not allocating enough resources to a single institution to enable it to run adequate courses in a difficult language. I have subsequently tried to follow up on this work by cooperating in any way I could, especially with Japanologists at the Universities of Cambridge (where I was made an honorary fellow of Robinson College), of Stirling (where I was awarded an honorary doctorate and have chaired an advisory committtee for the Scottish Centre for Japanese Studies) and Sheffield, as well as with the School of Oriental and African Studies (SOAS) at London University.

UK-JAPAN 2000 GROUP

In my last year as Ambassador in Tokyo at the Embassy we discussed how we could broaden Anglo-Japanese relations and talked with a number of businessmen of the possibility of establishing something on the lines of the Anglo-German Koenigswinter conferences. The outcome of these discussions was the formation of the UK-Japan 2000 Group with Jim (Lord) Prior as chairman of the UK side and KatoTadao, former Japanese Ambassador in London, as chairman of the Japan side. As Ambassador in Tokyo I had backed suggestions for such a group. I argued strongly that it should not be just a talking shop but should discuss specific aspects of Anglo-Japanese relations and make proposals for action.

I was not invited to be a member of the group at the outset. I suspect that this may have been due to the emphasis I had placed on the group discussing practical matters rather than debating general issues. After a couple of years, however, I was invited to join and I attended some seven annual conferences held in Japan and the UK.

UK-JAPAN HIGH TECHNOLOGY INDUSTRY FORUM

I took part from the beginning in the annual conferences of the UK-Japan HighTechnology Industry Forum which began in 1985 with LouisTurner as the enthusiastic British organizer, ably supported by industrialists such as Brian Newbould, then with ICI pharamaceuticals.While the Gaimusho were the Ministry in Tokyo with a watching brief for the UK-Japan 2000 Group, MITI were closely involved in the meetings of the forum, the Japanese side being led by the Japan Economic Foundation, a MITI-sponsored body. The participants on both sides were overwhelmingly from the private sector who put up the necessary funds. The meetings held alternately in Britain and Japan lasted two full days but were supplemented by industrial visits and other meetings.

While many of the subjects discussed were of both general and technical interest I think that the main value of the meetings lay in the informal talks which arose out of the meetings and the opportunities provided for the development of business links. Certainly those who took part on the British side were able to deepen their understanding of Japan and the way in which business and technology worked in a Japanese environment.

WRITING

I spent a good deal of time doing some amateur historical research and writing. My first task on my return to Britain was to complete *Dr Willis in Japan: British Medical Pioneer 1862-1877* and find a publisher. This latter task was not easy as the book was designed for a limited and specialist audience. Glaxo and Chugai pharmaceuticals gave valuable help and in 1985 the book was published by Athlone. While working on Dr Willis I became interested in the Japanese aspects of the life of A.B.Mitford, the first Lord Redesdale. With the help of the original letters written home by Mitford, which the then Lord Redesdale in 1985 allowed me to borrow and copy, I produced my edition of his writings about Japan. This was also published by Athlone in 1985 with help from NYK; I dedicated the book to the memory of Ariyoshi Yoshiya, former President and Chairman of NYK, and the Grand Old Man of Japanese shipping. Mitford's accounts of Japan in 1868 were an exciting and interesting supplement to Ernest Satow's descriptions in *A Diplomat in Japan*.

These two monographs led me to become increasingly interested in the role which English people had played in the Treaty Ports and in the development of Meiji Japan. Elizabeth and I began to collect books written by travellers and one-time residents and scoured the second-hand bookshops for interesting and relevant material. The outcome was my book *Victorians in Japan*. This was published in 1987 by Athlone with help from Tokyo Electric Power. All three volumes published by Athlone were translated into Japanese by Nakasuga Tetsuro and published by Chuokoronsha.

One British visitor to Japan in 1889 and 1892 was the author

Rudyard Kipling. His comments on Japan were, I thought, worth republishing. George Webb, an expert on Kipling, had also found Kipling's accounts of his visits to Japan more than just ephemera. George, a former colleague in the Diplomatic Service, and I got together. The result was *Kipling's Japan: Collected writings* which we jointly edited and which was published in 1988 by Athlone. Two other books which I edited for publication in 1991 were *Building Japan 1868-1876* by Richard Henry Brunton, published by Japan Library, and Sir Alfred East's *A British Artist in Meiji Japan*, which was published by Inprint.

I spent a great deal of time both in research and in writing a history of Japan to which I gave the title *The Japanese Achievement* which was commissioned by Sidgwick and Jackson for their Great Civilizations of the World series. This appeared in 1990 and went into a second edition and a paperback. One other book which I was commissioned to write, this time by Macmillans, was *Modern Japan: A Concise Survey.* This appeared in 1993 in Britain and in early 1994 in Japan where it was published by *The Japan Times*. It soon became out of date as the LDP lost power and the bursting of the bubble forced changes in institutions and practices. A book such as this should probably be prepared by a series of experts, not a single author, and brought up to date annually.

In 1991 I wrote a history of the Japan Society for the centenary volume of the Society, *Britain and Japan, 1859-1991, Themes and Personalities* published that year by Routledge and edited jointly by Gordon Daniels of Sheffield University and me. This publication led on to *Britain and Japan: Biographical Portraits* edited by Ian Nish and published by Japan Library in 1994. I contributed two pieces to this volume and four essays to the subsequent volume published in early 1997.

I also wrote occasionally for Japanese journals including the *Nihon Keizai Shimbun, Sankei Shimbun* and *The Japan Times*. My main contribution to the *Nihon Keizai* was a series of brief essays published once a week in 1985 in the evening edition's column 'Asu e no wadai' (which might be translated as 'a subject for discussion tomorrow'). These were later republished with some other articles and speeches by Chuokoronsha under the title 'Higashi no Shi-

maguni, Nishi no Shimaguni; zokuhen' (Eastern island country, Western island country; a continuation). I was indebted to Jerry Matsumura of the British Embassy's economic department for the translation of my pieces into Japanese.

I have contributed essays on a fairly regular basis to *Sankei Shimbun*. My pieces on a wide variety of topics, often critical of aspects of modern Japan, have appeared in the paper's *Seiron* column. *Sankei* has the reputation in Japan of being a conservative journal, but many of my articles were not in line with the policies advocated by the paper. Since 1996 I have been writing fairly regular pieces for *The Japan Times*. I have also written every year since 1984 one or sometimes two articles about Japanese artists or museums for *Arts of Asia*, a bi-monthly glossy magazine published in Hong Kong. I have been asked to review books about Japan for various publications, in particular for *The Proceedings of the Japan Society* and for *Asian Affairs*, published by the Royal Society of Asian Affairs.

In 1990, for my writings on Japan, I was awarded the Yamagata Banto prize by the Osaka authorities. My wife and I were invited to Osaka for me to receive the prize and give a speech in Japanese before an invited audience. We were also taken on an interesting tour of Osaka sights selected by us. I do not claim to be a scholar and was much gratified that I had been nominated for this prestigious prize.

THE JAPAN SOCIETY

I have spent a great deal of time on Japan Society affairs. I was elected Chairman of the Council in 1985 and remained so until 1995. When I took over the chairmanship, the Society, if not moribund, was out of touch with younger people and relatively inactive. I did my best to reactivate the Society. The Society needed more members and more funds, but to persuade more people to join we had to provide a better and fuller programme of events. This was difficult in the absence of any endowment. We had to do more even if this meant running a small deficit and running down our limited reserves. Unless we did so we would not attract the members we needed. It was a 'chicken and egg' situation. It soon became clear that there were strict limits to what we could do with only a part-time secretary and assistant.

The Society in pre-war days had made significant contributions to knowledge in Britain about Japan and its *Proceedings* contained many valuable articles and records of lectures to the Society. The level of *The Proceedings* had to be raised and we needed both a more professional editor and a higher standard of lectures to attract a larger audience. But the Society is more than just a lecture society. It had to be ready to lay on receptions, lunches and dinners for visiting Japanese dignitaries, including Prime Ministers and members of the Imperial family. The annual dinner was also an important occasion. All these require a great deal of organization.

A number of members shared my views about the Society and worked hard to reorganize and revivify it. Among these were Haruko Fukuda, then Vice Chairman of Nikko Europe, and Lew Radbourne, formerly of Dodwells in Japan. They were elected joint chairmen of the council in 1995 and have been very active with new initiatives including one to establish an endowment fund for the Society.

JAPAN FESTIVAL IN THE UNITED KINGDOM 1991

In 1987 I was asked to lunch by Sir Ian Hunter and Martin Campbell White of Harold Holt and Company, concert promoters. They had been organizing a German Festival and wanted my advice about the possibility of organizing a Japan Festival. I responded enthusiastically. I stressed that if it was to have any impact it needed to be on a large scale and suggested that it be held to coincide with and celebrate the Japan Society's centenary beginning in the autumn of 1991. They asked me whether I would be willing to act as chairman of an organizing committee. I said that in my view they needed someone with wider business connections but that I would do all I could to help and would be happy to act as Vice-Chairman. We agreed that an organization with more resources than the Japan Society was needed to back the proposal and we accordingly approached Robert (Lord) Armstrong in his capacity as chairman of the European Arts

Foundation suggesting that the Japan Society and the Foundation jointly back the proposed Festival. We then discussed the proposal with Patrick (Lord) Jenkin as chairman of the UK side in the UK Japan 2000 Group and agreed that the best person to be chairman would be Sir Peter Parker. He readily agreed to take on what proved a very onerous task.

As one of the Vice-Chairmen I took on responsibility for the exhibitions committee, for lectures and for the Kyoto garden which was built in Holland Park as a permanent memorial to the Japan Society's centenary. I also did what I could to help with events such as the Sumo performances at the Royal Albert Hall which proved so successful.

One event of particular importance to the Society was the reception offered to the Society by the Lord Mayor and Corporation of London. This was held at the Guildhall soon after the opening of the Festival and was attended by the Japanese Crown Prince, one of the two Royal Patrons. I also attached special significance to the Kyoto Garden at Holland Park which was opened by the Prince of Wales, the other Royal patron. I had at first despaired of getting the funds needed for a garden, but when I suggested that it should be a Kyoto Garden this spurred the Kyoto Chamber of Commerce and Industry to collect the necessary funds.

The Festival could not have taken place without the active support of Martin Campbell White and Jasper Parrott and their organizations. Nor could it of course, have ever taken place without the Festival office run by David Barrie with the enthusiastic help of many others including Graham McCallum and Joe Earle.

The Festival was, in my view, a great success and redounded to the credit of the Japan Society. My only regret was that by concentrating on funds for the Festival we had to put back fund-raising for the Society.

Did the Festival have any lasting impact? It is difficult to give a categoric answer. I believe that the Festival helped to increase interest in Japan and Japanese culture. The Japan Educational Trust established at the time has certainly found increasing interest in what it can offer schools. More Japan Societies have been formed and Japan-related exhibitions and performances attract good audiences. If the impact of the Festival is not to be dissipated there must, however, be more follow-up.

In the spring of 1995 I was awarded the Grand Cordon of the Sacred Treasure for my work on Anglo-Japanese relations. I felt deeply honoured to receive this award from the Japanese Ambassador in London, Mr Fujii Hiroaki. When we went to Japan in the autumn of 1995 we were received by the Emperor and Empress who invited us to an informal luncheon in their private palace in Tokyo.

Elizabeth and I have enjoyed our life (in retirement?) between our small house in London and our old farmhouse in East Sussex. I have kept myself busy but have made time to work on my vegetable garden and have found this very therapeutic. Fortunately, we have been able to see more of our family than we did when we were in the Diplomatic Service. We have also enjoyed opera at Glyndebourne which is not far from our Sussex home and in London mainly at the English National Opera. We frequent bookfairs in search of old volumes related to Japan and I find it difficult to resist buying a book or two if I go into or even pass by a bookshop.

CHAPTER SEVEN

Japan: A Reassessment 1998

—————————————— oOo ——————————————

S ince I retired from the Diplomatic Service in 1984, I have
been visiting Japan regularly and have done my best to keep
in touch with developments there. Of course, I have not had the
same political access as I had when I was Ambassador and have
not had the benefit of advice from Embassy experts. However, I
thought it might be interesting, at least to myself, to try to summarize what I might say in my farewell despatch if I were retiring
from the British Embassy in Tokyo in the middle of 1998. Perhaps
I should give this summary the same rather pompous title I gave
to the first of my two farewell despatches sent home in early 1984
namely 'Japan, Yesterday, Today and Tomorrow' (c.f Chapter Five
pages 210 et seq).

Over the last fourteen years Japan has changed hugely. Some
of these changes, such as new buildings, bridges and roads, have
been superficial, but there have been more fundamental changes.
Some of these changes have been beneficial, such as a growing
appreciation of the role women can play in society and an accel-
erating groundswell amongst the Japanese people reacting

against corruption; on the other hand, some changes have been bad, such as increases in crime, especially among juveniles, and a deepening political apathy which poses a potential threat to Japanese democracy. In some respects Japan hardly seems to have changed at all. The Liberal Democratic Party (LDP) is back in power, money and the pork barrel still rule Japanese politics. The politicians often seem to emulate the Emperor Nero who played the fiddle while Rome burnt. There is still a great deal of male chauvinism in Japanese society and corruption is still a canker in politics and in some sectors of the economy such as construction and transport.

The political reforms brought about by the Hosokawa government in January 1994 were seen abroad as a major step towards the development of a two-party system in Japan. The hope was that the new mixed electoral system of 300 single-member constituencies and 200 members elected on a regional proportional representation basis would reduce the politicians' need for money for electoral purposes. In fact, if only because the new constituencies were so large, politicians wanted more money to ensure their reelection, but Keidanren and the banks had decided, following the scandals which led to the demise of the LDP government in 1993, to stop making party political contributions. This suggested a break-up of the 'iron triangle' between politicians, business and the civil service. It inevitably infuriated the politicians who, as a consequence, have been only too delighted to humiliate the bankers and to squeeze businessmen by threatening to undermine entrenched positions, for example, by advancing deregulation and other measures if ways of resuming political contributions were not found.

The LDP which is neither liberal, nor democratic nor a proper political party, faced with a major threat to its hold on power in 1993/4, fought back and showed that it had not lost its ability to out-manoeuvre its oponents. The Japan Socialist Party which renamed itself the Social Democratic Party had lost credibility with the electorate and looked set to disappear. However, in a cynical desire to taste power before its demise, the party agreed to work with their historical enemies in the LDP who for their part were ready to 'sup with the devil' to force from power the 'traitors' from the LDP who had got together to form the first non-LDP government for some 40 years. The socialists had to give up almost all their principles including opposition to the US-Japan Security Treaty, but in return the LDP conceded the post of Prime Minister for a couple of years to the socialist leader Murayama Tomiichi. When the LDP felt strong enough they dumped Murayama, but as they did not have a majority in the upper house they could not totally dump the Socialists. However, they held almost all the cards and the Socialists under the inadequate leadership of Doi Takako have found themselves in an increasingly weak position.

The LDP have been helped by a feeble and divided opposition, with only the Communists really knowing what they want. It would be pointless to describe the numerous opposition parties which have come and gone or coalesced in the last few years. At one point it looked as if Ozawa Ichiro, who had led a breakaway from the LDP and who claimed to have a vision for Japan, would manage to weld the opposition groups together. But he was too tainted by his connections with the corrupt LDP leader Kanemaru and too dictatorial and abrasive in his dealings with the prima donnas in the opposition. He is also reputed to suffer from a heart problem. The latest figure to emerge as a potential opposition leader in 1998 was Kan Naoto. He had made a name for himself by dealing toughly with bureaucrats in the Ministry of Health and Welfare who had been responsible for allowing tainted blood to be given to haemophiliacs. But at the time of writing in mid-1998 he had not done much to show that he and his disparate colleagues had anything more to offer than a few platitudes.

It is hardly surprising that the Japanese public are fed up with Japanese politicians and show their contempt by the low level of voting in most elections. This apathy is dangerous for the health of Japanese democratic institutions.

In the years since 1984 the Japanese economy has been through boom and bubble to bust. In the late 1980s Japanese asset prices, especially of land, reached astronomic levels. It was absurdly suggested at one time that the value of the land occupied by the Imperial Palace in Tokyo was equivalent to the value of all the land in California. Japanese companies began to buy up prestige properties in the USA. Japanese exports boomed and Japanese technology and management were praised inordinately. America was said to be in decline and Japan was not only 'Number One' but the twenty-first century would be the Asian century led by Japan. All this hype led to some arrogant outbursts by Japanese politicians, and top Japanese bureaucrats found it difficult to avoid showing their contempt for non-Japanese ways.

Of course, what goes up has to come down and in the first half of the 1990s the bubble burst. The Bank of Japan (BOJ) adopted a much tighter monetary policy and interest rates were raised. This provided the prick which burst the bubble, but the bubble was in fact unsustainable. The American economy demonstrated that it had great resilience and American and other foreign companies, having learnt a thing or two from Japan, showed that Japanese management was not invincible. Japanese banks and companies which had invested heavily in North America and Europe were increasingly attracted to the closer Asian markets, especially China, and poured resources into the 'tiger' economies. Japanese readily echoed the vacuous assertions of leaders, such as Lee Kwan Yew and Dr Mahathir, about the superiority of Asian values which few could define except in vague neo-Confucian terms with the emphasis on 'discipline'. As 1997 showed, the Asian bubble, too, had to burst. With Japanese banks and manufacturing companies deeply involved in Asia the Japanese economy was inevitably badly affected.

One of the biggest problems in the Japanese economy was the state of the banks which had been overregulated and protected for far too long by the powerful Ministry of Finance (MOF). Bank lending, backed largely by collateral in the form of land and buildings, had been allowed to soar. The banks, with large unrealized gains on their share portfolios and their client base among *keiretsu* companies, saw no reason to worry about such things as BIS ratios and paid insufficient attention to risk assessment. Their depositors and clients also did not see any need for concern about the risks they were accepting. The MOF, through its so-called 'convoy system', would ensure that financial institutions did not go bankrupt and depositors saw the deposit insurance system operated in Japan as a firm guarrantee that they would not lose. This created a serious moral hazard. As the bubble burst share prices fell precipitously and properties if they could be sold at all fetched prices way below the value of the bank's loans.

The potential losses from bad loans had to be hidden by non-transparent accounting techniques approved by the MOF, and a rescue package developed to cover the loans to housing associations, the so-called *jusen*. The provision of public money for this purpose was highly controversial and public anger with the banks made it difficult for the government to force through the necessary measures. But the package, when eventually approved, did not solve the problems of Japan's financial institutions. Japan's partners called for transparency and accountability and a Japan premium was demanded by banks lending to Japanese financial institutions. The Japanese government, realizing that Tokyo's position as an international financial centre was threatened, increased the pace of deregulation of financial institutions and proposed a financial 'big bang' beginning with the abolition of exchange control on 1 April 1998.

Meanwhile, the Bank of Japan (BOJ), in the absence of adequate fiscal measures to stimulate the economy and to prevent systemic failure, operated a very loose monetary policy. Interest rates were reduced to record low levels and in order to sustain liquidity the BOJ began to print money at an unprecedented rate. But the pressures on some of the weaker institutions became too great and Sanyo and Yamaichi Securities as well as Hokkaido Takushoku Bank were sacrificed by the MOF in late 1997 to market pressures and forced to cease trading. A number of other banks in difficulties such as Yasuda Trust, Hokuriku, Ashikaga and Hiroshima Banks withdrew from operations overseas. It seemed as though the convoy system was being allowed to die, but when further public money was needed in early 1998 to prop up the banks and ensure conformity with BIS ratios, the strong and the weak all had to accept public money whether they needed capital or not, presumably to disguise the plight of the weaker institutions.

By 1998 it was apparent that the structure of the Japanese banking system needed a radical overhaul. The dividing lines between city banks, long-term credit banks and trust banks were fast breaking down. Japan was overbanked and mergers and acquistions, including foreign take-overs, looked essential before a healthy banking system could be reestablished. Because of Japanese traditions and corporate philosophies the process of change seemed certain to be fraught with difficulties. In June 1998 the spotlight was on the Long Term Credit Bank (LTCB) which seemed to be in difficulties.

The problems of Japanese financial institutions, including the MOF and BOJ, were compounded in 1997/8 by revelations of various scandals including pay-offs to *sokaiya* and the offering and acceptance of 'excessive' entertainment to officials at the MOF and BOJ in return for information and favours. These scandals gave the prosecutors the opportunity to demonstrate their power with maximum publicity. Some senior bankers and securities company officers were arrested and arraigned as well as a number of relatively junior officials of the MOF and the BOJ. In accordance with Japanese tradition, the Minister of Finance, the Governor of the Bank of Japan and Presidents and Chairmen of some of the banks and companies most closely involved accepted responsibility and resigned. It was noteworthy, however, that senior officials were generally not arraigned and there was only one arrest of a *sokaiya*. Some observers regarded the whole series of sordid episodes as scenes in a theatrical play, in other words more for show than reality, although those arrested no doubt did not enjoy the roles they were forced to play in the drama.

As is so often the case in Japan, the reaction to the drama has been an excessive swing away from Japan's long-established corporate culture where the wheels are oiled by sometimes lavish entertainment including invitations to golf. Civil servants will be banned from accepting presents or entertainment costing more than yen 5000. The restaurant and entertainment business, already suffering from the slump, will certainly feel the pinch.

However, although politicians will be banned from receiving favours for services rendered to companies and organizations the rules applying to civil servants will not apply to politicians and it is doubtful whether the death knell has sounded yet for the entertainment districts of Akasaka, Yanagibashi and elsewhere in Tokyo. It would take more than a few public scandals to destroy the culture of the *zenecon* (general contractors) and their shady associates among the *yakuza* (gangsters) and politicians.

The Japanese bureaucracy is not as good as it is sometimes claimed to be, but it does contain some of Japan's best brains and until recently at least it had a reputation for honesty. It is almost certainly not as corrupt as some parts of the media allege. Its greatest fault has been its blinkered approach to problems. Many civil servants seem unable or unwilling to see that the problems of their particular section or Ministry are not the most important for Japan's future. They have indeed often become much too beholden to members of the Diet representing special interests, the so-called *zoku-giin* who by a call to the personnel section chief can blight a civil servant's chance of promotion if he thwarts the politician's wish.

Over many years there has been pressure from the Americans and others, as well as from influential Japanese economists, to move from an export-led recovery to a reflation of internal demand. The Japanese government have responded by a series of packages of investment in public works. Unfortunately, some of the contents of these packages has been more for show than for real (i.e. *tatemae* rather than *honne*) and have consisted of bringing forward already planned expenditure. Economists have demanded more substance or 'real water' (*mamizu*). But even when the packages contain real substance many of the construction projects have consisted of bridges and toll roads which look most unlikely ever to pay their way. One Japanese friend of mine, to whom I described such projects as 'bridges to nowhere', replied succinctly 'bridges from nowhere to nowhere'.

The Japanese Government, understandably worried about Japan's ageing population and the burgeoning budget deficit and wrongly believing that the worst was over, increased the sales tax from 3% to 5% in April 1997. In theory this was not unreasonable as Japan has for too long over relied on direct taxes, but the government totally miscalculated the timing of the change. In the first three months of 1997 the economy had been growing quickly, led by consmer spending anticipating the sales tax rise. After the tax rise consumer spending declined sharply. The Japanese Government again misjudged the position, arguing that this was a mere blip and that spending would resume in the second half of the year. It did not and the Japanese economy began to go into deflationary mode. The government refused to recognize what was happening and indeed compounded it by announcing changes in contributions for pensions and medical expenses which frightened consumers already worried about their jobs. As a result, temporary income tax cuts were saved rather than spent. A permanent income tax cut, which was obstinately resisted by the government which had committed itself to an early end to deficit financing, might have led to increased spending, but, predictably, the Japanese Government's response was 'too little and too late'. Instead of admitting quickly that they had misjudged the situation, the government produced a series of seven packages of measures, but it was clear to most observers that the government had no real policies with which to reinvigorate the economy. They seemed primarily concerned to save face by sticking to the policy of fiscal reform. (In principle admirable but in practice untimely.) Instead of the tax reforms which Japan so badly needs (reducing rates of income and corporation taxes), public works were the chosen instrument for the government who claimed that these were appropriately Keynesian.

Much, of course, could and should be done to improve the environment in Japan by, for example, putting telephone and electricity wires underground rather than spoiling Japan's beautiful countryside by more hideous dams and roads, but such projects are not as visible to voters or as beneficial to the general contractors who have continued to be able to charge prices above those prevailing in other countries as a result of the *dango* system of allocating contracts. Many contracting companies have run up huge losses by investing in real estate at the wrong time and are being propped up by their political friends anxious to maintain their access to funds. The politicians also argue that support for the construction sector is an important element in ensuring that Japanese unemployment does not rise too fast.

The manufacturing sector in Japan has not escaped unscathed from the downturn in the economy. Small and medium-scale companies in traditional sectors and sub-contractors have been the first to suffer and there have been significant increases in the number and frequency of bankruptcies. The pressures on the banks to reduce their exposure to potentially non-performing loans had led by 1998 to serious concerns about a drying up of loans (*kashi-shiburi*). All this has meant a significant increase in unemployment. Japanese unemployment statistics are difficult to compare with those of other developed countries because of the use of different definitions, but rising unemployment had become a matter of significant concern by 1998. This concern is compounded by the inadequacy of Japan's safety net for the unemployed. Japanese cities have not had comparable cardboard cities for the homeless such as those in other developed countries, but in 1998 they were becoming an increasingly familiar phenomenon.

The larger Japanese companies who derive a significant part of their profits from exports and who have developed outstanding research and development have weathered the economic downturn better than other sectors, but even some major companies such as Mitsubishi Electric have had to declare large losses. This has been due partly at least to over-investment in plant and facilities as a result of the availability of cheap loans and the absence of shareholder pressures.

In 1998 it seemed that Japanese companies, if they were to survive and thrive in an increasingly global market, would have to pay much more attention to corporate governance including especially transparency in their accounts and greater accountability to shareholders. While progress has been slow there has been some winding down of cross-shareholdings of *keiretsu* companies. Some share buy-backs have been announced and share options are being offered by more companies. So far, however,

ROE (return on equity) is not given the sort of attention which will be needed in the future. Outside directors and independent corporate accountants and compliance officers were still rare in 1998. Japanese companies continued to seem like self-perpetuating oligarchies. The new entrepreneurs of Japan were more likely to come from new companies greedy for business with younger managers with flare and a willingness to take risks than from the corporate giants where it sometimes seemed that corporate loyalty and ability to cooperate smoothly with colleagues were more important than thrust and push.

Deregulation has been slow in retailing, distribution and transport, but its impact has begun to be felt. The mid-1990s were increasingly difficult ones for firms in these sectors. But the consumer has benefited from deregulation and the process cannot now be halted.

One of the main issues in 1998 was not whether the Japanese economy and especially financial services would be deregulated, but how quickly effective deregulation would be achieved. Companies which could suffer as a result of deregulation and the consequent increase in competition were continuing to lobby hard in 1998 for a slowing down of the process and for exceptions to be made in particular cases. Bureaucrats also found it difficult to give up their powers entirely. For instance, although foreign exchange controls have in theory been abolished, transfers of over 2 million yen have to be reported to the MOF. The ostensible excuse is that this is to ensure that there is no money laundering, but this is not convincing. As one Japanese economist put it to me, Japan needs psychological deregulation as well as real economic deregulation. Despite the weakening of the yen, deregulation measures and removal of barriers to imports Japan remains a relatively high-cost economy. The main reason for this is that deregulation has been too slow and too restricted in scope. Japan still lacks really effective consumer lobbies.

Foreign observers are impressed or dismayed by Japan's high rate of saving. They do not realize that this is at least partly due to the inadequacy of Japanese pension schemes and their inadequate funding. It also reflects the very low rate of return available to Japanese savers. Before the bubble burst they were attracted towards equities. Now, understandably, few private investors are tempted by the very low dividend payments and are afraid that they may face capital losses. Some older people say that they have all the electrical appliances they can use and do not need yet another car to drive in a traffic jam. They would like better and more spacious housing but for this they need more land and a more competitive building industry. Afraid for their jobs, fearing inadequate provision for their old age and receiving little or no interest on their savings it is not surprising that many Japanese prefer to save rather than spend any temporary income-tax cuts. The only way they can hope to use these savings effectively is to invest abroad. This suggests a weakening of the yen, but savers then have to face exchange-rate risks.

In 1998, Japan's balance of trade and current account surplus were causes for concern in America, Europe and Japan. So long as Japan is able and willing to recycle its current account surplus this should not matter, but the US Congress, with its inward-looking attitude and under strong protectionist pressures, is unfortunately likely see things differently. The threat by some short-sighted Japanese politicians that Japan would pull out of US treasuries (in 1998 Japan was no longer the largest holder of such bonds) if the Americans become too rough in trade negotiations was silly and unrealistic. American mercantilism and protectionism is mirrored by Japanese attitudes. Another trade battle may be avoided, but it will require common sense and vision on both sides. The Japanese authorities would be wise to work ever harder on deregulation and removing barriers. Japan's real interests lie in the maximum freedom for trade and investment, but not many Japanese politicians seem to understand this.

Politics and the state of the economy were not the only issues of concern about Japan in 1998. Japanese cities were still safer places in which to work and live than those of other developed countries. But the Japanese can no longer afford to be complacent over law and order. The Aum Shinrikyo sarin attack in the Tokyo underground in 1995 showed that there were relatively well educated men and women in Japan who were so disaffected with modern society that they were willing to follow the dictates of an uncharismatic and mad leader. A relatively small number of serious crimes by juveniles has highlighted the lack of adequate family supervision. The number of cases of serious bullying in schools has also drawn attention to inadequate school and family supervision and the instilling into children of ethical principles.

The failure of the police to arrest those responsible for the murders of, among others, a Sumitomo Bank Nagoya branch manager and a senior managing director of Fuji Photo Film Company, allegedly by gangsters (*yakuza*), and the lack of significant arrests of *yakuza*, *sokaiya* and their apparent allies in right-wing groups has suggested that the police and prosecutors are either incompetent or afraid to act. Reports in 1998 of gangsters intimidating American companies buying up bad loans of Japanese banks and attempting to foreclose on property controlled by gangsters have been received with alarm abroad. Low Japanese crime rates sometimes seem a facade behind which extortion is effected on a growing scale. The recent increase in the availability of narcotics and guns is generally assumed to be due to the activities of the gangsters.

Unfortunately, the Japanese media, especially the daily press, have not demonstrated the determination to conduct effective investigative journalism to probe such reports. This is probably due at least in part to the cosy relationships developed by the journalists groups (*kisha kurabu*) concentrating on particular organizations. There is understandably no 'club' concentrating on the *yakuza*.

I did not think fourteen years ago that the small but noisy groups of extreme rightists posed a significant threat to Japanese democracy. I have not changed this view, but I am concerned by reports of their connections to the *sokaiya* and *yakuza*. It has been reported that one way of intimidating a Japanese company is for the *sokaiya* to call up a few right-wing speaker vans to appear outside the company's offices and blare slogans, martial music and denunciations of the company management. It puzzles many observers that the police do not take action to prevent the rightist groups from bombarding the public with their objectionable sounds. Japan has noise pollution rules which the rightists ignore all the time. The police probably say that they do not take action because they will be accused of interfering with free speech, but could it be that they do not take action because they are afraid?

Fears are often expressed about the Japanese justice system. How well are human rights and basic freedoms protected when such a high proportion of those accused in Japan confess and are convicted? Defendants do not have access to lawyers while being interrogated. The police may no longer use strong-arm tactics in quite the same way as they did pre-war, but interrogations are not videoed and psychological pressures to confess are apparently frequent. Detention in prison is never going to be other than traumatic for a defendant, but Japanese prison regimes are reputed to be worse than in many other developed countries.

A basic problem about Japan's system of criminal justice is the inordinate time it takes to reach decisions. This does not inspire confidence in the system. The Japanese lawyers Association (*Nichibenren*) has for far too long operated a closed shop and limited the intake of lawyers into what is one of Japan's most lucrative professions. Sadly, Japanese lawyers, with a few exceptions, do not criticize the Japanese legal system under which they operate. They should be Japan's most active lobbyists for the protection of human rights and freedoms.

There is much to be said for a fully independent prosecution service, but the actions of the prosecutors in 1998 have suggested similarities with the pre-war *tokko* (special investigative force).

Japan still retains the death penalty and this is carried out in secret, the names of those executed being released only after the event. In Britain the death penalty was abolished many decades ago and its retention in the USA and elsewhere arouses concern.

Despite these reservations, I would still rather live in Japan than in some other countries claiming to be democratic. The Japanese courts do sometimes demonstrate independence from the executive.

In 1984, I expressed my concerns about Japanese education. Unfortunately, despite the various official recommendations for reform, little has changed. The Japanese educational system still produces numerate and literate young people stuffed with knowledge and technically qualified, but they are not taught or encouraged to ask questions and argue. It is depressing to give a speech or a lecture in Japanese and in provocative terms to an audience of university students who do not react and can rarely be persuaded to put a question. It still seems that for many students their years at university are a comparative rest after the examination hell (*shikenjigoku*) to get into university. One problem is the traditional pressures for consensus and the attitude of mind summed up in the Japanese proverb that 'the nail which sticks out gets hammered'. Another is the attitude of the Japanese teachers' union with their opposition to anything smacking of meritocracy (silly considering that Japan is very much of a meritocracy) and their over-emphasis on equality rather than equality of opportunity. Japanese government universities, especially the top institutions, such as the Universities of Tokyo and Kyoto, are world class but the same cannot be said of some of the lesser government universities. The staff who are classed as officials with tenure are not always as good as they should be and the relationship between these universities and business is often tenuous at best. It is not surprising that parents who can afford to send their children to private schools and universities are increasingly doing so.

Since 1984, Japanese cultural manifestations abroad have proliferated and Japanese literature, theatre and the arts are increasingly seen not merely as part of global culture but as manifestations of a civilized and cultured people. A few foreigners may still think of Japanese culture as 'exotic' but such prejudices are much less manifest than they used to be. Japanese conductors and soloists as well as orchestras, dancers and singers are received with acclaim outside Japan.

The cultural scene in Japan has flourished and shown much vitality especially in the visual arts and in cinema. New concert halls, museums and art galleries have been built in almost every prefecture. The main problem has been to find and buy appropriate objects to put in these new facilities. Some museums, such as one devoted to the *Manyōshū* which I visited in Toyama prefecture in 1998 was full of gimmicks and one young Japanese friend described it as a Nintendo-type museum designed for children rather than adults.

The Japanese language continues to change not always for the better. The cult of foreign words in *katakana* has thrived and many adverts seem to consist solely of such foreign words, but Japanese culture has always been eclectic and has generally managed to give foreign influences a Japanese slant and flavour.

Much lip-service is paid to the protection of the environment in Japan and certainly air and water pollution have much decreased since 1984. But the rape of the Japanese countryside continues. Planning regulations seem to be used more often to control plot ratios and protect farming interests than to impose design standards so that new buildings conform to local patterns and that colours used blend easily with their surroundings.

In a country like Japan, which is prone to earthquakes and typhoons, building standards need to be strict. But they were not strict enough when Kobe was hit by a major earthquake in 1995. It was alleged by some that construction companies building roads had skimped in their work in the interests of profit and that inspections had been inadequate. This may or may not be true, but it was certainly the case that the Japanese Government's management of the crisis was woefully inadequate. The lesson seems to have been learnt that in events of this kind the Prime Minister must be able and willing to act immediately.

☐

The most significant development in Japanese foreign policy between 1984 and 1998 was the adoption of the Peace Keeping Operations Law following Japan's sorry showing in relation to the Gulf War. The law is inadequate, but represents a step forward in Japan's assumption of her international responsibilities. It seems likely to be further amended in due course and provides a necessary backing for the Japanese wish to achieve permanent membership of the UN Security Council. This wish is now supported by the major powers, but there has been no progress in achieving an amendment to the UN charter to enable Japan to achieve its ambition and because of opposition from other powers aspiring to similar status it is impossible to say when the charter may be amended.

Debate about possible changes to the Japanese post-war constitution has continued in a desultory way. There is probably now more of a consensus in favour of a limited change to Article 9 (the 'no war' clause) than there was fourteen years ago, but the impetus for change is lacking and the supporters of the present article are not about to give up their opposition to a constitutional amendment.

The Japanese relationship with the United States remains crucial for the Japanese economy as well as for Japanese security. US bases in Okinawa have continued to be a cause of friction. There is no easy answer to this problem. Trade relations seem certain to become more difficult if the yen continues to weaken and US economic growth were to falter.

Japanese relations with China seemed in 1998 to have become warmer. A crucial factor in Japan-China relations remains the problem of Taiwan. So long as the Chinese Government do not resort to force or the threat of force to solve the Taiwan problem, or to put pressure on countries in South East Asia, political relations should remain relatively calm and friendly. The smooth growth of the Chinese economy poses opportunities for Japanese business, but could also pose significant challenges. These will need to be managed carefully.

The maintenance of peace in the Korean peninsula is crucial for Japan. The recovery of the South Korean economy and for a *modus vivendi* at least with the North are important to Japanese interests.

With Russia, little real progress seems to have been made over the northern islands (the so-called 'Northern Territories') and the conclusion of a peace treaty, but Prime Minister Hashimoto Ryutaro and President Yeltsin appeared in 1998 to have achieved some kind of personal rapport which might perhaps eventually lead to some progress.

Japanese economic interests in South East Asian countries

have grown greatly in the last fourteen years. The Japanese have accordingly been particularly concerned by the Asian currency crises. Japanese investment in both Thailand and Indonesia has been put at serious risk and the Japanese are particularly worried about potential instability in Indonesia.

Europe is important to Japan not only as a market but also as a counterweight to the United States. The Japanese will be carefully watching the development of EMU. They recognize that a strong Euro will pose problems and opportunities for Japanese companies. There can be no doubt that if the Euro is successful the Japanese with their large investments in the United Kingdom will want and expect Britain to join EMU sooner rather than later.

Despite continuing efforts to diversify energy supplies the Middle East remains important to Japan, but there is little they can or are willing to do to help the Israeli-Arab peace process. The Japanese decision to co-sponsor the British resolution over Iraq in March 1998 was a welcome sign of Japanese willingness to cooperate where they can.

Latin America is important to Japan not only as a market but also because of the presence in many Latin American countries of peoples of Japanese ethnic origin.

Japanese foreign policy has matured in the last fourteen years, but Japan remains a somewhat reluctant player on the international stage. The island mentality of many Japanese politicians remains a constraining factor.

British relations with Japan were generally good in 1998. The state visit of the Emperor and Empress to Britain in May which might have taken place earlier but for the continuing demands for compensation by ex-prisoners of war who had suffered grievously at the hands of members of the Japanese imperial forces was a symbol of the good relations existing between the two countries. The British have wisely devoted much effort to expanding exports to Japan and attracting Japanese investment into Britain. Both policies have been generally successful and have helped to reduce trade and economic friction. Trade relations are, of course, now a matter for the European Commission and this ensures that issues such as Japanese non-tariff barriers and

European charges against Japanese companies of dumping are no longer bilateral problems. Cultural relations have grown much closer. The Japan Festival in Britain in 1991 and the British year in Japan in 1998 have highlighted the extent of cultural interchange. Grassroots exchanges have developed significantly, although the opposition of the British Home Office to a working holiday visa arrangement for young people has demonstrated a lack of vision on the part of an inward-looking part of the British bureaucracy. The UK-Japan 2000 group has been a useful talking shop since it was created in 1995 but it needs to rethink its objectives and modalities. Exchanges on political issues are now regarded as a matter of course. Both governments speak rather glibly about a special relationship, but the British need to remember that Britain is only one of a number of European states important to Japan in economic, political and cultural terms.

If I were Ambassador in Japan today I do not think I would recommend any significant changes in our policies towards Japan. I would essentially urge more of the same. I would, however, warn against complacency and urge our new political leaders to get to know Japan better.

□

The pages above are inevitably a superficial attempt to encapsulate my view of Japan 'yesterday and today'. How, then, do I view Japan 'tomorrow' or in other words 'Whither Japan?' Futurology is largely a matter of guesswork influenced by prejudices and possibly wishful thinking. But whether we are in business trying to decide about an investment which will not pay off for many years or whether we are in government trying to assess what policy we should adopt we all have to make some tentative predictions about the future.

I found Mr Nakamae's scenarios for Japan in 2020, as reported in *The Economist* in March 1998, thought-provoking if not always convincing. In 1998 it seemed to me that Japan had reached a significant turning point. It could and most probably would attempt to muddle through or manoeuvre through the economic downturn. It might succeed for a while but postponing difficult decisions about the economy and its ability to survive, let alone thrive, in the increasingly global world of the twenty-first century could well lead to a particularly difficult situation in the first decades of the new century. This will be especially so if the Chinese economy manages to grow quickly and overcome its numerous problems, including those involving the uneconomic state sector. Japan's economic problems will inevitably be exacerbated by the decline in the working population of Japan as Japanese society ages. The provision of adequate pensions and health-care will become even more serious issues for Japan and a decline in the Japanese ability to compete internationally looks inevitable. Japan could, in this scenario, cease to be the major economic power in Asia and become like other advanced nations, including Britain, a second or even third-rate power. Britain, at least, should remain a member of the European Union which could well become the second force in the world after the United States. An Asian Union, whether political or economic, is hardly to be envisaged in the first half of the next century.

An alternative scenario, which would be painful for Japan, but possibly more beneficial in the long run, would be a major economic crisis involving further bankruptcies of financial institutions and companies and a significant increase in unemployment. Such a crisis could conceivably trigger a revolution in attitudes in Japan. As a result, a healthier and more internationally-competitive Japan in services as well as manufacturing could emerge. This 'revolution' would require the financial 'big bang' to be forced through quickly, despite the pain in terms of bankruptcies and unemployment involved, and would lead to a major restructuring of Japanese financial institutions including significant mergers and acquisitions. It would also mean the speedy running down of *keiretsu* holdings and the adoption by companies of policies involving better corporate governance and an emphasis on ROE. Japanese companies might still be self-perpetuating oligarchies, but they would become more responsive to shareholders and to other outside pressures.

In view of the ageing of Japanese society, Japanese companies will need to concentrate on adding intellectual value. This means that a major priority will have to be significant reforms in Japanese education. This may be the hardest task in any 'revolution' resulting from a real economic crisis.

Despite my reservations about Japan's legal system and the operation of Japanese democratic institutions, I am reasonably optimistic about the survival of Japanese democracy. I am also confident that Japanese culture will continue to flourish.

The alternative scenarios outlined above take little account of possible changes in the world outside Japan. It would be impossible in a brief overview to consider properly the possibility that, for instance, the United States might decide to withdraw from Asia or that China developed expansionist policies which threatened Japan's prosperity and integrity. Nor can I take account of the possibility that Japan might be hit by some huge natural disaster such as a repeat of the Kanto earthquake of 1923. Hopefully, none of these possibilities will happen.

In all probability, Japan will not follow either of the alternatives set out above but will develop somewhere between the two courses I have described. The result will not be clear-cut, but I hope that real changes for the better will be effected which will ensure a better life for all my Japanese friends in their old age.

If any researcher comes across this chapter in twenty or thirty years time he will doubtless be tempted to remark on my lack of perspicacity!

JUNE 1998

Postscript

——————————— oOo ———————————

Looking back on my career, I do not regret that I tried so hard to join the Foreign Service, nor that I remained in the Service until I had to retire. Nevertheless, I would not, without reservations, recommend young men or women to join a Service which has been so undermined by post-war governments, Conservative and Labour.

There were obviously times of frustration and tedium during my 35 years in the Service, but that surely is true of other walks of life. I had strong views and did not find it at all easy to disguise these. On the whole, however, with a few exceptions I was normally able to persuade myself that the policies I had to advocate were by and large right for Britain. At any rate, I never had any real difficulty in standing up for British interests abroad.

Every aspiring diplomat soon learns that his job is to pursue the national interest, but he should try to ensure that his political masters take a long-term rather than a short-term view of where these interests lie. It cannot, in my view, ever be in the long-term interest of any country, particularly not of a democratic country, to pursue policies which are not morally justifiable in terms of the accepted norms of his or her society.

A British diplomat should not normally have to face up to moral dilemmas in his work because most British politicians do not generally behave immorally or if they do they rightly face criticism and possibly condemnation in the House of Commons and in the media. But politicians for short-term electoral reasons may be prepared to fudge issues and in so doing accept an element of moral hazard as was for instance the case over exports of equipment of possible military value to Iraq which was the subject of the Scott report of 1996. It must have been very difficult for civil servants whose job it is to carry out government policies to know when and how to blow the whistle in a case like this, not least when British jobs might be at risk if such exports were prevented. Nevertheless, civil servants cannot escape their moral responsibility in such matters any more than those who commit war crimes can plead that they were only acting under orders.

I can only think of two occasions when as a diplomatic officer I faced what I thought was a serious moral dilemma. The first was over Suez when I found it very difficult to support publicly the British case for taking the action we did. Fortunately, I was a very junior officer at the time. I was unaware of the secret negotiations with France and Israel and had no direct involvement or responsibility for our policies in this conflict. I did not accordingly see any need to resign. My main concern at the time was that our action at Suez took the spotlight off Soviet suppression of the Hungarian uprising.

The second was over Vietnamese refugees where I thought that the line initially taken by Mrs Thatcher was immoral but where Lord Carrington ensured that in the end Britain accepted the moral obligation to give asylum to a reasonable quota of Vietnamese refugeees (see page 142).

I am glad that I have never been directly involved in asylum policy. I consider that the policies pursued by the Home Office under Michael Howard as Home Secretary were to some extent at least immoral. Nor was I directly involved in the arguments during the Governorship of Chris Patten over passports for citizens of Hong Kong. I thought and still think that the line taken by the Home Secretary was wrong and demonstrated a singularly cynical attitude regarding our historical obligations towards the people of Hong Kong. This was especially true in the case of people of Indian origin who were stateless. Fortunately, in the end, the British Government of John Major overrode the Home Secretary in this latter case. I still think that, having given British citizenship to the inhabitants of Gibraltar and the Falklands, we have a moral obligation to give similar rights to those few who still live in our remaining colonies such as St Helena.

I did not find it at all easy to advocate and defend some of the economic policies of the Labour Governments in the 1970s, but the moral dilemma for the diplomat in this case lay in how to avoid being 'too economical with the truth' in his advocacy of these policies. I do not endorse Sir Henry Wotton's much-quoted view that 'an Ambassador is an honest man sent to lie abroad for his country'. If a diplomat lies abroad he will soon be found out and his country's interests will in the long run be harmed rather than helped.

I was glad to see that the Labour Government, elected in 1997, emphasized that the upholding of universal human rights and support for democratic institutions and procedures would be an important priority for British foreign policy. It will not be easy to maintain this line if it means stopping exports and thus leading to a loss of jobs. There will always be advocates of such exports who argue that employment should be our top priority and that in any case if we do not export the items in question some other less scrupulous foreign firm with its government's backing will do so. It will require courage and determination to enforce these principles in the conduct of foreign policy. In this context I have watched with some disgust the way in which the Western powers in their anxiety to pick up valuable commercial scraps in the vast and growing Chinese market have seemed willing to overlook and condone the Chinese Government's trampling on human rights.

I have never belonged to any political party. While I was a civil servant I was precluded from playing any part in politics. I suppose that politically, like most sensible British people, I abhor extremism. I would describe myself as a 'liberal' in the dictionary sense of being 'favourable to democratic reform and individal liberty'. I am convinced that 'free trade' is much more conducive to world economic prosperity than managed trade or protectionism. I consider that nationalism and racialism remain threats to international peace and that we should pursue internationalist policies. Although at heart an idealist I am also an international realist. It follows from this that I have watched with concern the way in which British policies in the post-war world, especially in relation to Europe, have developed. It took far too long for our political masters to recognize that Britain was no longer a world power or even a first-rate power. Many attached too much importance to the 'special relationship' with America and deluded themselves that Britain as the predominant power in the Commonwealth could continue to lead the world. I cannot subscribe to the Eurosceptic line which must in the long run lead to Britain withdrawing from Europe and becoming a small and unimportant island off-shore from the European continent. This does not mean that I currently advocate a federal Europe. At least in the foreseeable future, neither European governments nor peoples are ready for such a move. Nor do I advocate excessive European-wide regulation. We need less not more regulation. This said, Britain must, in my view, work with rather than against the other members of the European Union.

I cannot say that I have found many politicians (British, Japanese, German or American) particularly congenial. I suppose that this may be at least partly due to the fact that I cannot accept that any one party is invariably right. I often had to suppress my feelings pretty hard in dealing with politicians. I was, I know, at times, an undiplomatic diplomat. I often wondered how someone so different from the possibly mythical type of suave and urbane diplomat who never showed his true feelings managed to be appointed to as senior a post as Ambassador at Tokyo. Perhaps it was just good luck.

My life in diplomacy has been interesting to me but in comparison with the life of people in some other walks of life it may not have been as exciting. Nor in comparison with the life of most British diplomats was it particularly varied. The focus was almost always on Japan. I do not regret this as I always found dealing with Japan interesting and challenging if from time to time frustrating. At least the focus on Japan ensured that I was more than a superficial generalist.

From time to time I ask myself, or I am asked, if I really understand Japan and the Japanese. This question makes me wonder whether I would claim to understand my own country or British people all the time. As for Japan and the Japanese I have to admit that I do not always understand all Japanese responses to particular problems. *Haragei* (literally stomach art, but implying the conveying of meaning without being verbally explicit) is not easy for the non-Japanese to understand, especially for someone like me who tends to be frank and finds it difficult to dissemble. I have to admit that, while I understand why Japanese try to avoid saying 'no' and give vague answers which might be misinterpreted as implying acquiescence, I do find such responses at best awkward and that, perhaps out of wishful thinking, I may misinterpret some Japanese responses. I am inclined to tell my Japanese friends that I am no good at *tatemae* (the official stance which disguises the truth) and prefer to stick to *honne* (the real truth).

Japanese diplomats and officials generally sometimes seem to have turned silence into a diplomatic art-form. In negotiations I found many Japanese were adept at making the other side do the talking. We British hate silences and are often tempted to offer compromises which the Japanese take and then demand more. It took me a long time to learn this simple lesson; I am not sure that I have yet learnt it fully.

The Japanese *shirankao* (literally 'don't know face') is far from a universal Japanese characteristic. In my experience Japanese are just as capable of displaying or hiding their emotions as the British. The Japanese way of giggling in order to hide embarrassment is, however, rather difficult for the foreigner to appreciate.

I was often asked, especially in the years immediately following the end of the war, whether I really liked the Japanese. This has always struck me as a silly question. The only possible answer is that as in any country there are people I like, people I dislike and people to whom I am indifferent.

Similarly, I have also often been asked whether I have any real Japanese friends. The answer is, of course, 'yes'. Cross-cultural friendships are inevitably more difficult to achieve than those with people of similar backgrounds and it requires a special effort to keep up with friends when one lives so far apart as Britain and Japan. The Japanese sense of personal obligation may sometimes be embarrassing, but it does help to ensure that friendships are maintained. Japanese humility is an attractive characteristic, but Japanese flattery can be cloying especially when the compliments are so clearly untrue. One of the most irritating types of Japanese flattery is to be told that one speaks Japanese better than a Japanese. One knows that this is not and cannot be true. For me, the most difficult Japanese (or non-Japanese for that matter) are the arrogant ones or those who suffer from inferiority complexes or conceit.

For real friendship, it is necessary to have common interests beyond work. Unfortunately, many Japanese businessmen are so wrapt up in their work that they have no other interests except golf and perhaps mahjong, neither of which I play.

Japanese have sometimes been described as the Prussians of East Asia and as 'workaholics' lacking a sense of humour. Japanese often pride themselves on being serious people (*majime-ningen*) dedicated to their work. This does not necessarily make them into 'workaholics' The habit of working long hours in offices is not unique to Japan. In Japan the tradition of not leaving the office before your boss has become ingrained and is due in part to the competitive nature of most Japanese companies. The office worker thinks that in order to get on he must prove that he is at least as conscientious and loyal as his fellow workers, even if this means going out drinking with his colleagues and neglecting his home life. This is something I am not prepared to do. I could not, however, have enjoyed life in Japan if I had thought the Japanese generally lacking in a sense of humour. Some Japanese do not perhaps have a very well developed sense of humour when it comes to laughing at themselves, but many of us are like that.

Japanese novels are often very introspective and melancholic, but Japanese humour has a long history. Unfortunately, in Japanese literature comic writing tends to be regarded as populist and inferior to serious literature.

Another myth about the Japanese which some Japanese and Americans have worked hard to perpetuate is that Japanese people are unique and special. My immediate reaction to this is that we are all unique. Personally, I am bored and bemused by the discussions of what is termed the *Nihonjinron*. One of the most ludicrous examples of the nonsense perpetrated under this theory was the attempt to justify Japanese opposition to importing foreign rice on the grounds that Japanese rice was peculiarly suited to Japanese intestines which were longer than Caucasian intestines. Even sillier was the suggestion that imported skis were dangerous because they were not adapted to the quality of Japanese snow.

The arguments have usually been rather more sophisticated than this. They stress the uniqueness of the Japanese ethical system with its emphasis on loyalty and consensus although these could simply be construed as a Japanese adaption of Confucian values.

Arguments based on the alleged ethnic purity of the Japanese people are more dangerous. Such assertions cannot be sustained by any objective reading of Japanese history.

Japanese nationalism may not be worse than extreme forms of nationalism elsewhere, but recent Japanese history must make us all extremely wary of Japanese nationalist politicians, particularly those who have tried to suppress unpleasant facts and pervert history for their own ends. I do not believe that the Japanese or any other people have innate qualities. Cruelty, for instance, is sadly a characteristic found in most human beings, but the instinct needs to be recognized and suppressed. Unfortunately, if it is condoned as it was in the pre-war Japanese military it leads to the sort of behaviour which resulted in the maltreatment of prisoners-of-war and the Nanking massacre. (Of course, we all need to avoid 'holier than thou' attitudes and exercise that useful Japanese concept *jiko-hansei* or 'self reflection'.)

The contention that the Japanese are unique is a threat to Japanese national interests as such claims suggest to some foreigners that if Japanese are different then special (i.e.discriminatory) measures against Japan are justified.

I retain my admiration and liking for Japanese art and literature and my interest in Japanese history. I have tried to do what I can to promote understanding of Japanese culture in Britain, but I dislike cultural nationalism (British or Japanese). It is necessary to understand something of the nature of foreign cultures in order to evaluate better your own country's contribution to world civilization.

Over the years, I have come to appreciate the part which Buddhism, epecially Zen Buddhism, has played in the development of Japanese culture. I have also come to realize better the Japanese approach to nature which finds an expression in some forms of Shinto. But I was brought up as a Christian and still regard myself as a Christian, although I am not a regular churchgoer and find aspects of organized Christianity today antipathetic. In particular, I cannot accept the intolerance which seems to have become ingrained in many aspects of Church doctrines. Holiness is a quality which some Buddhists as well as Christians achieve.

It is more than fifty years since I first went to Japan. Over the last half century Japan has changed hugely and will doubtless change just as much in the next fifty years. The Japan which I first saw in 1946 was on the verge of starvation and in a state of shock following its defeat in the Second World War. Today, Japanese living standards are among the highest in the world even if appearances are not always the same as reality. I have seen the economic bubble grow and burst. Some thought that the Japanese were economic miracle-makers, but this was another myth. Japanese management achieved some real successes in manufacturing and advanced technology, but managements have found it difficult to make the restructuring required to adjust to faltering growth

Japanese society has altered almost as much but will have to undergo further major changes to cope with Japan's ageing society. Unfortunately, an isolationist or island mentality has inhibited the growth of more appropriate internationalist attitudes.

Nevertheless, there has also been a significant element of continuity. We may wish to ignore history and argue that history does not repeat itself, but Japan and the Japanese, like Britain and the British today, have been moulded by their history. We may not always find the study of history congenial or enlightening but it is essential if we are to understand one another better.

In conclusion, I must stress that while I have been unable to avoid making generalizations about Japan and the Japanese I am conscious that most generalizations about the Japanese or any other people are at best only partly true. When I am asked whether the Japanese are this or that I reply that there are over 126 million Japanese who, like other human beings, are all different.

Index

(of some of the principal personal and place names mentioned)

oOo